DATA STRUCTURES

DATA STRUCTURES

N.K. Tiwari
Director
Bansal Institute of Science & Technology
Bhopal (MP)

Jitendra Agrawal
Assistant Professor
Department of Computer Science & Engineering
Rajiv Gandhi Proudyogiki Vishwavidyalaya
Bhopal (MP)

Shishir K. Shandilya
Dean (Academics) and Professor & Head
Department of Computer Science & Engineering
Bansal Institute of Research & Technology
Bhopal (MP)

TECHSAR™
NEW DELHI

Published and Printed by
Techsar Pvt. Ltd.
4435-36/7, Ansari Road, Daryaganj,
New Delhi - 110002
E-mail: tech_info@techarworld.com
Website: www.techsarworld.com

ISBN: 978-93-84588-92-2

Reprint 2025

Preface

This is an introductory book for data structures as a core subject recommended for beginners. This book focuses on data structures and algorithms for manipulating them. Data structures for storing information in tables, lists, trees, queues and stacks are covered. As a subject, Data Structures will be suitable for B.E./B. Tech students of Computer Science & Engineering and for M.C.A. students. It is also useful for working software professionals and programmers for understanding commonly used data structures and algorithm techniques. Familiarity with C programming is assumed from all readers. To understand the material in this book one should be comfortable enough in a programming language to be able to work with and write their own variables, arithmetic expressions, if-else conditions, loops, subroutines, pointers, class structures, and recursion modules.

The purpose of this book is to provide all the important aspects of the subject. Attempt has also been made to illustrate the working of algorithms with self-explanatory examples.

Outline

Organized in ten chapters, each chapter includes problems and programming examples also.

N.K. Tiwari
Jitendra Agrawal
Shishir K. Shandilya

Contents

1

INTRODUCTION

In computer science, a data structure is a way of storing data in computer so that it can be used efficiently. Often a carefully chosen data structure will allow a more efficient algorithm to be used. The choice of the data structure often begins with the choice of an abstract data structure. A well-designed data structure allows a variety of critical operations to be performed, using as little resources, both during execution time and memory space allocation, as possible. After the data structures are chosen, the algorithms to be used often become relatively obvious. Sometimes things work in the opposite direction - data structures are chosen because certain key tasks have algorithms that work best with a particular data structure.

This insight has given rise to many formalized design methods and programming languages in which data structures, rather than algorithms, are the key organizing factors. Most languages feature some sort of a module system, allowing data structures to be safely reused in different applications by hiding their verified implementation details behind controlled interfaces. Object-oriented programming languages such as C++ and Java in particular use objects for this purpose. Since data structures are so crucial to professional programs, many of them enjoy extensive support in standard libraries of modern programming languages and environments, such as C++ Standard Template Library, the Java API, and the Microsoft .Net framework.

1.1 INFORMATION

Computer science is fundamentally the study of information. The information is associated with an attribute or a set of attributes of a situation or an object; for example, the number of students in a class, the length of a hall, and the make of a computer. But to explain and transmit these abstract properties they are represented in the same way and these representations convey the knowledge or information. As a result of frequent and well-understood use, these representations have come to be accepted as being the information they convey.

The basic unit of information is the data; information is a collection of data. When data is processed or organized, it gives a meaningful and logical knowledge, and it becomes information.

1.2 BASIC TERMINOLOGIES

Data and Data Types

Data are simply values or sets of values. A data item refers to a single unit of value. Data is a raw form of information. Data is plural and 'datum' is singular form. Data items that are divided into sub-items are called group items; those are not called elementary items. For example, a student's name may be divided into three sub-items - first name, middle name and last name. Data can be numerical, character, symbol or any other kind of information.

A data type consists of a domain (a set of values), and a set of operations. A data type is a term which refers to kinds of data that variables may hold in the programming language. The data is stored in the memory at some location. By using the name of the variable, one can access the data from that memory location easily. For example in 'C', the data types are `int` (integer value), `float` (floating point value), `char` (character), `double` (real value of large range) etc.

Data types are divided into the following categories: built in data types (primitive data) and user defined data types (non-primitive data). Generally, a programming language supports a set of built in data types and allow a user to define a new type which are called user defined data types.

1. **Built in data type:** These are basic data that are directly operated upon machine instructions. These have different representations on different computers. Such as `int, float, char,` double which are defined by the programming language itself.
2. **User defined data type:** These are more sophisticated data, which are derived from the primitive data. The user defined data emphasize on structuring of a group of homogeneous or heterogeneous data items. With the set of built in data types a user can define his own data type such as arrays, lists, stacks, queues, file, etc.

Example: Consider the data type fraction. How can we specify the domain and operations that define fractions? It seems straightforward to name the operations; fractions are numbers so all the normal arithmetic operations apply, such as addition, multiplication and comparison. In addition, there might be some fraction-specific operations such as normalization of a fraction by removing common terms from its numerator and denominator. For example, if we normalize 6/9 we'd get 2/3.

But how do we specify the domain for fractions, i.e. the set of possible values for a fraction?

Structural and Behavioral Definitions

There are two different approaches to specifying a domain: we can give a structural definition or a behavioral definition. Let us see what these two are like.

Structural Definition of the domain for 'fraction'

The value of a fraction is made of three parts (or components):

- A sign, which is either + or –
- A numerator, which may be any non-negative integer
- A denominator, which may be any positive integer (not zero, not negative).

A structural definition defines the values of a type by imposing an internal structure on them. This is called a structural definition because it defines the values of the type fraction by imposing an internal structure on them (they have three parts). The parts themselves have specific types, and there may be further constraints. For example, we could have insisted that a fraction's numerator and denominator have no common divisor (in that case we wouldn't need the normalization operation - 6/9 would not be a fraction by this definition).

Behavioral definition of the domain for 'fraction'

The alternative approach for defining the set of values for fractions does not impose any internal structure on them. Instead, it just adds an operation that creates fractions out of other things, such as

CREATE_FRACTION (N, D)

Where N is any integer, D is any non-zero integer.

The values of the type fraction are defined to be the values that are produced by this function for any valid combination of inputs.

The parameter names were chosen to suggest its intended behavior: CREATE_FRACTION (N, D) should return a value representing the fraction N/D (N for numerator and D for denominator).

CREATE_FRACTION could be any old random function. How do we guarantee that CREATE_FRACTION (N, D) actually returns the fraction N/D?

The answer is that we have to constrain the behavior of this function by relating it to the other operations on fractions. For example, one of the key properties of multiplication is:

NORMALIZE ((N/D) * (D/N)) = 1/1

This turns into a constraint on CREATE_FRACTION:

NORMALIZE (CREATE_FRACTION (N, D) * CREATE_FRACTION (D, N)) = CREATE_FRACTION (1, 1)

CREATE_FRACTION cannot be any old function, its behavior is highly constrained, because we can write down a lot of constraints like this.

In this type of definition, the domain of a data type - the set of permissible values -plays an almost negligible role. Any set of values will do, as long as we have an appropriate set of operations to go along with it.

1.3 COMMON STRUCTURES

Let us stick with structural definitions for the moment, and briefly survey the main kinds of data types, from a structural point of view.

Atomic Data Types

First of all, there are atomic data types. These are data types that are defined without imposing any structure on their values. Boolean, our first example is an atomic data type. So are characters, as these are typically defined by enumerating all the possible values that exist on a given computer.

Structured Data Types

The opposite of atomic is structured. A structured data type has a definition that imposes a structure upon its values. As we saw above, fraction normally are structured data types.

In many structured data types, there is an internal structural relationship, or organization, that holds between the components. For example, if we think of an array as a structured type, with each position in the array being a component, then there is a structural relationship of 'followed by': we say that component N is followed by component N + 1.

Structural Relationships

Not all structured data types have this sort of internal structural relationship. Fractions are structured, but there is no internal relationship between the sign, numerator and denominator. But many structured data types do have an internal structural relationship, and these can be classified according to the properties of this relationship.

Linear Structure

The most common organization for components is a linear structure. A structure is linear if it has these two properties:

Property P1

Each element is 'followed by' at most one another element.

Property P2

No two elements are 'followed by' the same element.

An array is an example of a linearly structured data type. We generally write a linearly structured data type like this: A → B → C → D (this is one value with 4 parts).

- Counter example 1 (violates P1): A points to B and C. B ← A → C
- Counter example 2 (violates P2): A and B both point to C. A → C ← B

Dropping Constraint P1:

If we drop the first constraint and keep the second, we get a tree structure or hierarchy: no two elements are followed by the same element. This is a very common structure too, and extremely useful.

Counter example 1 is a tree, but counter example 2 is not.

Dropping both P1 and P2:

If we drop both constraints, we get a graph. In a graph, there are no constraints on the relations which we can define.

Cyclic Structures

All the examples we have seen are acyclic. This means that there is no sequence of arrows that leads back to where it started. Linear structures are usually acyclic, but cyclic ones are not uncommon.

Example of a cyclic linear structure: A B C D A

Trees are virtually always acyclic.

Graphs are often cyclic, although the special properties of acyclic graphs make them an important topic of study.

Example: Add an edge from G to D and from E to A.

1.4 ABSTRACT DATA TYPE

An abstract data type is a triple of D-Set of domains, F-Set of functions and A-Axioms in which only what is to be done is mentioned but how is to be done is not mentioned.

In ADT, all the implementation details are hidden. In short

ADT = Type + Function names + Behaviors of each function

We can minimize this cost - and therefore buy as much freedom as possible to change the implementation whenever we like - by minimizing the amount of code that makes use of specific details of the implementation.

This is the idea of an abstract data type. We define the data type - its values and operations without referring to how it will be implemented. Applications that use the data type are oblivious to the implementation: they only make use of the operations defined abstractly. In this way, the application, which might be millions of lines of code, is completely isolated from the implementation of the data type. If we wish to change the implementation, all we have to do is to re-implement the operations. No matter how big our application is, the cost in changing the implementation is the same. In fact, often we do not even have to re-implement all the data type operations, because many of them will be defined in terms of a small set of basic core operations on the data type.

Substitutivity of Implementations

An abstract data type is written with the help of the instances and operations. We make use of the reserved word **Abstract Data Type** while writing an ADT. Let us understand the concept of ADT with the help of some example.

Array as ADT

In ADT, instances represent the elements on which various operations can be performed. The basic operations that can be performed on array are `store ()` and `display ()`. Hence -

```
AbstractDataType Array
{
//Instance: An array A of some size, index i and total number of elements in the array n.
store () - This operation stores the desired elements at each successive location.
display () - This operation displays the elements of the array.
}
```

ADT is useful to handle the data type correctly. Always what is to be done is given in ADT but how it is to be done is not given in ADT. Note that we have only given what are the operations (arrays) in above example. But how is to be done is not given. Thus, while using ADT only abstract representation of the data structure is given.

In a real application, we would like to experiment with many different implementations, in order to find the implementation that is most efficient - in terms of memory and speed - for our specific application. And, if our application changes, we would like to have the freedom to change the implementation so that it is the best for the new application.

Equally important, we would like our implementation to give us simple implementations of the operations. It is not always obvious from the outset how to get the simplest implementation; so, again, we need to have the freedom to change our implementation.

What is the cost we must pay in order to change the implementation? We have to find and change every line of code that depends upon the specific details of the implementation (e.g.

available operations, naming conventions, details of syntax – for example, the two implementations of fractions given above differ in how you refer to the components: one uses the dot notation for structures, and the bracketed index notation for arrays). This can be very expensive and can run a high risk of introducing bugs.

Programming with Abstract Data Types

By organizing our program this way i.e., by using abstract data types – we can change implementations extremely quickly. All we have to do is re-implement three very trivial functions no matter how large our application is.

In general terms, an abstract data type is a specification of the values and operations that has two properties:

- It specifies everything you need to know in order to use the data type.
- It makes absolutely no reference to the manner in which the datatype will be implemented.

When we use abstract datatype, our program divides into two pieces as shown in Figure 1.1.

The Application: The part uses the abstract data type.

The Implementation: The part that implements the abstract data type.

These two pieces are completely independent. It should be possible to take the implementation developed for one application and use it for a completely different application with no changes.

If programming is done in teams, the implementers and application writers can work completely independently once the specification is set.

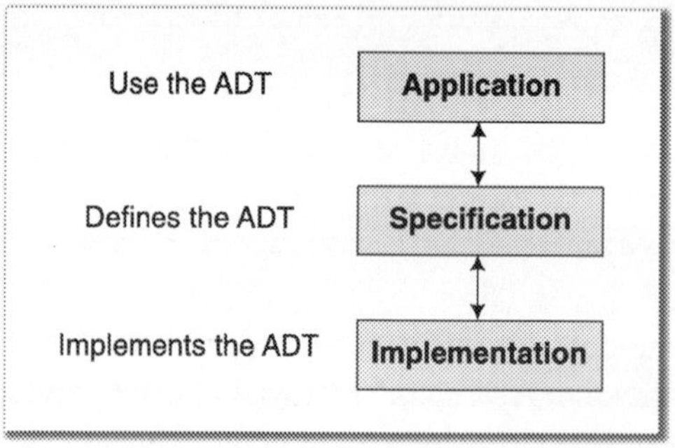

Figure 1.1 Parts of an abstract data type.

1.5 SPECIFICATION

Let us now look in detail at how we specify an abstract data type. We will use 'stack' as an example.

The data structure stack is based on the everyday notion of stack, such as a stack of books, a stack of plates or stack of folded towels. The defining property of a stack is that you can only access the top element of the stack. All the other elements are underneath the top one and these can't be accessed except by removing all the elements above them one at a time.

The notion of a stack is extremely useful in computer science, and it has many applications. It is so widely used that microprocessors often are stack-based or at least provide hardware implementations of the basic stack operations.

We will briefly consider some of the applications later. First, let us see how we can define, or specify, the abstract concept of a stack. The main point to notice here is how we specify everything needed in order to use the stacks, without any mention of how the stacks will be implanted.

Pre- & Postconditions

Preconditions

These are properties about the inputs that are assumed by an operation. If they are satisfied by the inputs, the operation is guaranteed to work properly. If the preconditions are not satisfied, the behavior of the operation is unspecified. It might work properly (by chance), it might return an incorrect answer, or it might crash.

Postconditions

These specify the effects of an operation. These are the only things that you may assume as have been done by the operation. They are only guaranteed to hold if the preconditions are satisfied.

Note: the definition of the values of type 'stack' makes no mention of an upper bound on the size of a stack. Therefore, the implementation must support stacks of any size. In practice, there is always an upper bound - the amount of computer storage available. This limit is not explicitly mentioned, but is understood - it is an implicit precondition on all operations that there is storage available, as needed. Sometimes this is made explicit, in which case it is advisable to add an operation that tests if there is sufficient storage available for a given operation.

Operations

The operations specified on the handout are core operations - any other operation on stacks can be defined in terms of these ones. These are the operations that we must implement in order to implement 'stack'. Everything else in our program can be independent of the implementation details.

It is useful to divide operations into four kinds of functions:

1. Those that create stacks out of non-stacks, e.g. CREATE_STACK, READ_STACK and CONVERT_ARRAY_TO_STACK.
2. Those that 'destroy' stacks (opposite of create) e.g. DESTROY_STACK
3. Those that 'inspect' or 'observe' a stack, e.g. TOP, IS_EMPTY and WRITE_STACK
4. Those that take stacks (and possibly other things) as input and produce other stacks as output, e.g. PUSH and POP.

A specification must say what the inputs and outputs of an operation are, and definitely must mention when an input is changed. This falls short of completely committing the implementation to procedures or functions (or whatever other means of creating 'blocks' of code might be available in the programming language). Of course, these details eventually need to be decided in order for the code to be actually written. But these details do not need to be decided until the code-generation time. Throughout the earlier stages of program design, the extract interface (at the code level) can be left unspecified.

Checking Pre- & Postconditions

It is very important to state in the specification whether each precondition will be checked by the user or by the implementer. For example, the precondition for POP may be checked either by the procedure(s) that call POP or within the procedure that implements POP.

User Guarantees Preconditions

The main advantage, if the user checks preconditions - and therefore guarantees that they will be satisfied when the core operations are invoked - is efficiency. For example, consider the following:

```
Push(s, 1);
Pop(s);
```

It is obvious that there is no need to check if S is empty - this precondition of POP is guaranteed to be satisfied because it is the postcondition of PUSH.

Implementation Checks Preconditions

There are several advantages of having the implementation check its own preconditions:

1. It sometimes has access to information which is not available to the user (e.g. implementation details about space requirements), although this is often a sign of a poorly constructed specification.
2. Programs won't bomb mysteriously - errors will be detected (and reported) at the earliest possible moment. This is not true when the user checks preconditions, because the user is human and occasionally might forget to check, or might think that checking was unnecessary when it was needed in fact.
3. Most important of all, if we ever change the specification, and wish to add, delete, or modify preconditions, we can do this easily, because the precondition occurs in exactly one place in our program.

There are arguments on both sides. This textbook specifies that procedures should signal an error if their preconditions are not satisfied. This means that these procedures must check their own preconditions. That's what our model solution will do too. We will thereby sacrifice some efficiency for a high degree of maintainability and robustness.

1.6 LAYERED SOFTWARE

Recall Figure 1.1 that already showed you earlier:

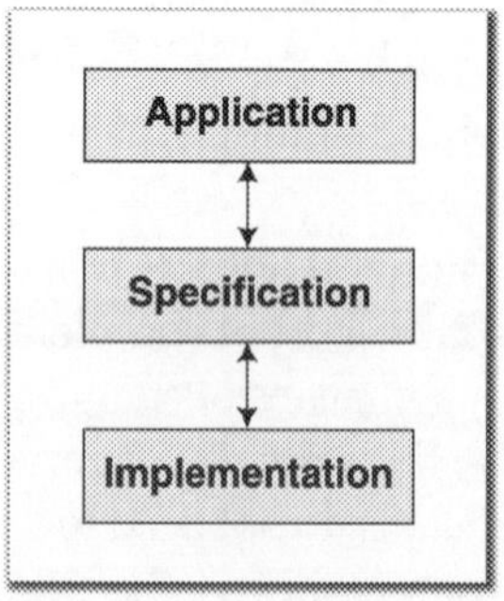

Figure 1.2 Layers of software.

It illustrates an important, general idea: the idea of a layered software. In this figure, (Figure 1.2) there are two layers: the application layer and the implementation layer. The critical point - the property that makes these truly separated layers – is that the functionality of the upper layer and the code that implements that functionality are completely independent of the code of the lower layer. Furthermore, the functionality of the lower layer is completely described in the specification.

We have already discussed how this arrangement permits very rapid, bug-free changes to the code implementing an abstract data type. But this is the not the only advantage.

Reusability

Another great advantage is that the abstract data type (implemented in the lower layer) can be ready reused: nothing in it depends critically on the application layer (neither its functionality nor its coding details). An abstract type like 'stack' has extremely diverse uses in computer science, and the same well-specified, efficient implementation can be used for all of them (although always keep in mind that there is no universal, optimally-efficient implementation: so efficiency gains by re-implementation are always possible).

Abstraction in Software Engineering

Libraries of abstract data type are a very effective way of extending the set of data type provided by a programming language, which themselves constitute a layer of 'abstraction' – the so called virtual machine, above the actual data types supported by the hardware. In fact, in an ordinary programming environment there are several layers of software layers in the same strong sense as above.

The use of a strictly layered software is a good software engineering practice, and is quite common in certain software areas. Operating systems themselves have a long tradition of layering, starting with a small kernel and building up the functionality layer-by-layer. Communications (software/hardware) also conform to a well-defined layering.

Bottom-up Design

The concept of a layered software suggests a software development methodology which is quite different from the top-down design. In the top-down design, one starts with a rather complete description of the required global functionality and decomposes this into sub-functions that are simpler than the original. The process is applied recursively until one reaches functions simple enough to be implemented directly. This design methodology does not, by itself, tend to give rise to layers – coherent collections of sub-functions whose coherence is independent of the specific application under development.

The alternative methodology is called 'bottom-up' design. Starting at the bottom – i.e. the virtual machine provided by the development environment, one builds up successively more powerful layers. The uppermost layer, which is the only one directly accessible to the application developer, provides such powerful functionality that writing the final application is relatively straightforward. This methodology emphasizes flexibility and reuse, and of course, integrates perfectly with the bottom-up strategies for implementation and testing. Throughout the development process, one must bear in mind the needs of the specific application being developed, but, as said above, most of the layers are quite immune to large shifts in the application functionality, so one does not need a 'final', 'complete' description of the required global functionality, as is needed in the top-down methodology.

1.7 DATA STRUCTURE

A data structure can be defined as the organization of data or elements and all possible operations which are required for those set of data. In other words, data may be organized in different ways. The logical or mathematical model of a particular organization of data is known as a **data structure**. Some of the data structures are arrays, stacks, queues, linked lists, trees and graphs etc.

A data structure is a set of domains D, a set of functions F and set of axioms A. This triple set (D, F, A) denotes the data structure d.

A data structure can be viewed as an interface between two functions or as an implementation of methods to access storage that is organized according to the associated data type.

Example:

Consider a set of elements which are required to store an array. Various operations such as reading of the elements and storing them at appropriate index can be performed. If we want to access any particular element then that element can be retrieved from the array. Thus traversing, inserting, printing, searching would be the operations required to perform these tasks for the elements. Thus, the data object integer elements and set of operations form the data structure Array.

Basic Operation of Data Structures

The data or elements appearing in our data structures are processed by means of certain operations. In fact, the particular data structure that one chosen for a given situation depends largely on the frequency with which specific operations are performed.

The following four operations play a major role in data processing on data structures:

1. **Traversing:** Accessing each record exactly once so that certain items in the record may be processed. This accessing and processing is sometimes called visiting the record.
2. **Inserting:** Adding a new record to the structure.
3. **Deleting:** Removing a record from the structure.
4. **Searching:** Finding the location of a record with a given key value, or finding the locations of all records which satisfy one or more conditions.

Sometimes two or more of the operations may be used in a given situation. The following two operations, which are used in special situations, are:

1. **Sorting:** Arranging the records in some logical order.
2. **Merging:** Combining the records in two different sorted files into a single sorted file.

Classification of Data Structures

Data structures are normally divided into two broad categories. Figure 1.3 shows various types of data structures. Linear data structures are the data structures in which data is arranged in a straight sequence, consecutive or in a list. For example, Arrays, Stacks, Queues and List. Non-linear data structures are the data structures in which the data may be arranged not in a sequence or hierarchical manner. For example, Trees and Graphs.

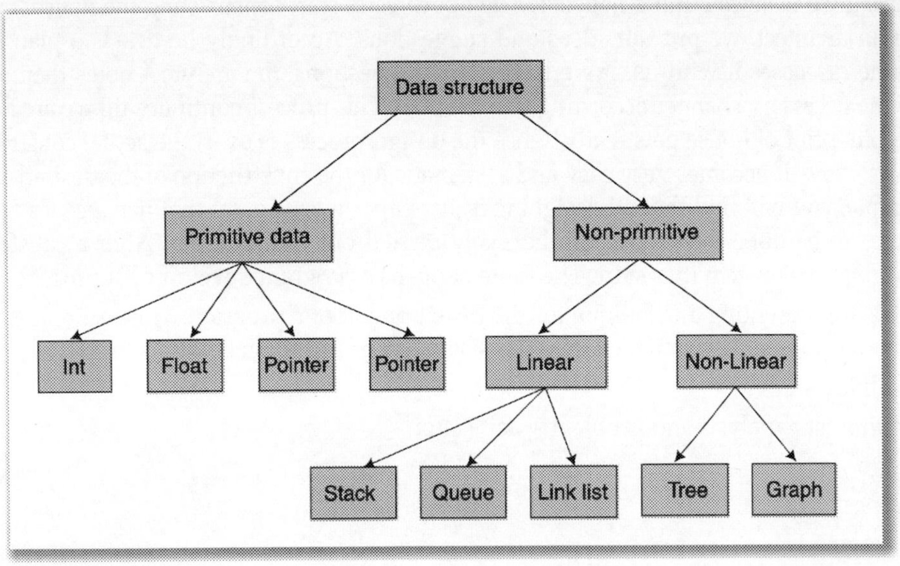

Figure 1.3 Classification of data structures.

1.8 ALGORITHMS

An algorithm is composed of a finite set of steps, each of which may require one or more operations. An algorithm is a finite set of instructions that, if followed, accomplishes a particular task. An algorithm must satisfy the following criteria:

1. **Input:** Zero or more quantities are externally supplied.
2. **Output:** At least one quantity is produced.
3. **Definiteness:** Each instruction is clear and unambiguous.
4. **Finiteness:** If we trace out the instructions of algorithm, then for all cases the algorithm terminates after a finite number of steps.
5. **Effectiveness:** Every instruction must be very basic so that it can be carried out, in principle, by a person using only pencil and paper.

A program is the expression of an algorithm in a programming language. Sometimes words such as procedure, function and subroutine are used synonymously for a program.

Implementation of Algorithm

Any program can be created with the help of two things – algorithm and data structures. To develop any program, we should first select a proper data structure, and then we should develop an algorithm for implementing the given problem with the help of the data structure which we have chosen.

In computer science, developing a program is an art or skill. And we can have mastery on the program development process only when we follow certain method. Before actual implementation of the program, designing a program is a very important step.

Suppose, if we want to build a house, we do not directly start constructing the house. Instead we consult an architect, we put our ideas and suggestions. Accordingly he draws a plan of the house, and he discusses it with us. If we have some suggestions, the architect notes them down and makes the necessary changes accordingly in the plan. This process continues till we are happy. Finally, the blueprint of house gets ready. Once the design process is over, the actual construction activity starts. Now, it becomes very easy and systematic for the construction of the desired house. In this example, you will find that all designing is just paper work and at that instance if we want some changes to be done then those can be easily carried out in the paper. After a satisfactory design, the construction activities start. The same happens a program development process.

Here, we are presenting a technique for the development of a program. This technique called the program development cycle which involves several steps as shown below.

1. Feasibility study.
2. Requirement analysis and problem specification.
3. Design.
4. Coding.
5. Debugging.
6. Testing.
7. Maintenance.

Let us discuss each step one by one.

Feasibility study

In the feasibility study, the problem is analyzed to decide whether it is feasible to develop some program for the given problem statement. If we find that it is really essential to develop some computer program for the given program then only the further steps will be carried out.

Requirement analysis and problem specification

In this step, the programmer has to find out the essential requirement for solving the given problem. For that, the programmer has to communicate with the user of his software. The programmer then has to decide what are the inputs needed for this program, in which form the inputs are to be given, the order of the inputs, and what kind of output should be generated. Thus, the total requirement for the program has to be analyzed. It is also essential to analyze what could be the possible in the program. Thus, after deciding the total requirements for solving the problem, one can make the problem statement specific.

Design

Once the requirement analysis is done, the design can be prepared using the problem specification document. In this phase of development, some layout for developing a program has to be decided. In this step, the algorithm has to be designed for the most suitable data structure. Then the appropriate programming language has to be implemented for the given algorithm. The design of algorithm and selection of data structures are the two key issues in this phase.

Coding

When the design of the program is ready then coding becomes a simpler job. If we have already decided the language of implementation then we can start writing the code simply by breaking the problem into small modules. If we can write functions for these modules and interface functionalities in some desired order then the desired code gets ready. The final step in coding is the well-document, well formed output.

Debugging

In this phase we compile the code and check for errors. If any error is there then we try to eliminate it. The debugging needs a complete scan of the program.

Testing

In the testing phase, certain set of data is given to the program as an input. The program should show the desired results as the output. The output should vary according to the input of the program. For the wrong input, the program should terminate or it should display some error message, it should not be in a continuous loop.

Maintenance

Once the code is ready and is tested properly, then if the user requires some modifications in the code later then those modifications should be easily carried out. If the programmer has to rewrite the code then it is because of poor design of the program. The modularity in the code has to be maintained.

Documentation

The documentation is not a separate step in the program development process but it is required at every step. Documentation means providing help or some manual which will help the user to make use of the code in the proper direction. It is a good practice to maintain some kind of document for every phase of the compilation process.

We have already discussed the fundamentals of algorithm. Writing an algorithm is essential step in the program development process. The efficiency of algorithm is directly related to efficiency of the program. In other words, if the algorithm is efficient then the program becomes efficient.

Analysis of Programs

The analysis of the program does not mean simply working of the program but to check whether for all possible situations program works or not. The analysis also involves working of the program efficiently. Efficiency in the following sense:

1. The program requires less amount of storage space.
2. The programs get executed in very less amount of time.

The time and space are factors which determine the efficiencies of the program. Time required for execution of the program cannot be computed in terms of seconds because of the following factors:

1. The hardware of the machine.
2. The amount of time required by each machine instruction.
3. The amount of time required by the compilers to execute the instruction.
4. The instruction set.

Hence, we will assume that time required by the program to execute means the total number of times the statements get executed.

Complexity of an Algorithm

The analysis of algorithms is a major task in computer science. In order to compare algorithms, there must be some criteria to measure the efficiency of an algorithm. An algorithm can be evaluated by a variety of criteria – the rate of growth of the time or space required to solve larger and larger instance of a program.

The three cases one usually investigates in complexity theory are as follows:

1. **Worst case:** The worst case time complexity is the function defined by the maximum amount of time needed by an algorithm for an input of size, 'n'. Thus, it is the function defined by the maximum number of steps taken on any instance of size 'n'.
2. **Average case:** The average case time complexity is the execution of an algorithm having typical input data of size 'n'. Thus, it is the function defined by the average number of steps taken on any instance of size 'n'.
3. **Best case:** The best case time complexity is the minimum amount of time that an algorithm requires for an input of size 'n'. Thus, it is the function defined by the minimum number of steps taken on any instance of size 'n'.

Space Complexity: The space complexity of a program is the amount of memory it needs to run to completion. The space needed by a program is the sum of the following components:

- A fixed part that includes space for the code, space for simple variable and fixed size component variables.
- The variable part that consists of the space needed by a component variable where the size is dependent on the particular problem.

The space requirement S (P) of any algorithm P may therefore be written as

$$S(P) = c + S_p$$

where c is a constant and S_p denotes instance characteristics.

Time Complexity: The time complexity of an algorithm is the amount of computer time it needs to run to completion. The time T (P) taken by a program P is the sum of the compilation time and the run (or execution) time. The compilation time does not depened on the characteristics. We assume that a compiled program will run several times without recompilation. We concern ourselves with just time of a program. This run time is denoted by T_p (instance characteristics).

If we knew the characteristics of the compiler to be used, we could proceed to determine the number of additions, subtractions, multiplications, divisions, compares, stores and so on, that would be made by the code for *P*.

$$T_p(n) = c_a \text{ADD}(n) + c_s \text{SUB}(n) + c_m \text{MUL}(n) + \ldots\ldots\ldots\ldots$$

where n denotes the instance characteristics, and c_a, c_s, c_m and so on.

Efficiency of algorithms

If we have two algorithms that perform the same task, and the first one has a computing time of O(n) and the second of $O(n^2)$, then we usually prefer the first one.

The reason for this is that as n increases the time required for the execution of the second algorithm will get far more than the time required for the execution of the first. We will study various values for computing the function for the constant values.

$$\log_2 n > n > n \log_2 n > n^2 > n^3 > 2^n$$

Notice how the times O (n) and O (n $\log_2$ n) grow much slower than the others. For large data sets, algorithms with a complexity greater than O($n \log_2 n$) are often impractical. The very slow algorithm will be the one having the time complexity 2^n.

Algorithm complexity notations

To choose the best algorithm, we need to check the efficiency of each algorithm. The efficiency can be measured by computing the time complexity of each algorithm. Asymptotic notation is a shorthand way to represent the time complexity.

Using asymptotic notations we can give time complexity as 'fastest possible', 'slowest possible' or 'average time'.

Various notations such as Ω, Θ and O used are called asymptotic notions.

Big oh notation

The big oh notation is denoted by 'O'. it is a method of representing the upper bound of an algorithm's running time. Using the big oh notation we can give the longest amount of time taken by the algorithm to complete.

Definition

Let F (n) and g (n) be two non-negative functions.

Let n_0 and constant c are two integers such that n_0 denotes some value of input, and $n > n_0$. Similarly, c is some constant such that $c > 0$. We can write

$$F(n) \leq g(n)$$

Then F (n) is big oh of g (n). It is also denoted as F (n) Є O (g (n)). In other words if F (n) is less then g (n) is multiple of some constant c.

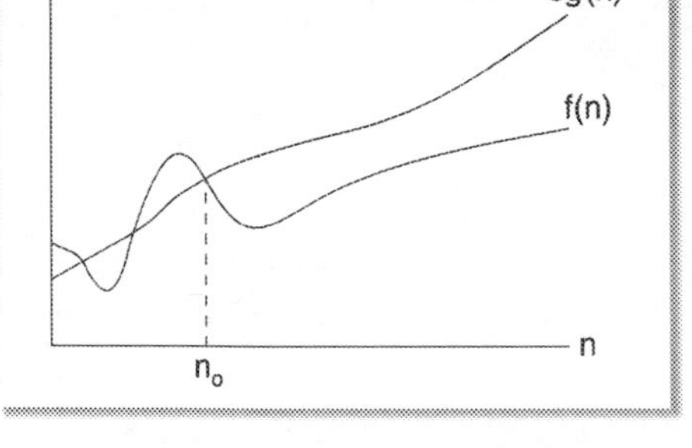

Example: Consider the function F (n) = 2n + 2 and g (n) = n^2.

Then we have to find some constant c, so that $F(n) \leq c * g(n)$. As F (n) = 2n + 2 and g (n) = n^2 then we find c for n = 1 then

$$F(n) = 2n + 2$$
$$= 2(1) + 2$$
$$F(n) = 4$$

and $g(n) = n^2$
$$= (1)^2$$
$$g(n) = 1$$

i.e. $F(n) > g(n)$

if n = 2 then,

$$F(n) = 2n + 2$$
$$= 2(2) + 2$$
$$F(n) = 6$$

and $g(n) = n^2$
$$= (2)^2$$
$$g(n) = 4$$

i.e. $F(n) > g(n)$

if n = 3 then,

$$F(n) = 2n + 2$$
$$= 2(3) + 2$$
$$F(n) = 8$$

and $g(n) = n^2$
$$= (3)^2$$
$$g(n) = 9$$

i.e. $F(n) < g(n)$ is true.

Hence, we can conclude that for $n > 2$, we obtain,

$$F(n) < g(n)$$

Thus, always upper bound of existing time is obtained by the big *O* notation.

Omega Notation

Omega notation is denoted by 'Ω'. This notation is used to represent the **lower bound** of the algorithm's running time. Using the omega notation we can denote the shortest amount of time taken by an algorithm.

Definition

A function F (n) is said to be in Ω (g (n)) if F (n) is bounded below by some positive constant multiple of g (n) such that

$$F(n) \geq c * g(n) \text{ for all } n \geq n_0$$

It is denoted as $F(n) \in \Omega(g(n))$. The following graph illustrates the curve for the Ω notation.

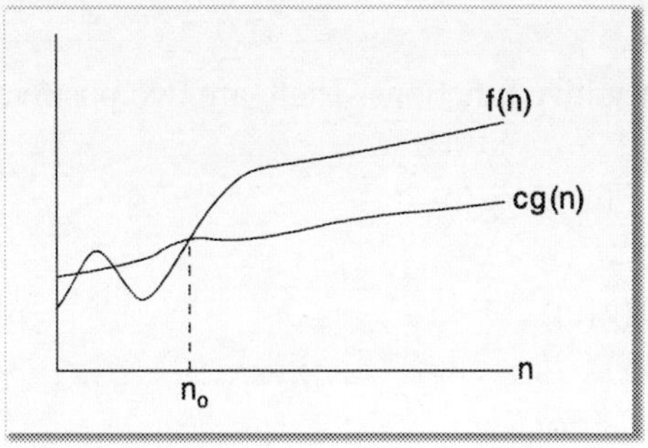

Example: Consider $F(n) = 2n^2 + 5$ and $g(n) = 7n$

Then if $n = 0$

$F(n) = 2(0)^2 + 5$

$= 5$

$g(n) = 7(0)$

$= 0$ i.e. $F(n) > g(n)$

But if $n = 1$

$F(n) = 2(1)^2 + 5$

$= 7$

$g(n) = 7(1)$

$= 7$ i.e. $F(n) = g(n)$

If $n = 2$ $n = 2$

$F(n) = 2(2)^2 + 5$

$= 13$

$g(n) = 7(2)$

$= 14$ i.e. $F(n) < g(n)$

If $n = 3$ $n = 3$

$F(n) = 2(3)^2 + 5$

$= 23$

$g(n) = 7(3)$

$= 21$ i.e. $F(n) > g(n)$

Hence, we can conclude that for the $n > 3$, we obtain $F(n) > c * g(n)$. It can be represented as $2n^2 + 5 \in \Omega(n)$.

Thus, always the lower bound of the existing time is obtained by Ω notation.

'Θ' Notation

The theta notation is denoted by Θ. By this method, the running time is between the upper bound and lower bound.

Definition

Let F (n) and g (n) be two non-negative functions. There are two positive constants, namely, c_1 and c_2 such that

$$c_1 g(n) \leq F(n) \leq c_2 g(n)$$

Thus, we can say that

$$F(n) \in \Theta(g(n))$$

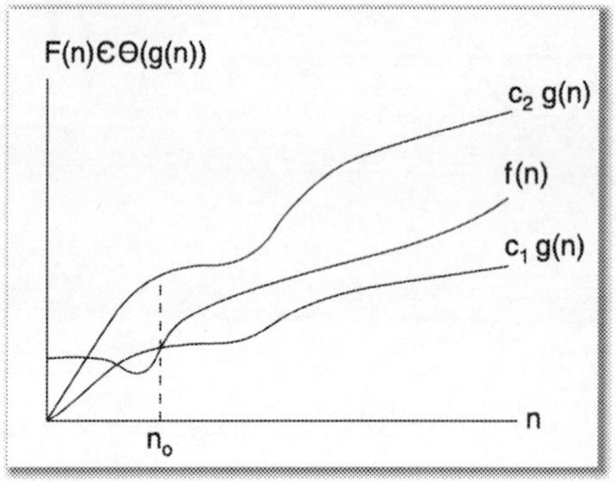

Example: Consider F (n) = 2n + 8 and g (n) = 7n, where n ≥ 2.

Similarly, $F(n) = 2n + 8$

$g(n) = 7n$

i.e. $5n < 2n + 8 < 7n$ For $n \geq 2$

Here $c_1 = 5$ and $c_2 = 7$ with $n_0 = 2$.

The theta notation is more precise with big oh and omega notations.

2

ARRAY

2.1 INTRODUCTION

In computer programming, an array, (also known as a vector or list) is one of the simplest data structures. Array is a non-primitive data structure or linear data structure. An array holds a series of data elements, usually of the same size and data type. Individual elements are accessed by an index using a consecutive range of integers, as opposed to an associative array. Some arrays are multi-dimensional, i.e. they are indexed by a fixed number of integers, for example by a quadruple of four integers. Generally one and two-dimensional arrays are the most common.

The fundamental data types are char, int, float, and double. Although these types are very useful, they are constrained by the fact that a variable of these types can store only one value at any given time. Therefore, they can be used to handle limited amounts of data. In many applications, however, we need to handle a large volume of data in terms of reading, processing and printing. To process such large amounts of data, we need a powerful data type that would facilitate efficient storing, accessing and manipulation of data items. C supports a derived data type known as Array that can be used for such applications.

Most programming languages have arrays as built in data type. Some programming languages (such as Fortran, C, C++, and Java) generalize the available operations and functions to work transparently over arrays as well as scalars, providing a higher-level multiplication than most other languages, which require loops over all the individual members of the arrays.

2.2 USES

Although useful in their own right, arrays also form the basis for several more complex data structures, such as heaps, hash tables and lists and can represent strings, stacks and queues. They also play a minor role in many other data structures. All of these applications benefit from the compactness and locality of arrays.

One of the disadvantages of array is that it has a single fixed size, and although its size can be arrived in many environments, this is an expensive operation. Dynamic arrays are arrays which automatically perform this resizing as late as possible, when the programmer attempts to add an element to the end of the array and there is no more space. To average the high cost of resizing over a long period of time, they expand the array again, it just uses more of this reserved space.

In the C programming language, one-dimensional character arrays are used to store null terminated strings, so called because the end of the string is indicated with a special reserved character called the null character.

2.3 ARRAY DEFINITION

An array is a linear data structure. It is a collection of all the elements with similar data types. Arrays are the collection of a finite number of homogenous data element such that the elements of the array are referenced respectively by an index set consisting of n consecutive numbers and stored respectively in successive memory locations. The arrays can be represented as one dimensional, two dimensional or multidimensional.

Advantages of sequential organization of data structure

1. Elements can be stored and retrieved very efficiently sequentially in sequential organization with the help of an index or memory location.
2. All the elements are stored at the continuous memory location. Hence, searching of an element from the sequential organization is easy.

Disadvantages of sequential organization of data structure

1. Insertion and deletion of elements becomes complicated due to their sequential nature.
2. Memory fragmentation occurs if we remove the elements randomly.
3. For storing the data, large continuous free block of memory is required.

2.4 REPRESENTATION OF ARRAY

The syntax of declaring an array is

Data_type name_of_array [size];

For example, `int a [20]; float b [10]; double c [10][5];`

Here 'a' is the name of the array inside the square bracket where the size of the array is given. This array is of integer type – all the type elements are of integer type in array 'a'. The number n of elements is called the **length** or **size** of array. The size or length of an array can be obtained as follows:

$$\text{Length} = \text{UB} - \text{LB} + 1$$

Where, UB = Upper bound (largest index) and LB = Lower bound (smallest index).

The elements of an array are stored in consecutive memory locations. Hence, the computer does not need to keep track of the address of every element in an array, but needs to track only of the address of the first element of the array.

Let, A be a linear array in the memory of a computer. The address of the first element in A is denoted by **Base** (A) and is called the **Base address** of A.

2.4.1 One-dimensional Arrays

A list of elements can be given one variable name using only one subscript and such a variable is called a single-subscripted variable or a one-dimensional array. The subscript can begin with number 0, that is, A[0] is allowed. For example, if we want to represent a set of five numbers, say (12, 23, 33, 45, 54) by an array variable A, then we may declare it as

```
int A[5];
```

And the computer reserved five storage locations as shown below:

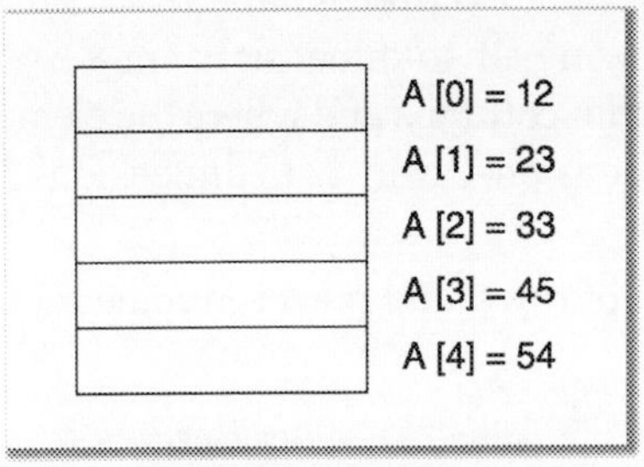

Figure 2.1 One-dimensional array.

Now let us see how to handle this array. We will write a simple C++ program in which we are simply going to store the elements and then we will print those stored elements.

```
#include<iostream.h>
#include<conio.h>
main( )
{
 int a[5];
clrscr( );
cout<< " Enter the element which want to store"<<endln;
for ( int i = 0; i < 5; i++)
{
cin>> a[i];
}
cout<<"Print the stored element in array"<<endln;
for ( int i = 0; i < 5; i++)
{
cout<< a[i] <<endln;
}
getch( );
}
```

2.4.2 Two-dimensional Arrays

Two-dimensional arrays are declared as follows:

Type array_name [row_size][column_size];

Two dimensional arrays are called **matrices** in mathematics and **tables** in business application. Hence, two-dimensional arrays are also called matrix arrays.

A two-dimensional $m \times n$ array A is a collection of $m * n$ data elements such that each element specified by a pair of integers I and J, called subscript such that

$$1 \le I \le m \text{ and } 1 \le J \le n$$

The element of A with first subscript I and second subscript K will be dented by

$$A [I, J] \text{ or } A_{I,J}$$

There is a standard way of drawing a two-dimensional $m \times nA$ where the elements of A form a rectangular array with **m rows** and **n columns** and where the element A[I, J] appears in row I and column J. One such type of two-dimensional array with dimensions 3 rows and 4 columns is shown in Figure 2.2.

A [3, 4] where m = 3 is number of rows, and n = 4 is number of columns.

	Columns			
Rows	0	1	2	3
0	A [0,0]	A [0,1]	A [0,2]	A [0,3]
1	A [1,0]	A [1,1]	A [1,2]	A [1,3]
2	A [2,0]	A [2,1]	A [2,2]	A [2,3]

Figure 2.2 3 × 4 array – two-dimensional.

The length of any dimension in a multidimensional array can be calculated as follows:

Length = Upper bound - Lower bound +1

For example, an array A [3, 4] can be represented as follows:

A [0...2, 0....3]. The array has three rows (0,1and 2) four columns (0,1,2 and 3).

Thus, the length of the row will be:

$$\text{Row} = \text{Upper bound} - \text{Lower bound} + 1$$
$$= 2 - 0 + 1 = 3$$

and length of the column will be:

$$\text{Column} = \text{Upper bound} - \text{Lower bound} + 1$$
$$= 3 - 0 + 1 = 4$$

Row Major Representation

If the elements are stored in a row-wise manner then it is called row major representation. It means that the complete first row is stored and then the complete second row is stored and so on.

Example: If we want to store elements 10, 20, 30, 40, 50, 60, 70, 80, 90 then the elements will be filled up by row-wise manner as follows (consider the array A [3,4]).

Address of elements in Row Major Implementation

For an array A, the base (A) is the address of the first element of the array. That is, it is declared by

```
int A [m, n];
```

where m and n are the ranges of the first and second dimensions, respectively, base (A) is the address of A [0,0].

	0	1	2
0	10	20	30
1	40	50	60
2	70	80	90
.			
9			

Figure 2.3 Row major store in array.

To calculate the address of the first of an arbitrary element A [I, J], first compute the address of the first element of row I and then add the quantity J * size. Therefore, the address of A [I, J] is:

Base (A) + (I * n + J) * size

For example, the array A [3, 4] is stored as in Figure 2.3. The base address is 200. Here m =3, n = 4 and size = 1. Then the address of A [1, 2] is computed as

= 200 + (1 * 4 + 2) * 1

= 206

Column major representation

If the elements are stored in a column-wise manner then it is called column major representation. It means that the complete first column is stored and then the complete second column is stored and so on.

Example: If we want to store elements 10, 20, 30, 40, 50, 60, 70, 80, 90,100,110,120 then the elements will be filled up in a column-wise manner as follows (consider the array A [3,4]).

	0	1	2	3
0	10	20	30	40
1	50	60	70	80
2	90	100	100	120

Figure 2.4 Column major store in array.

Address of Elements in Column Major Implementation

For an array A, base (A) is the address of the first element of the array. That is, it is declared by

```
int A [m, n];
```

where m and n are the ranges of the first and second dimensions, respectively, base (A) is the address of A [0,0].

Address of element A [I, J] = base address + (m (J – L_2) + (I – L_1)) * size

where m is the number of rows, L_1 is the lower bound of the row, and L_2 is the lower bound of the column.

For example, the array A [3,4] is stored as in Figure 2.3. The base address is 200. Here m =3, n = 4 and size = 1. Then the address of A [1, 2] is computed as

= 200 + (3 (2 – 0) + (1 – 0)) * 1

= 207

Example 2.1: Consider the integer array int A [3,4] declared. If the base address is 1000, find the address of the element A [2, 3] with row major and column major representation of array.

Solution:

Row major representation

Given that base address = 1000, the size is integer = 2 byte, m = 3, n = 4, I = 2, J = 3.

Then A [2, 3] = Base (A) + (I * n + J) * size

= 1000 + (2 * 4 + 3) * 2

= 1022

Column major representation

Given that base address = 1000, the size is integer = 2 byte, m = 3, n = 4, I = 2, J = 3, $L_1 = 0$, $L_2 = 0$.

Then A [2, 3] = base address + (m (J – L_2) + (I – L_1)) * size

= 1000 + (3 (3-0) + (2 -0)) * 2

= 1022

We will write a simple C++ program in which we are simply going to store the elements and then we will print those stored elements in two- dimensional array and perform the addition.

Program:

```
#include<iostream.h>
#include<conio.h>
void main()
{
int a[3][3],b[3][3],c[3][3],i,j;
clrscr();
cout<<"enter the value of first matrix"<<endl;
for(i=0;i<=2;i++)
{ for(j=0;j<=2;j++)
{ cin>>a[i][j];
}
}
cout<<"first matrix is"<<endl;
for(i=0;i<=2;i++)
{ for(j=0;j<=2;j++)
{ cout<<a[i][j];
}
cout<<endl;
```

```
}
cout<<"enter second matrix"<<endl;
for(i=0;i<=2;i++)
{ for(j=0;j<=2;j++)
{ cin>>b[i][j];
}
}
cout<<"second is"<<endl;
for(i=0;i<=2;i++)
{ for(j=0;j<=2;j++)
{ cout<<b[i][j];
}
cout<<endl;
}
cout<<"addition of matrix"<<endl;
for(i=0;i<=2;i++)
{ for(j=0;j<=2;j++)
{ c[i][j]=a[i][j]+b[i][j];
}
}
for(i=0;i<=2;i++)
{ for(j=0;j<=2;j++)
{ cout<<c[i][j]<<" ";
}
cout<<endl;
}
getch();
}
```

Output of the Program

```
Enter the value of first matrix
1
2
3
4
5
6
7
8
9
First matrix is
1 2 3
```

```
4 5 6
7 8 9
Enter second matrix
14
10
12
13
11
25
23
26
22
Second is
14 10 12
13 11 25
23 26 22
Addition of matrix
15 12 15
17 16 31
30 34 31
```

2.4.3 Analysis of Arrays

There are two basic operations which can be performed on arrays and these are:

1. Storing the elements in an array.
2. Retrieval of the elements from the array.

Basic operation in one-dimensional arrays –

```
int i, n, a[10];
cout << "how many elements to store?";          Execute for O(n) time
cin >> n; Execute for O(n) time
for ( i =0; i <n; i++)
cin >> a[i];
cout << "element are.....";                     Execute for O(n) time
for ( i=0; i<n; i++)
cout <<a[i];
```

In the above C++ code, the for loop is used to store the elements in an array. By this the elements will be stored from location 0 to n-1. Similarly, for retrieval of elements again a for loop is used.

```
int i, m, n, a[10][3];
cout << "how many rows and columns";
cin >> m,
```

```
cin >>n;
for ( i =0; i <m; i++)
for ( j=0; j<n; j++)
cin >> a[i][j];
cout << "element are.....";
for ( i =0; i <m; i++)
for ( j=0; j<n; j++)
cout <<a[i][j];
```

Execute for $O(n^2)$ time

The above code takes overall $O(n^2)$ time.

2.5 ORDERED LIST

Ordered list is nothing but a set of elements. Such a list is sometimes called as linear list. More abstractly, we can say that an ordered list is either empty or it can be written as ($a_1, a_2, a_3, a_4 \ldots\ldots a_n$) where the a_i are atoms from set S.

Examples

1. List of one digit numbers (0, 1, 2, 3, 4, 5, 6, 7, 8, 9)
2. Days in a week (Sunday, Monday, Tuesday, Wednesday, Thursday, Friday, Saturday)

Operation on ordered list

Following operations can be done on an ordered list.

1. Display of the list.
2. Searching a particular element from the list.
3. Insertion of any element in the list.
4. Deletion of any element from the list.
5. Read the list from left-to-right or right-to-left.

2.5.1 Polynomials

One classic example of an ordered list is a polynomial. A polynomial is the sum of term consisting of variable, coefficient and exponent.

Various operations which can be performed on a polynomial are:

1. Addition of two polynomials
2. Multiplication of two polynomials.
3. Evaluation of polynomials.

An array structure can be used to represent the polynomial.

Representation of array polynomial using single dimensional array

For representing a single-variable polynomial one can make use of one-dimensional array. In a single-dimensional array the index of an array will act as the exponent and the coefficient can be stored at that particular index which can be represented as follows:

Example: $3x^4 + 5x^3 + 7x^2 + 10x - 19$

This polynomial can be stored in single dimensional array.

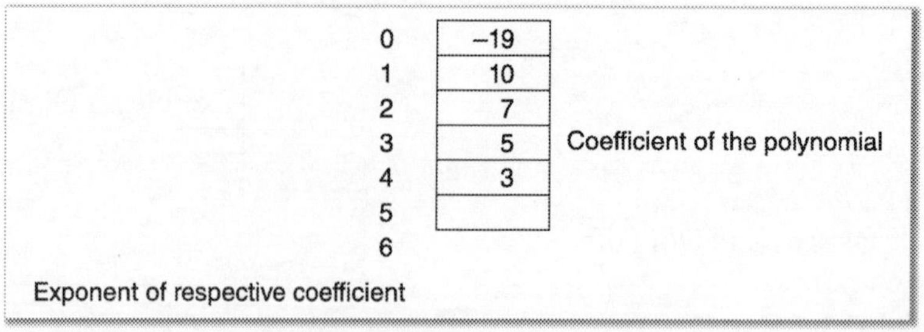

Figure 2.5 Polynomial representation.

2.6 SPARSE MATRICES

Matrices play a very important role in solving many interesting problems in various scientific and engineering applications. It is therefore necessary for us to design efficient representation or matrices. Normally matrices are represented in a two-dimensional array. In a matrix, if there are m rows and n columns then the space required to store the numbers will be $m \times n \times s$ where s is the number of bytes required to store the value.

Suppose, there are 10 rows and 10 columns and we have to store the integer values then the space complexity will be in bytes.

$$10 \times 10 \times 2 = 200 \text{ bytes}$$

Here 2 bytes are required to store an integer value and the time complexity will be $O(n^2)$ because the operations that are carried out on matrices need to scan the matrices one row at a time and the individual columns in that row result in use of two nested loops.

Definition

A sparse matrix is that matrix which has a very few non-zero elements, as compared to the size $m \times n$ of the matrix or matrices with a relatively high proportion of zero entries are called **sparse matrices** or **sparse array**.

Example: If the matrix is of size 100×100 and only 10 elements are non-zero then for accessing these 10 elements one has to make 10000 times scan. Also only 10 spaces will be with non-zero elements, the remaining spaces of the matrix will be filled with zero only. We will have to allocate the memory of $100 \times 100 \times 2 = 20000$.

2.6.1 Representation of Sparse Matrix

The representation of a sparse matrix will be a triplet only in the sense that basically the sparse matrix means very few non-zero elements having in it. Rest of the spaces have the value zero which are basically useless values or simply empty values.

Consider the matrix

$$A = \begin{vmatrix} 0 & 0 & 6 & 0 & 9 & 0 & 0 \\ 2 & 0 & 0 & 7 & 8 & 0 & 4 \\ 10 & 0 & 0 & 0 & 0 & 0 & 0 \\ 0 & 0 & 12 & 0 & 0 & 0 & 0 \\ 0 & 0 & 0 & 0 & 0 & 0 & 0 \\ 0 & 0 & 0 & 3 & 0 & 0 & 5 \end{vmatrix}$$

Figure 2.6 Sparse matrix.

2.7 STORAGE POOL

A storage pool is a collection of all the memory blocks that are allocated by the application programs, and which are in use. When an object allocated some blocks of memory then that allocation is returned to the storage pool.

The storage pool contains all nodes that are not currently being used. This pool cannot be accessed by the programmer except through the *getnode* and *freenode* operations. The *getnode* option removes a node from the pool, whereas the *freenode* return a node to the pool. The most natural form for this pool to take is that of a linked list acting as a stack. The list is linked together by the next field in each node. The *getnode* operation removes the first node from this list and makes it available or use. The *freenode* operation adds a node to the front of the list, making it available for reallocation by the next *getnode*. The list of available nodes is called available list.

2.8 GARBAGE COLLECTION

When some object is created and is not used for a long time then such an object is called **garbage**. Garbage collection is the method of detecting and reclaiming free nodes or objects. In this method, on object no longer in use remains allocated and undetected until all available storage has been allocated but are no longer in use once recovered.

Garbage collection is carried out in two phases. In first phase called the marking phase, all nodes that are accessible from an external pointer are marked. The second phase, called the collection phase, involves proceeding sequentially through the memory and freeing all nodes that have not been marked. The second phase is trivial when all nodes are of a fixed size.

3

RECURSION

3.1 INTRODUCTION

Recursion is a programming technique that allows the programmer to express operations in terms of themselves. In C++, this takes the form of a function that calls itself. A useful way to think of recursive functions is to imagine them as a process being performed where one of the instructions is to 'repeat the process'. This makes it sound very similar to a loop because it repeats the same code, and in some ways it is similar to looping. On the other hand, recursion makes it easier to express ideas in which the result of the recursive call is necessary to complete the task. It must be possible for the 'process' to sometimes be completed without the recursive call. One simple example is the idea of building a wall that is ten feet high. If I want to build a ten feet high wall, and then I will first build a 9 feet high wall, and then add an extra foot of bricks. Conceptually, this is like saying the 'build wall' function takes a height and if that height is greater than one, first calls itself to build a lower wall, and then adds one foot of bricks.

3.2 RECURSION

Recursion is a programming technique in which the function calls itself repeatedly for some input. Recursion is a process of doing the same task again and again for some specific input.

Recursion is:

- A way of thinking about problems.
- A method for solving problems.
- Related to mathematical induction.

A method is **recursive** if it can call itself, either **directly**:

```
void f( ) {
 ... f( ) ...
          }
```

or **indirectly**:

```
void f( ) {
 ... g( ) ...
      }
void g( ) {
 ... f( ) ...
      }
```

A recursion is said to be **direct** if a subprogram calls itself. It is **indirect** if there is a sequence of more than one subprogram call which eventually calls the first subprogram: such as a function f calls a function g, which in turn calls the function f.

3.2.1 Recursive Functions

Many mathematical functions can be defined recursively:

- Factorial
- Fibonacci
- Euclid's GCD (greatest common denominator)
- Fourier Transform

Many problems can be solved recursively, games of all types from simple ones like the 'Towers of Hanoi' problem to complex ones like chess. In games, the recursive solutions are particularly convenient because, having solved the problem by a series of recursive calls, you want to find out how you got to the solution.

3.2.2 Factorial Function

One of the simplest examples of a recursive definition is that for the factorial function. For example, if 6 factorial has to be calculated then, it will be = 6*5*4*3*2*1 = 720, which is defined for positive integers N by the equation

$$N! = N \times (N-1) \times (N-2) \times \ldots \times 2 \times 1$$

factorial (n)
if (n = 0) then 1
else
n * factorial(n-1)

A natural way to calculate factorials is to write a recursive function which matches this definition:

```
function factorial(int n)
 {
 if (n == 0) return 1;
 else
 return n*factorial(n-1);
 }
```

Note how this function calls itself to evaluate the next term. Eventually, it will reach the termination condition and exit.

We can trace this computation in the same way that we trace any sequence of function calls.

factorial(6)
  factorial(5)

factorial(4)
 factorial(3)
  factorial(2)
   factorial(1)
    return 1
   return 2*1 = 2
  return 3*2 = 6
 return 4*6 = 24
return 5*24 = 120
return 6*120 = 720

Our `factorial( )` implementation exhibits the two main components that are required for every recursive function.

The base case returns a value without making any subsequent recursive call. It does this for one or more special input values for which the function can be evaluated without recursion. For `factorial( )`, the base case is N = 1.

The reduction step is the central part of a recursive function. It relates the function at one (or more) inputs to the function evaluated at one (or more) other inputs. Furthermore, the sequence of parameter values must converge to the base case. For `factorial()`, the reduction step is N*factorial(N - 1) and N decreases by one for each call, so the sequence of parameter values converges to the base case of N = 1.

A Factorial program in C++

```
#include<iostream.h>
#include<conio.h>
void main()
{
        int n,fact;
        int rec(int); clrscr();
        cout<<"Enter the number:->";
        cin>>n;
        fact=rec(n);
        cout<<endl<<"Factorial Result are:: "<<fact<<endl;
        getch();
}
rec(int x)
{
        int f;
        if(x==1)
                return(x);
        else
        {
                f=x*rec(x-1);
                return(f);
        }
}
```

Output of Program

```
Enter the number :-> 6
Factorial Result are:: 720
```

3.2.3 Fibonacci Function

Another commonly used example of a recursive function is the calculation of Fibonacci numbers. The Fibonacci series is the sequence of integers.

0	1	2	3	4	5	6	7	8	9
0	1	1	2	3	5	8	13	21	34

Each number in this sequence is the sum of two preceding elements. The series can be formed in this way:

0^{th}element + 1^{st}element = 0 + 1 = 1

1^{st}element + 2^{nd}element = 1 + 1 = 2

2^{nd}element + 3^{rd}element = 1 + 2 = 3 so on.

Following the definition:

fibo(n) = if (n = 0) then 1
if (n = 1) then 1
else
fibo(n-1) + fibo(n-2)

We can define the recursive definition of Fibonacci sequence by the recursive function

```
function fibo( int n )
  {
  if ( (n == 0) || (n == 1) ) return 1;
  else
 return fibo(n-1) + fibo(n-2);
  }
```

A Fibonacci program in C++

```
#include<iostream.h>
#include<conio.h>
fibo(int);
void main()
{
 clrscr();
 int n,i;
 cout<<"Enter the total elements in the series : ";
 cin>>n;
 cout<<"\nThe Fibonacci series is:\n";
 for(i=0;i<n;i++)
 {
  cout<<fibo(i)<<" ";
```

```
  }
getch();
}
fibo(int n)
{
 if(n==0)
 return 0;
 else if(n==1)
 return 1;
 else
 return fibo(n-1) + fibo(n-2);
}
```

Output of Program

```
Enter the total elements in the series: 6
The Fibonacci series is:
0 1 1 2 3 5
```

3.2.4 Tail and Head Recursions

If the recursive call occurs at the end of a method, it is called a tail recursion. Tail recursion is similar to loop. The method executes all the statements before jumping into the next recursive call.

If the recursive call occurs at the beginning of a method, it is called a head recursion. The method saves the state before jumping into the next recursive call. Compare these:

```
public void tail(int n)
{
 if(n == 1)
   return;
else
   print(n);
   tail(n-1);
}
```

```
public void tail(int n)
{
 if(n == 0)
   return;
else
   head(n-1);
   Print(n);
}
```

A function with a path with a single recursive call at the beginning of the path uses a head recursion. The factorial function of a previous exhibit uses a head recursion. The first thing it does once it determines that recursion is needed is call itself with the decremented parameter.

A function with a single recursive call at the end of a path uses a tail recursion. Most examples of head and tail recursion can be easily converted into a loop. Most loops will be naturally converted into head or tail recursion.

3.2.5 Differences Between Iteration and Recursions

S.No.	Iteration	Recursion
1.	The iterative methods are more efficient because of better execution speed.	The recursive methods are less efficient.

2.	A recursive problem can be solved iteratively.	Not all problems have recursive solution.
3.	It is a process of executing a statement or a set of statements, until some specified condition is specified.	It is the technique of defining anything in terms of itself.
4.	Memory utilization by iteration is less.	Memory utilization is more in recursion.
5.	It is simple to implement.	It is complex to implement.
6.	The line of code is more when we use iteration.	Recursive methods bring compactness to the program.

3.3 TOWER OF HANOI

The **Tower of Hanoi** (also called the **Tower of Brahma** or **Lucas' Tower** and sometimes pluralized) is a mathematical game or puzzle. The puzzle was first publicized in the West by the French mathematician Édouard Lucas in 1883. There is a history about an Indian temple in Kashi Vishwanath which contains a large room with three time-worn posts in it, surrounded by 64 golden disks. Brahmin priests, acting out the command of an ancient prophecy, have been moving these disks, in accordance with the immutable rules of the Brahma, since that time. The puzzle is therefore also known as the Tower of Brahma puzzle. According to the legend, when the last move of the puzzle will be completed, the world will end. It is not clear whether Lucas invented this legend or was inspired by it. If the legend were true, and if the priests were able to move disks at a rate of one per second, using the smallest number of moves, it would take them $2^{64} - 1$ seconds or roughly 585 billion years or 18, 446, 744, 073, 709, 551, 615 turns to finish, or about 45 times the life span of the sun.

The problem of the 'Towers of Hanoi' consists of three rods, and a number of disks of different sizes which can slide onto any rod. The puzzle starts with the disks in a neat stack in ascending order of size on one rod, the smallest at the top, thus making a conical shape as shown in Figure 3.1.

The objective of the puzzle is to move the entire stack to another rod, obeying the following rules:

- Only one disk may be moved at a time.
- Each move consists of taking the upper disk from one of the rods and sliding it onto another rod, on top of the other disks that may already be present on that rod.
- No disk may be placed on top of a smaller disk.

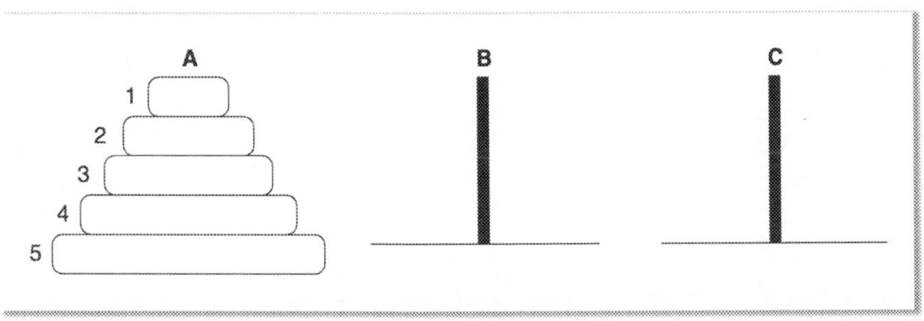

Figure 3.1

The solution of this problem is very simple. The solution can be stated as

1. Move top n-1 disks from A to B using C as auxiliary.
2. Move the remaining disk from A to C.
3. Move the n-1 disks from B to C using A as auxiliary.

The above is a recursive algorithm: to carry out steps 1 and 3, apply the same algorithm again for $n-1$. The entire procedure is a finite number of steps, since at some point the algorithm will be required for $n = 1$. This step, moving a single disc from peg A to peg B, is trivial.

We can convert it to

Move disk 1 from A to B.

Move disk 2 from A to C.

Move disk 1 from B to C.

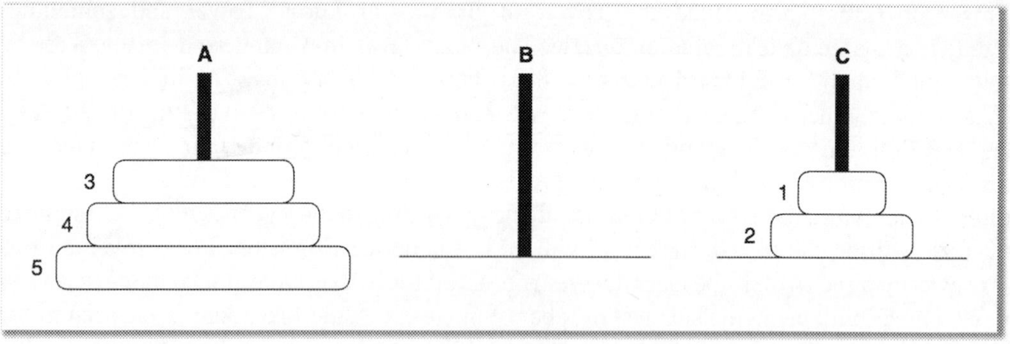

Figure 3.2

Move disk 3 from A to B.

Move disk 1 from C to A.

Move disk 2 from C to B.

Move disk 1 from A to B.

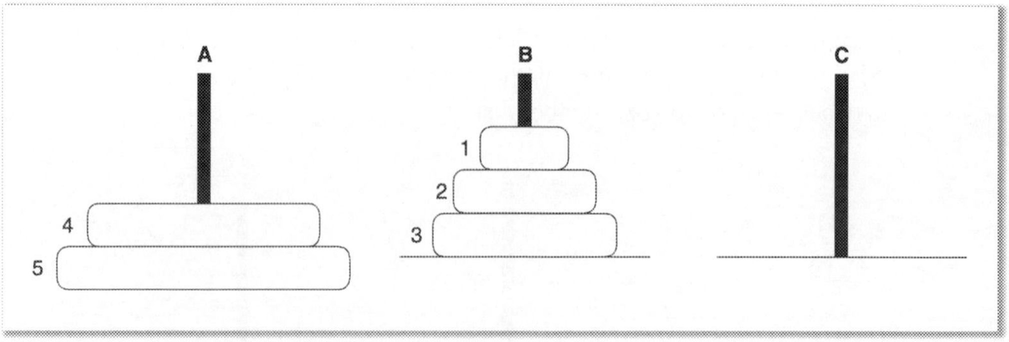

Figure 3.3

Move disk 4 from A to C.
Move disk 1 from B to C.
Move disk 2 from B to A.
Move disk 1 from C to A.
Move disk 3 from B to C.

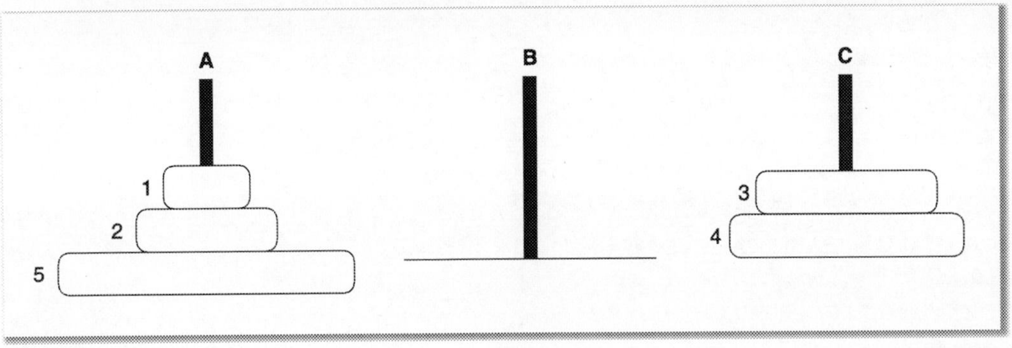

Figure 3.4

Move disk 1 from A to B.
Move disk 2 from A to C.
Move disk 1 from B to C.

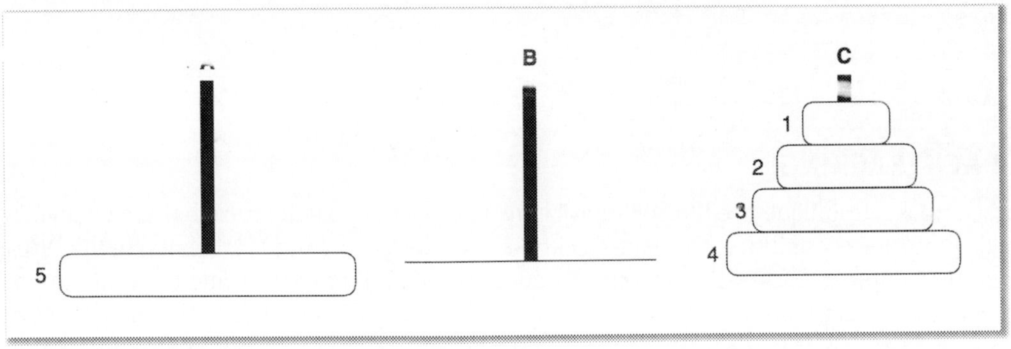

Figure 3.5

Actually we have moved n -1 disk from peg A to C. in the same way we can move the remaining disks from A to C.

Code for Program of Tower of Hanoi in C++

```
#include <iostream.h>
#include <conio.h>
void tower(int a,char from,char aux,char to){
 if(a==1){
```

```
        cout<<"\t\tMove disc 1 from "<<from<<" to "<<to<<"\n";
        return;
    }
    else{
        tower(a-1,from,to,aux);
        cout<<"\t\tMove disc "<<a<<" from "<<from<<" to "<<to<<"\n";
        tower(a-1,aux,from,to);
    }
}
void main(){
        clrscr();
        int n;
        cout<<"\n\t\t*****Tower of Hanoi*****\n";
        cout<<"\t\tEnter number of discs : ";
        cin>>n;
        cout<<"\n\n";
        tower(n,'A','B','C');
        getch();
}
```

Output of Program

```
*****Tower of Hanoi*****
Enter number of discs: 2
Move disk 1 from A to B.
Move disk 2 from A to C.
Move disk 1 from B to C.
```

3.4 BACKTRACKING

Backtracking is a technique used to solve problems with a large search space that systematically tries and eliminates possibilities. The name backtrack was first coined by D.H. Lehmer in the 1950s. A standard example of backtracking would be going through a maze. At some point in a maze, you might have two options of which direction to go. One strategy would be to try going through portion A of the maze. If you get stuck before you find your way out, then you *'backtrack'* to the junction. At this point in time you know that portion A will NOT lead you out of the maze, so you then start searching in portion B. Clearly, at a single junction you could have even more than two choices. The backtracking strategy says to try each choice, one after the other, if you ever get stuck. *'Backtrack'* to the junction and try the next choice. If you try all choices and never find a way out, then there is no solution to the maze.

3.4.1 Eight Queens Problem

The problem is specified as follows:

Find an arrangement of eight queens on a single chess board such that no two queens attack one another. In chess, queens can move all the way down any row, column or diagonal (so long as no pieces are in the way). Due to the first two restrictions, it's clear that each row and column of the board will have exactly one queen.

The backtracking strategy is as follows:

(1) Place a queen on the first available square in row 1.

(2) Move onto the next row, placing a queen on the first available square there (that doesn't conflict with the previously placed queens).

(3) Continue in this fashion until either (a) you have solved the problem, or (b) you get stuck. When you get stuck, remove the queens that got you there, until you get to a row where there is another valid square to try.

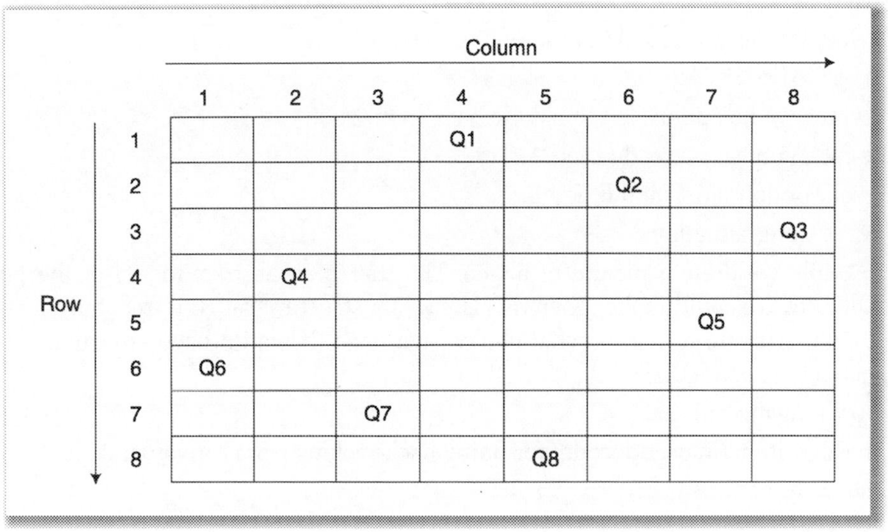

Figure 3.6 8-queen problem.

3.4.2 Backtracking is a Form of Recursion

The usual scenario is that you are faced with a number of options, and you must choose one of these. After you make your choice you will get a new set of options. What set of options you get depends on what choice you made. This procedure is repeated over and over until you reach a final state. If you made a good sequence of choices, your final state is a goal state. If you didn't, it isn't.

Conceptually, you start at the root of a tree. The tree probably has some good leaves and some bad leaves, though it may be that the leaves are all good or all bad. You want to get to a good leaf. At each node, beginning with the root, you choose one of its children to move to, and you keep this up until you get to a leaf.

Suppose you get to a bad leaf. You can backtrack to continue the search for a good leaf by revoking your most recent choice, and trying out the next option in that set of options. If you run out of options, revoke the choice that got you here, and try another choice at that node. If you end up at the root with no options left, there are no good leaves to be found.

This needs an example.

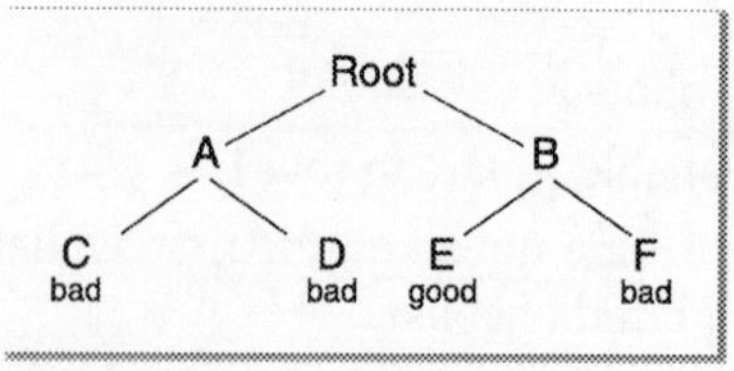

1. Starting at the root, your options are A and B. You choose A.
2. At A, your options are C and D. You choose C.
3. C is bad. Go back to A.
4. At A, you have already tried C, and it failed. Try D.
5. D is bad. Go back to A.
6. At A, you have no options left to try. Go back to the root.
7. At the root, you have already tried A. Try B.
8. At B, your options are E and F. Try E.
9. E is good. Congratulations!

In this example we drew a picture of a tree. The tree is an abstract model of the possible sequences of choices we could make. There is also a data structure called a tree, but usually we don't have a data structure to tell us what choices we have (If we do have an actual tree data structure, backtracking on it is called depth-first tree searching.).

The backtracking algorithm:

Here is the algorithm (in pseudocode) for doing backtracking from a given node n:

```
boolean solve(Node n) {
    if n is a leaf node {
        if the leaf is a goal node, return true
        else return false
 } else {
    for each child c of n {
        if solve(c) succeeds, return true
    }
     return false
  }
}
```

Notice that the algorithm is expressed as a Boolean function. This is essential to understanding the algorithm. If solve(n) is true, that means that node n is part of a solution–that is, node n is one of the nodes on a path from the root to some goal node. We say that n is solvable. If solve(n) is false, then there is no path that includes n to any goal node.

How does this work?

- If any child of n is solvable, then n is solvable.
- If no child of n is solvable, then n is not solvable.

Hence, to decide whether any non-leaf node n is solvable (part of a path to a goal node), all you have to do is test whether any child of n is solvable. This is done recursively, on each child of n. In the above code, this is done by the lines

```
for each child c of n {
    if solve(c) succeeds, return true
}
    return false
```

Eventually, the recursion will 'bottom' out at a leaf node. If the leaf node is a goal node, it is solvable. If the leaf node is not a goal node, it is not solvable. This is our base case. In the above code, this is done by the lines

```
if n is a leaf node {
    if the leaf is a goal node, return true
    else return false
}
```

The backtracking algorithm is simple but important. You should understand it thoroughly. Another way of stating it is as follows:

To search a tree:

1. If the tree consists of a single leaf, test whether it is a goal node,
2. Otherwise, search the subtrees until you find one containing a goal node, or until you have searched them all unsuccessfully.

4

STACK

One of the most useful concepts of data structure in computer science is that of stack. In this chapter, we shall define stack, algorithm and procedures for insertion and deletion and see why stack plays such a prominent role in the area of programming. We shall also describe prefix, postfix and infix expression. The stack method of expression evaluation was first proposed by early German computer scientist F.L. Bauer, who received the IEEE Computer Society Pioneer Award in 1988 for his work on computer stacks.

4.1 DEFINITION AND EXAMPLES

The stack is a kind of ordered list but the access, insertion and deletion of elements are restricted by following certain rules. In a stack, operations are carried out in such a way that the last element which is inserted will be the first one to come out. In computer science, a stack is a data structure that works on the principle of **Last In First Out** or **(LIFO).** This means that the last item put on the stack is the first item that can be taken off, like a physical stack of coins. The coins can be arranged one on another. When we add a new coin it is always placed on the previous coin and while removing the coin the recently placed coin can be removed.

A stack is a linear or non-primitive data structure. It is an ordered list in which addition (insertion) of a new data item and deletion of an already existing data item is done from only one end, called the TOP. Since, all the insertion and deletion in a stack are made from the top of the stack, the last added item will be the first to be removed from the stack.

The most accessible information in a stack is at the top of stack and the least accessible information is at the bottom. When an item is added to a stack, we say that we **push** it onto a stack, and when an item is removed from stack, we say that **pop** it from the stack. For example, if we have to make stack of elements 2, 4, 6, 8, 10, then 2 will be the bottommost element and 10 will be the topmost element in a stack. A stack is shown in Figure 4.1.

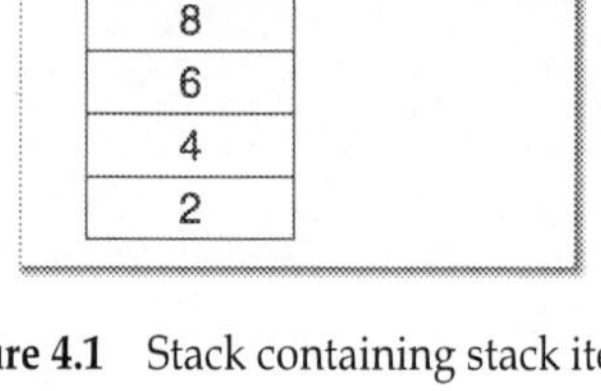

Figure 4.1 Stack containing stack items.

4.2 DATA STRUCTURE OF STACK

A stack is a special case of an ordered list, i.e. it is an ordered list with some restrictions on the way in which we perform various operations on a list to create a stack in the memory. Creation of a stack can be either done by arrays or linked list. It is therefore quite natural to use sequential representation for implementing a stack. We need to define an array of the maximum size. We need an integer variable top which will keep track of the top of the stack as more and more elements are inserted into and deleted from the stack. The declarations in C are as follows.

```
# define size 100
   int stack [size];
   int top = -1;
```

In the above declaration, the stack is nothing but an array of integers. And the most recent index of that array will act as the top.

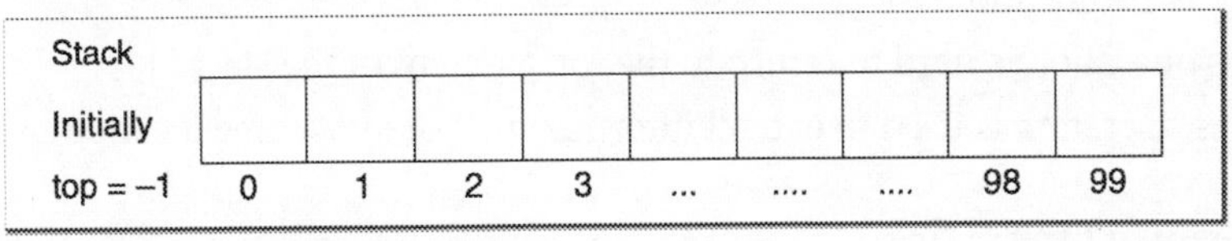

Figure 4.2 Stack using one-dimensional array.

The stack is of the size 100. As we insert the numbers, the top will get incremented. The elements will be placed from 0th position in the stack.

The stack can also used in a database. For example, if we want to store marks of all students of third semester we can declare the structure of the stack as follows:

```
# define size 60
typedef struct student
{
        int rollno;
        char name [30];
        float marks;
} stud;
        stud S1 [size];
        int top = -1;
```

The above stack will look like this

	rollno	name	marks
59			
.			
top = 3 →	40	Mita	66
2	30	Rita	91
1	20	Geeta	88.3
0	10	Sita	75.6

S1

Thus, we can store the data about the whole class in our stack. The above declaration means creation of a stack.

4.2.1 Basic Operations on Stack

The basic operations that we can perform on stack are as follows:

1. **CREATE:** This operation is used to create an empty stack.
2. **PUSH:** This operation is used to the process of inserting a new element to the top of stack. Each time a new element is inserted in the stack, the top is incremented by one before the element is placed on the stack.
3. **POP:** This operation is used to the process of deleting an element from the top of stack. After every pop operation the top is decremented by one.
4. **EMPTY:** This operation is used to check whether the stack is empty or not. It returns a true if the stack is empty and false otherwise.
5. **TOP:** This operation is used to return to the top element of the stack.
6. **PEEP:** This operation is used to extract information stored at some location in a stack.

4.2.2 Stack Empty Operation

Initially the stack is empty. At that time, the top should be initialized to – 1 or 0. If we set the top to – 1 initially then the stack will contain the elements from the 0th position and if we set top to 0 initially, the element will be stored form 1st position in the stack. The stack becomes empty whenever top reaches to – 1.

```
int stackempty ( )
{
 if (top = = -1)//stack empty
 return 1;
else
 return 0;
}
```

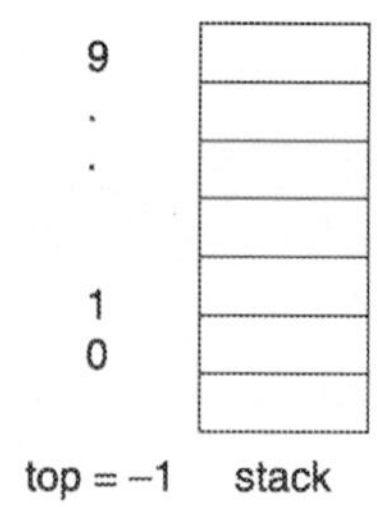

Figure 4.3 Stack empty condition.

Thus stackempty is a Boolean function: if the stack is empty it returns 1 otherwise it returns 0.

4.2.3 Stack Full Operation

In the representation of stack using arrays, the size of an array means the size of the stack. As we go on inserting the elements the stack get filled with the elements. So it is necessary before inserting the elements to check whether the stack is full or not. A stackfull condition is achieved when the stack reaches the maximum size of the array.

```
int stackfull ( )
{
if ( top > = size -1) // stack full
 return 1;
else
  return 0;
}
```

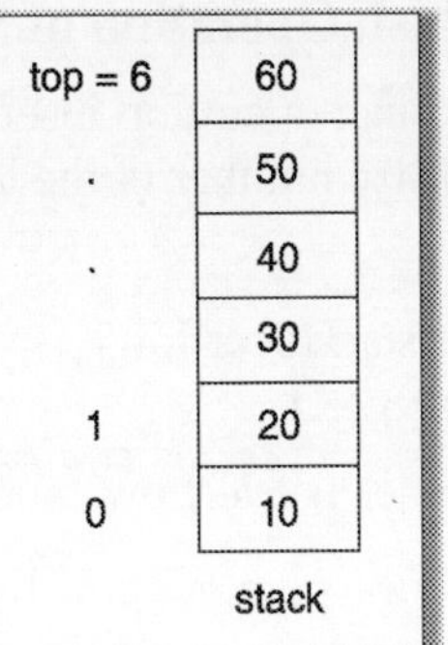

Figure 4.4 Stack full condition.

Thus stackfull is a Boolean function: if the stack is full it returns 1 otherwise it returns 0.

4.2.4 Stack Push Operation

This operation is used to the process of inserting a new element to the top of stack. Each time a new element is inserted in the stack, the top is incremented by one before the element is placed on the stack. The function is as follows:

```
void push (int item)
{
     top= top + 1;
     stack [top] = item;
}
```

The push function takes the parameter **item** which actually is the element which we want to insert into the stack, which means we are pushing the element onto the stack. In the function, we have checked whether the stack is full or not. If the stack is not full then only the insertion of the element can be achieved by means of a push operation.

A push operation can be shown by following Figure 4.5.

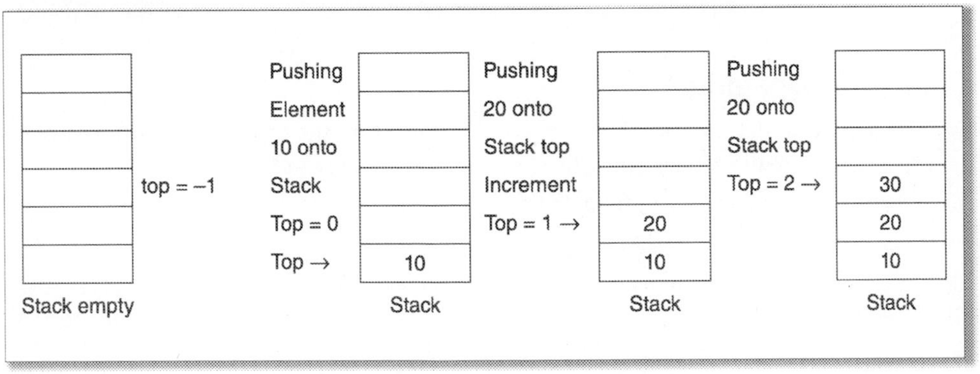

Figure 4.5 Performing push operation.

Algorithm for Push Operation of Stack

The algorithm for push operation inserts an item to the top of a stack, which is represented by S and it contains the size number of the item, with a pointer TOP denoting the position of top-most item in the stack.

Step 1: [Check for stack overflow]
if TOP > = Size -1
Output "Stack is overflow" and exit

Step 2: [Increment the pointer value by one]
TOP = TOP + 1

Step 3: [Perform insertion]
S [TOP] = item

Step 4: Exit

The function for the stackpush operation is as follows –

```
void push ( )
{
int item;
if (top = = (size-1))
{
cout << " the stack is full"<< endl;
}
else
{
cout <<" Enter the element to be pushed" << endl;
cin >> item;
top = top + 1;
S [top] = item;
}
}
```

4.2.5 Stack POP Operation

This operation is used to the process of deleting an element from the top of stack. After every pop operation the top is decremented by one. The function pop is as given below.

Note that always top element can be deleted.

```
void pop ( )
{
   int item;
   item = stack [top] ;
   top= top - 1; }
```

In the choice of pop, it invokes the function 'stackempty' to determine whether the stack is empty or not. If it is empty, then the function generates an error as stack underflow. If not then the pop function returns the element which is at the top of the stack. The value at the top is stored in some variable as an item and it then decrements the value of the top.

The pop operation can be shown by following Figure 4.6.

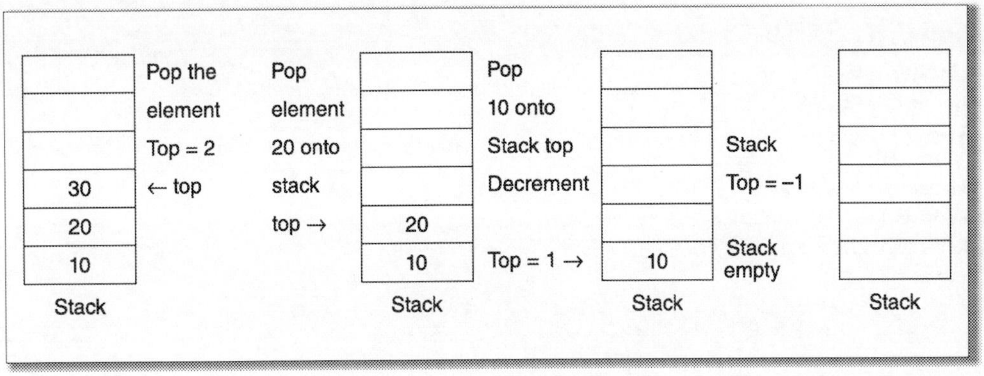

Figure 4.6 Performing a pop operation.

Algorithm for Pop Operation of Stack

The algorithm for a pop operation deletes an item from the top of a stack, which is represented by S and contains the size number of the item, with a pointer TOP denoting the position of the top-most item in the stack.

Step 1: [Check for stack underflow]
if TOP = -1
Output "Stack is underflow" and exit

Step 2: [Perform deletion]
item = S [TOP]

Step 3: [Decrement the pointer value by one]
TOP = TOP - 1

Step 4: Exit

The function for the stackpush operation is as follows –

```
void pop ( )
{
int item;
if (top = = -1))
{
cout << " the stack is empty"<< endl;
}
else
```

```
{
item = S [top];
top = top - 1;
}
}
```

Program

```
# include<iostream.h>
# include<conio.h>
# define Maxsize 10
   void push( );
   int pop( );
   void traverse( );
   int top=-1;
   int stack[Maxsize];
   void main()
{
  int choice;
  char ch;
do
{
 clrscr ( );
 cout <<"1.Push"<<endl;
 cout <<"2.Pop"<<endl;
 cout <<"3.Traverse"<<endl;
 cout <<"enter your choice"<<endl;
 cin >> choice;
 switch(choice)
{
case 1: push();
        break;
case 2:
          cout  <<"The deleted element is"<<endl<<pop( );
          break;
case 3:
         traverse();
         break;
default:
         cout<<"your wrong choice"<<endl;
}
       cout<<"Do u wish to continue pres Y"<<endl;
      cin >>ch;
}
while (ch=='Y'|| ch=='Y');
}
  void push( )
{
     int item;
if(top==(Maxsize-1))
{
```

```
    cout<<"stack is full";
}
else
{
    cout<<"Enter the element to be inserted"<<endl;
    cin>>item;
    top=top+1;
    stack[top]=item;
}
}
   int pop()
{
   int item;
if(top==-1)
{
   cout<<"The stack is empty"<<endl;
}
else
{
    item=stack[top];
    top=top-1;
}
return (item);
}
   void traverse( )
{
    int i;
    if(top==-1)
{
    cout<<"The stack is empty";
}
else
{
    for(i=top;i>=0;i--)
{
    cout<<"Traverse the Element="<<stack[i];
    cout<<endl;
}
}
}
```

Output

```
1. Push
2. Pop
3. Traverse
Enter your Choice 1
Enter the element to be inserted
 19 21 23
```

```
1. Push
2. Pop
3. Traverse
Enter your Choice 3
Traverse the Element= 19 21 23
```

4.3 DISADVANTAGES OF STACK

1. The insertion and deletion of element can be performed by only one end.
2. The element being inserted first has to wait for longest time to get popped off.
3. Only the element at the top can be deleted at a time.

4.4 APPLICATIONS OF STACK

Various applications of stack are

1. Expression conversion
2. Expression evaluation
3. Parsing well formed parenthesis
4. Decimal to binary conversion
5. Reversing a string
6. Storing function calls
7. Recursion
8. Stack machine

4.5 EXPRESSIONS (POLISH NOTATION)

The method of writing the operators of an expression either before their operands or after them is called the **polish notation**. An expression is a string of operands and operators. Operands are some numeric values and operators are two types: unary operators and binary operators. Unary operators are '+' and '-' and binary operators are '+', '-', '*', '/' and exponential. In general, there are three types of expressions:

1. Infix Expression
2. Postfix Expression
3. Prefix Expression

One of the applications of stack is conversion of the expression. First of all, let us see these expressions with the help of examples:

1. Infix Expression:

When the operators exist between two operands then the expression is called an infix expression.

Infix expression = operand1 operator operand2

For example: 1. (A+B)

2. (A+B) * (C-D)

2. Prefix Expression:

When the operators are written before their operands then the expression is called a prefix expression.

Prefix expression = operator operand1 operand2

For example: 1. (+AB)

2. * +AB - CD

3. Postfix Expression:

When the operators are written after their operands then the expression is called a postfix expression.

Postfix expression = operand1 operand2 operator

For example: 1. (AB+)

2. AB + CD - *

4.5.1 Conversion from Infix to Postfix Expression

Algorithm

1. Read the infix expression for left to right, one character at a time.
2. If the input symbol read is an operand then place it in the postfix expression.
3. If the input symbol is an operator then:
   (a) Check if the priority of the operator in the stack is greater than the priority of the incoming (or input read) operator. If yes, then pop that operator from the stack and place it in the postfix expression. Repeat Step 3(a) till we get the operator in the stack which has a greater priority than the incoming operator.
   (b) Otherwise push the operator being read, onto the stack.
   (c) If we read the input operator as ')' then pop all the operators until we get '(' and append the popped operators to the postfix expression. Finally just pop '('.
1. Finally pop the remaining contents from the stack until the stack becomes empty. Append them to the postfix expression.
2. Print the postfix expression as a result.

The conversion of the given expression to postfix expression is as follows –

A - B - (C * D - F/ G) * E

= A - B - (C * D - FG/) * E

= A - B - (C D* - FG/) * E

= A - B - (C D* FG/-) * E

= A - B - C D* FG/- E*

= A - B C D* FG/- E* -

= A B C D* F G / - E * - - // this is a postfix expression of a given infix expression.

Using the given algorithm convert the given infix expression to a postfix expression.

Input character read	Stack	Postfix
A	Empty	A
–	–	A
B	–	AB
–	- -	AB
(	- - (	AB
C	- - (	ABC
*	- - (*	ABC
D	- - (*	ABCD
–	- - (-	ABCD*
F	- - (-	ABCD*F
/	- - (-/	ABCD*F
G	- - (-/	ABCD*FG
)	- -	ABCD*FG/-
*	- - *	ABCD*FG/-
E	- - *	ABCD*FG/-E
)	empty	ABCD*FG/- * - -

4.5.2 Conversion from Infix to Prefix Expression

Algorithm

1. Reverse the infix expression.
2. Read this reversed expression from left to right, one character at a time.
3. If the input symbol being read is an operand then place it in the prefix expression.
4. If the input symbol read is an operand then
   (a) Check if the priority of the operator in the stack is greater than the priority of the incoming (or input) operator from stack and place it in the prefix expression. Repeat Step 4(a) till we get the operator in the stack which has a greater priority than the incoming operator.
   (b) Otherwise push the operator being read.
   (c) If we read '(' as input symbol then pop all the operators until we get ')' and append the popped operator to the prefix expression.
1. Finally pop the reaming contents of the stack and append them to the prefix expression.
2. Reverse the obtained prefix expression and print it as a result.

Example: Convert the infix expression (a + b) * (c – d) into an equivalent prefix form.

Step 1: (a + b) * (c – d) must be reversed first. So we get) d – c – (*) b + a (. Now we will read each character from left to right one at a time.

) d – c – (*) b + a (operator) is read push it onto the stack

Input character read	Stack	Prefix
)	)	
d	)	d
–	) –	d
c	) –	dc
(	pop all content until get)	dc –
*	*	dc –
)	*)	dc –
b	*)	dc – b
+	*) +	dc –b
a	*) +	dc – ba
(	pop all content until get)	dc – ba + *

Now reverse the prefix expression. It will * + ab – cd. Print it as a result.

4.5.3 Conversion from Postfix to Infix Expression

Algorithm

1. Read the prefix expression from left to right, one character at a time.
2. If we read the operand then push it onto the stack.
3. If we read the operator then pop the first operand and concatenate it with '(', call it as str1. Then pop the second operand and concatenate it with str1, call it as str2. And then concatenate str2 with ')'. Thus and infix expression '(operand 1 operator operand 2' gets performed. Push this expression onto stack.
4. Go to Step1 until the complete input is read.

For example: Convert the postfix expression ab + cb - * into equivalent infix form.

Input character	Operation	Stack
a	Read the operand push the stack	a
b	Read the operand push the stack	ab
+	The operator is read then pop two operands and form an infix	(a + b)
c	Read the operand push the stack	(a + b) c

d	Read the operand push the stack	(a + b) c d
–	The operator is read then pop two operands and form an infix	(a + b) (c + d)
*	The operator is read then pop two operands and form an infix	(a + b) * (c + d)

4.5.4 Conversion from Postfix to Prefix Expression

Algorithm

1. Read the prefix expression from left to right, one character at a time.
2. If we read the operand then push it onto the stack.
3. If we read the operator then pop two operands. Call the first popped operand as OP2 and second popped operand as OP1 from the expression 'Operator OP1 OP2'. Then push this string onto the stack. Call this expression as the prefix expression.
4. Go to Step 1 until the complete input is read.

Example: Convert the postfix expression ab + cb – * into equivalent prefix form.

Input character	Operation	Stack
a	Read the operand push the stack	a
b	Read the operand push the stack	ab
+	The operator is read then pop two operands and concatenate + with OP1 and OP2	+ a b
c	Read the operand push the stack	+ a b c
d	Read the operand push the stack	+ a b c d
–	The operator is read then pop two operands and concatenate - with OP1 and OP2	+ a b – c d
*	The operator is read then pop two operands and concatenate * with OP1 and OP2	*+ a b – c d

4.6 EVALUATION OF POSTFIX EXPRESSION

Algorithm

1. Read the postfix expression from left to right, one character at a time.
2. If we read the operand then push it onto the stack.
3. If we read the operator then pop two operands. Call the first popped operand as OP2 and second popped operand as OP1. Perform an arithmetic operation. If the operator is

   + then result = OP1 + OP2

   – then result = OP1 – OP2

   * then result = OP1 * OP2

   / then result = OP1/OP2

↑ then result = OP1 ↑ OP2 so on.

4. Push the result onto the stack.
5. Repeat Steps 1-4 till the postfix expression is not over.

Example: The postfix expression is

3 2 ↑ 5 * 3 2 * 3 – / 5 +

Input symbol	OP1	OP2	Result	Stack
3	3			3
2		2		3,2
↑	3	2	9	9
5				9,5
*	9	5	45	45
3				45,3
2				45,3,2
*	3	2	6	45,6
3				45,6,3
–	6	3	3	45,3
/	45	3	15	15
5				15,5
+	15	5	20	20

The result of this postfix expression is 20.

4.7 DECIMAL TO BINARY CONVERSION

Let us take some decimal number as 8. Now its binary equivalent can be obtained by using a stack. What we can do is that just go on dividing that number by 2, and whatever is the remainder store it onto the stack. And, finally, pop the element from the stack and print it.

Divided by	Number	Remainder
2	8	0
2	4	0
2	2	0
2	1	1

Now stack is

stack
1
0
0
0

4.8 REVERSING THE STRING

To reverse a string a stack can be used. The simple mechanism is to push all the characters of a string onto the stack and then pop all the characters from the stack and print them. For example, if the input string is

P	R	O	G	R	A	M	\0

then push all the characters onto the stack till '\0' is encountered.

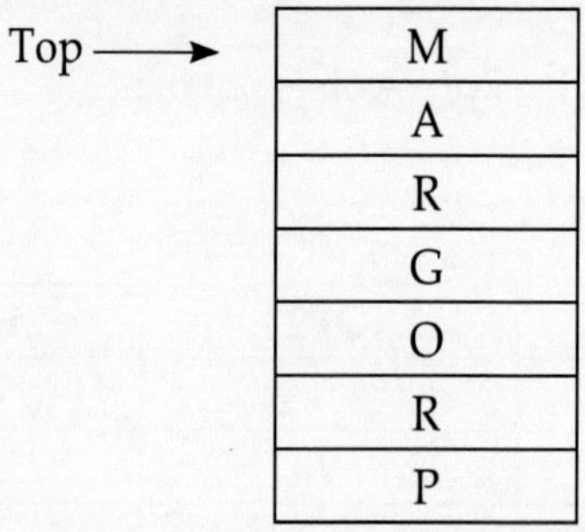

Now if we pop each character from the stack and print it we get,

M	A	R	G	O	R	P

This is a reversed string.

5

QUEUE

5.1 INTRODUCTION

A queue is a linear data structure in which additions are made only at one end of the list and from the other end of the queue you can delete the elements. The queue can be formally defined as an ordered collection of elements that has two ends named as **front** and **rear.** From the front end one can delete the elements and from the rear end one can insert the elements. This is a first in first out (FIFO) list since an element, once added to the rear of the list, can be removed only when all the earlier additions have been removed.

Example:

When a receptionist makes a list of the names of patients who arrive to see a doctor, adding each new name at the front of the list and crossing the top name off the list as a patient is called in, her list of names has the structure of a queue. The word 'queue' is also used in many other everyday examples. The typical example can be a queue of people who wait for railway ticket a ticket counter at a railway station. Any new person joins at one end of the queue. You can call it as the rear end. When one person gets ticket at the other end first, you can call it as the front end of the queue.

Figure 5.1 represents the queue of a few elements.

10	30	35	21	55	11	61
Front						Rear

Figure 5.1 Queue structure.

A queue is a linear list where additions and deletions may take place at either end of the list, but never in the middle. A queue which is both input-restricted and output-restricted must be either a stack or a queue.

5.2 OPERATIONS ON QUEUE

As we have seen, queue is nothing but a collection of items. Both the ends of the queue have their own functionality. The queue is also called as FIFO i.e. a first in first out data structure. All the elements in the queue are stored sequentially. Various operations on the queue are:

1. Create a queue
2. Check whether a queue is full or queue overflow.
3. Insertion of an element into the queue (at the rear).
4. Check whether a queue is empty or queue underflow.
5. Deletion of an element into the queue (at the front).
6. Read the front of an queue.
7. Display (print) of the queue.

5.3 STATIC IMPLEMENTATION OF QUEUE

If a queue is implemented by static means using arrays, we must be sure about the exact number of elements to be stored in the queue. A queue has two pointers, **front** and **rear**, pointing to the front and rear elements of the queue, respectively.

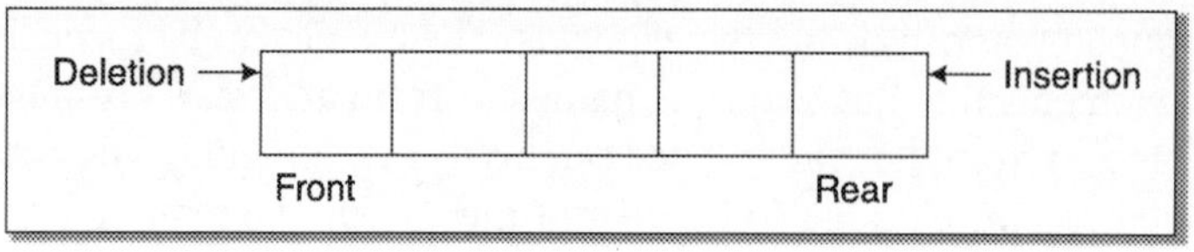

Figure 5.2

In this case, the beginning of the array will become the front for the queue and the last location of the array will act as rear for the queue. The total number of elements present in the queue is

Front – rear + 1

Let us consider that there only 10 elements in the queue at present as shown in Figure 5.3 (a). When we remove an element from the queue, we get the resulting queue as shown in Figure 5.3 (b) and when we insert an element in the queue we get the resulting queue as shown in Figure 5.3 (c). When an element is removed from the queue, the value of the front pointer is increased by 1 i.e.,

Front = Front + 1

Similarly, when an element is added to the queue the value of the rear pointer is increased by 1 i.e.,

Rear = Rear + 1

If rear < front then there will be no element in the queue or the queue will always be empty.

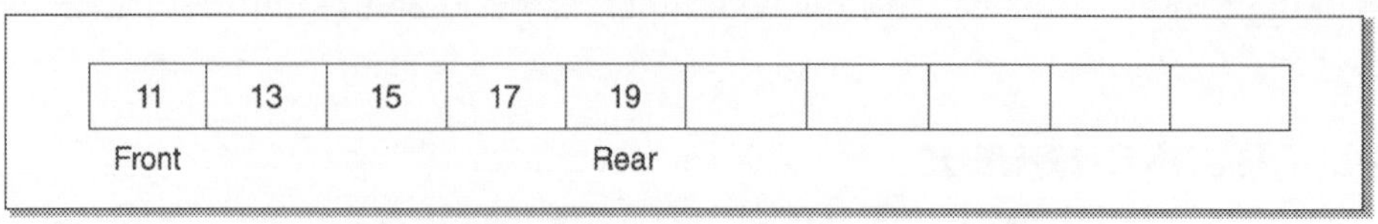

Figure 5.3(a) Queue in memory.

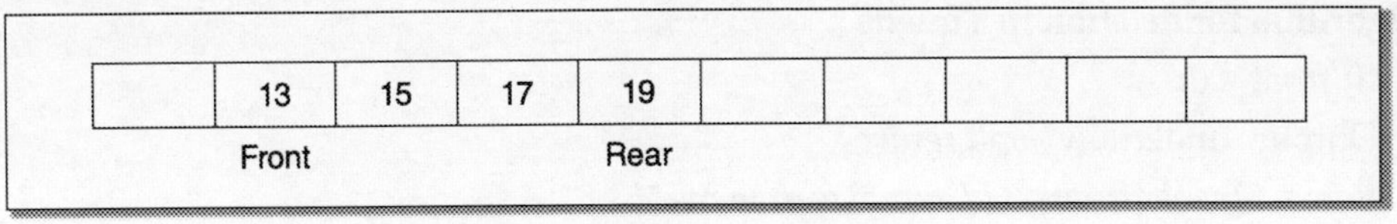

Figure 5.3(b) Queue after deleting the first element.

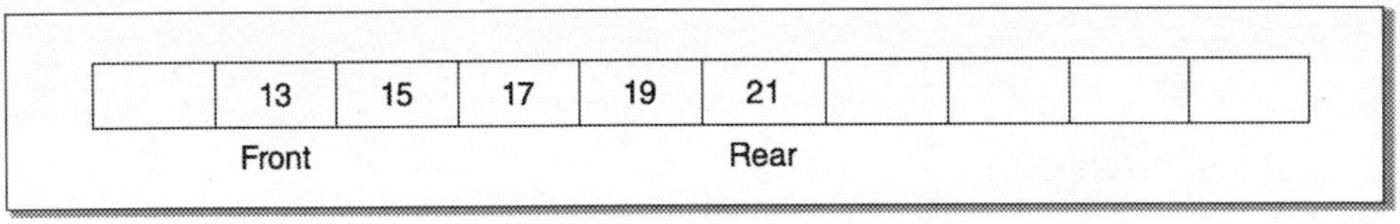

Figure 5.3(c) Queue after inserting an element.

5.3.1 Concept of Queue as ADT

AbstractDataType queue {

Instance:

A queue is a collection of elements in which an element can be inserted form one end called rear and elements get deleted from the other end called front.

Operation

Q_full() – checks whether a queue is full or not.

Q_Empty() – checks whether a queue is empty or not.

Q_insert () – insert the element in a queue from the rear end.

Q_delete () – delete an element in queue from the front end.

Thus, the ADT for a queue gives the abstract for what has to be implemented, which are the various operations on the queue. But it never specifies how to implement these operations.

5.3.2 Algorithms for Operation on Queue

Let a queue be an array of size MAXSIZE, then the insertion and deletion algorithms are as follows:

1. **Algorithm for insertion in a queue**

   (a) If Rear > = MAXSIZE

   Output "overflow" and return

   else

   Set Rear = Rear + 1

   (b) Queue [rear] = item // insert an item

   (c) If Front = -1 // set the front pointer

   Then Front = 0

   (d) Return

2. Algorithm for deletion in a queue

(a) If (front < 0)
    Output "underflow" and return
(b) Item = Queue [front] // remove an item
(c) If (Front = rear) // set the front pointer
    Then Front = 0
        Rear = – 1
    Else
        Front = front +1
(d) Return

Program for operation on queue in C++

```
#include<iostream.h>
#include<conio.h>
#include<stdlib.h>
using namespace std;

class queue
{
            int queue1[5];
            int rear,front;
      public:
            queue()
              {
                    rear=-1;
                    front=-1;
              }
            void insert(int x)
             {
                  if(rear >  4)
                   {
                      cout <<"queue over flow";
                      front=rear=-1;
                      return;
                   }
                   queue1[++rear]=x;
                   cout <<"inserted" <<x;
             }
            void delet()
             {
                  if(front==rear)
                    {
```

```
                    cout <<"queue under flow";
                    return;
                }
                cout <<"deleted" <<queue1[++front];
            }
        void display()
         {
             if(rear==front)
               {
                   cout <<" queue empty";
                   return;
               }
             for(int i=front+1;i<=rear;i++)
             cout <<queue1[i]<<" ";
         }
};
main()
{
     int ch;
     queue qu;
     while(1)
       {
         cout <<"\n1.Insert  2.Delete  3.Display  4.Exit\nEnter ur choice";
           cin >> ch;
           switch(ch)
             {
               case 1:   cout <<"enter the element";
                             cin >> ch;
                         qu.insert(ch);
                         break;
               case 2:  qu.delet();  break;
               case 3:  qu.display();break;
               case 4: exit(0);
               }
         }
return (0);
}
```

Output

```
1.Insert 2.Delete 3.Display 4. Exit
Enter ur choice1
enter the element21
```

```
inserted21
1.Insert 2.Delete 3.Display 4.Exit
Enter ur choice1
Enter the element22
inserted22
1.Insert 2.Delete 3.Display 4.Exit
Enter ur choice1
enter the element16
inserted16
1.Insert 2.Delete 3.Display 4.Exit
Enter ur choice3
21 22 16
1.Insert 2.Delete 3.Display 4.Exit
Enter ur choice2
deleted21
1.Insert 2.Delete 3.Display 4.Exit
Enter ur choice3
22 16
1.Insert 2.Delete 3.Display 4.Exit
Enter ur choice
```

5.4 CIRCULAR QUEUE

As we have seen, in case of linear queue the elements get deleted logically. This can be shown by following Figure 5.4.

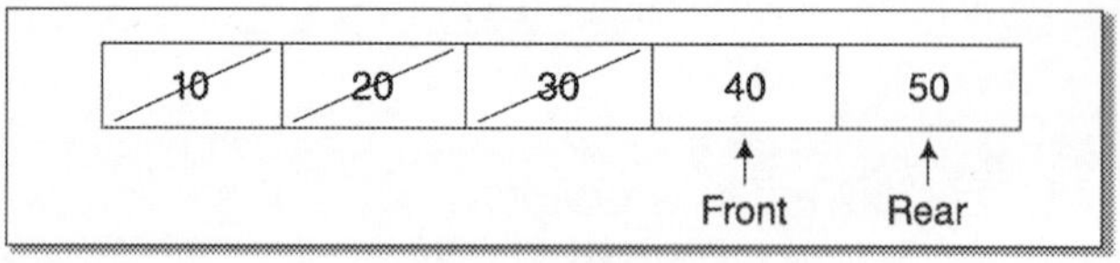

Figure 5.4 Linear queue.

We have deleted the elements 10, 20 and 30 means simply the front pointer is shifted ahead. We will consider a queue from the front to the rear always. And now if we try to insert any more elements then it won't be possible as it is going to give 'queue full' message. Although there is a space occupied by elements 10, 20 and 30 (these are the deleted elements), we cannot utilize them because the queue is nothing but a linear array.

This brings us to the concept or circular queue. The main advantage of a circular queue is that we can utilize the space of the queue fully. A circular queue shown in Figure 5.5.

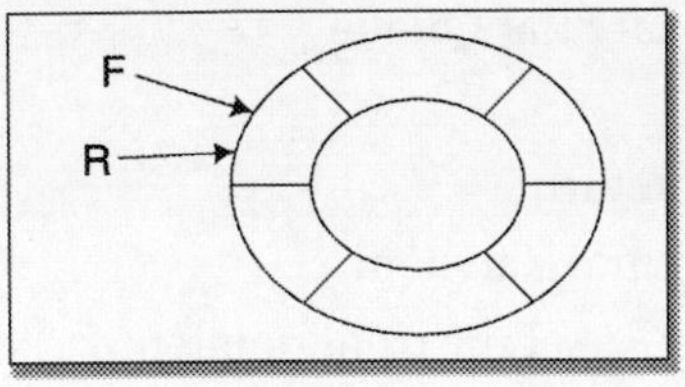

Figure 5.5 Circular queue.

A circular queue has a front and rear to keep the track of the elements to be deleted and inserted. The following assumption are made:

1. The front will always be pointing to the first element.
2. If front = rear, the queue is empty.
3. When a new element is inserted into the queue the rear is incremented by one (Rear = Rear + 1).
4. When an element is deleted from the queue the front is incremented by one (Front = Front +1).

Insertion in a circular queue will be the same as with a linear queue, but it is required to keep a track of front and rear with some extra logic. If a new element is to be inserted in the queue, the position of the element to be inserted will be calculated using the relation:

Rear = (Rear + 1) % MAXSIZE

If we add an element 30 to the queue the rear is calculated as follows:

Rear = (Rear + 1) % MAXSIZE
= (2 + 1) % 5
= 3

The deletion method for a circular queue also requires some modification as compared to a linear queue. The position of the front will be calculated by the relation:

Front = (Front + 1) % MAXSIZE

5.4.1 Algorithms for Operation on Circular Queue

Let a queue be an array of size MAXSIZE. The insertion and deletion algorithms are as follows:

1. **Algorithm for insertion in a Circular Queue**

   (a) If (front = = ((Rear + 1) % MAXSIZE)
   Output "overflow" and exit
   else
   take the value

   (b) If (front = = -1)
   Set front = rear = 0;
   Rear = (Rear + 1) % MAXSIZE

   (c) Queue [rear] = value
   End if
   exit

2. Algorithm for deletion in a Circular Queue

(a) If (front = = -1)
Output "underflow" and return

(b) Item = Queue [front] // remove an item

(c) If (Front = = rear) // set the front pointer
Then Front = –1
Rear = –1
Else
Front = (Front +1) % MAXSIZE
Exit

5.5 D-QUEUE (DOUBLE ENDED QUEUE)

In a linear queue, for insertion of elements we use one end called rear and for deletion of elements we use another end called front. But in a double-ended queue or D-queue the insertion and deletion operations are performed from both the ends. That means it is possible to insert the elements at the rear as well as at the front. Similarly, it is possible to delete the elements from the front as well as from the rear.

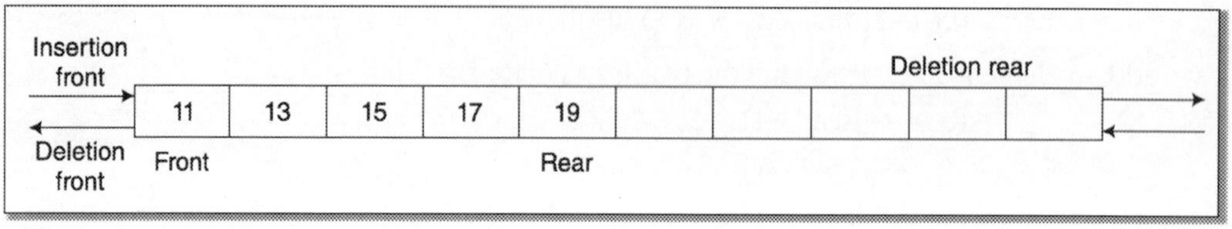

Figure 5.6 D-Queue.

There exists two variations of D-Queue

1. Input-restricted D-Queue
2. Output-restricted D-Queue.

Input restricted D-Queue: Input-restricted D-Queue allows insertion of an element at only one end, but it allows the deletion of an element at both of ends.

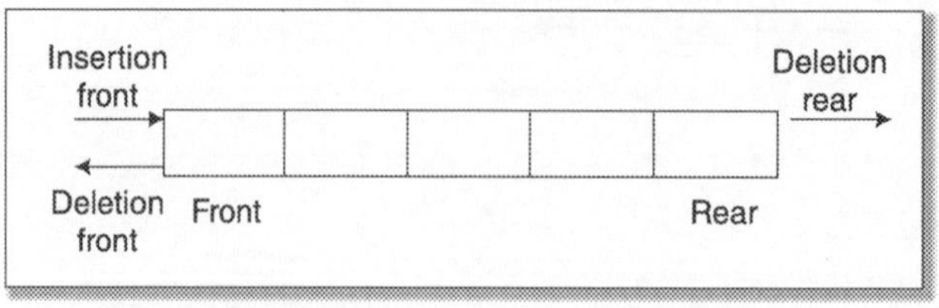

Figure 5.6(a) Input-restricted D-Queue.

Output-restricted D-Queue: Output-restricted D-Queue allows deletion of an element at only one end, but it allows the insertion of an element at both the ends.

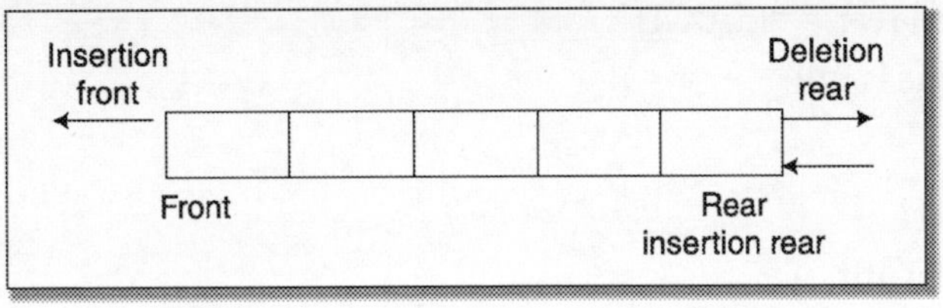

Figure 5.6(b) Output-restricted D-Queue.

In D-queue, if the element is inserted from the 'front-end' then the 'front' is decreased by 1. If it is inserted at the 'rear-end' then the rear is increased by 1. If the element is deleted from the front-end, then the front is increased by 1. If the element is deleted from the rear-end, then the rear is decreased by 1. When the front is equal to the rear before deletion then front and rear are both set to NULL to indicate that the queue is empty.

ADT for D-queue

Instances:

Deq[MAX] is a finite collection of elements in which the elements can be inserted from both the ends, rear and front. Similarly, the elements can be deleted from both the ends, front and rear.

Precondition

The front and rear should be within the maximum size MAX.

Before an insertion operation, whether the queue is full or not is checked.

Before a deletion operation, whether the queue is empty or not is checked.

Operation

1. Create ( ): The D-queue is created by declaring the data structure for it.
2. Insert_rear ( ): This operation is used for inserting the element from the rear end.
3. Delete_front ( ): This operation is used for deleting the element from the front end.
4. Insert_front ( ): This operation is used for inserting the element from the front end.
5. Delete_rear ( ): This operation is used for deleting the element from the rear end.
6. Display ( ): The elements of the queue can display from the front to the rear end.

Algorithm for DQEmpty

1. [check for empty Deque]
   If (front = = 0 and rear = =1)
   Then print "deque is empty"
2. [finished]
   Return

Algorithm for DQFull

1. [check for full Deque]
   If (front = = 0 and rear = =MAX-1)
2. Then print "deque is full"
   [finished]
   Return

Algorithm for insertFront

1. [If (front = = 0 and rear = =MAX-1)
   Then print "deque is full" and return
   Else
      front = front -1
      Deque [front] = value
2. Return.

5.6 PRIORITY QUEUE

The priority queue is a data structure having a collection of elements which are associated with a specific ordering. There are two types of priority queues:

1. Ascending priority queue
2. Descending priority queue

Ascending priority queue: It is a collection of items in which the items can be inserted arbitrarily but only the smallest element can be removed.

Descending priority queue: It is a collection of items in which the items can be inserted arbitrarily but only the largest element can be removed.

In a priority queue, the elements are arranged in any order and out of which only the smallest or largest element are allowed to be deleted each time.

ADT for Priority Queue

Various operations that can be performed on priority queue are:

1. Insertion
2. Deletion
3. Display

Instances

P_que[MAX] is a finite collection of elements associated with some priority

Precondition:

- The front and rear should be within the maximum size MAX.
- Before an insertion operation, whether the queue is full or not is checked.
- Before a deletion operation, whether the queue is empty or not is checked.

Operations

1. Create ( ) – The queue is created by declaring the data structure for it.
2. Insert ( ) – An element can be inserted in the queue.
3. Delete ( ) – If the priority queue is an ascending priority queue then only the smallest element is deleted each time.
4. Display ( ) – The elements of a queue are displayed from the front to rear.

Applications of Priority Queue

- In network communication, a priority queue is used to manage limited bandwidth for transmission.
- In simulation modeling, a priority queue is used to manage the discrete events.

5.7 APPLICATIONS OF QUEUE

Typical uses of queues are in simulations and operating systems.

- Operating systems often maintain a queue of processes that are ready to execute or that are waiting for a particular event to occur.
- Computer systems must often provide a 'holding area' for messages between two processes, two programs, or even two systems. This holding area is usually called a 'buffer' and is often implemented as a queue.
- Destination queues – Any queue that the sending application sends messages to or that the receiving application reads messages from.
- Administration queues – Queues used for acknowledgment messages returned by message queuing or connector applications.
- Response queues – Queues used by receiving applications to return response messages to the sending application.
- Report queues – Queues used to store report messages returned by message queuing.

Software queues have counterparts in real-world queues. We wait in queues to buy pizza, to enter movie theaters, to drive on a turnpike, and to ride on a roller coaster. Another important application of the queue data structure is to help us simulate and analyze such real-world queues.

6

LIST

6.1 LIMITATIONS OF STATIC MEMORY

Static memory allocation is done by arrays. In arrays the elements are stored sequentially. The elements can be accessed sequentially as well as randomly when we use arrays. But there are some drawbacks or limitations of using arrays as given below.

1. Once the elements are stored sequentially, it becomes very difficult to insert the element in between or to delete the middle elements. This is because, if we insert some element in between then we will have to shift down the adjacent elements. Similarly, if we delete some element from an array, then a vacant space gets created in the array. And we do not desire such vacant spaces in between in the arrays. Thus shifting of elements is time consuming and is not logical. The ultimate result is that the use of array makes the overall representation time and space inefficient.
2. Use of array requires determining the array size prior to its use. There are some chances that the pre-decided size of the array might be larger than the requirement. Similarly it might be possible that the size of array may be less than the required one. This results in either wastage of memory or shortage of memory. Hence, another data structure has come up which is known as linked list. This is basically a dynamic implementation.

6.2 LISTS

Lists, like arrays, are used to store ordered data. A list is a linear sequence of data objects of the same type. Real-life events such as people waiting to be served at a bank counter or at a railway reservation counter may be implemented using list structures. In computer science, lists are extensively used in database management systems, in process management systems, in operating systems, in editors, etc.

We shall discuss lists such as singly, doubly and circularly linked lists, and their implementation; using arrays and pointers.

In computer science, a list is usually defined as an instance of an abstract data type (ADT) formalizing the concept of an ordered collection of entities. For example, a single linked-list, with 3 integer values is shown in Figure 6.1.

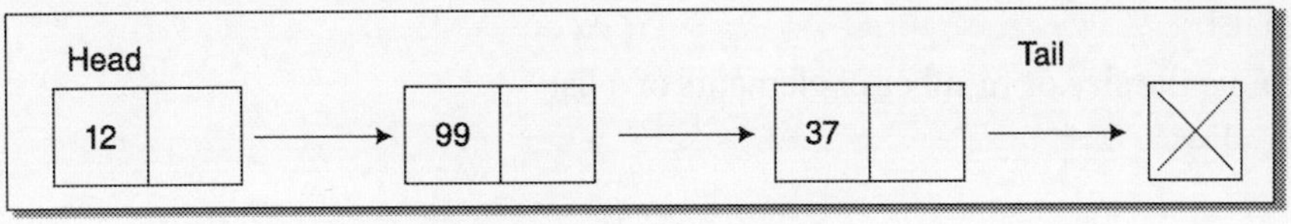

Figure 6.1 A single linked list.

In practice, lists are usually implemented using arrays or linked lists of some sort, as lists share certain properties with arrays and linked lists. Informally, the term list is sometimes used synonymously with linked list.

A linear list is an ordered set consisting of a variable number of elements to which addition and deletion can be made. A linear list displays the relationship of physical adjacency. The first element of a list is called **head** and the last element is called **tail** of the list. The next element to the head of list is called its **successor**. The previous element to the tail of the list is called its **predecessor**. A head does not have successor. Any other element of list has both one successor and one predecessor.

6.3 CHARACTERISTICS

Lists have the following properties:

- The size and contents of lists may or may not vary at runtime, depending on the implementations.
- Random access over lists may or may not be possible, depending on the implementation.
- In mathematics, sometimes equality of lists is defined simply in terms of object identity: two lists are equal if and only if they are the same object.
- In modern programming languages, equality of lists is normally defined in terms of structural equality of the corresponding entries, except that if the lists are typed then the list types may also be relevant.
- In a list, there is a linear order (called followed by or next) defined on the elements. Every element (except for one called the last element) is followed by one other element, and no two elements are followed by the same element.

6.4 OPERATIONS OF LIST

Following are some of the basic operations that may be performed on lists:

- Create a list
- Check for an empty list
- Search for an element in a list
- Search for a predecessor or a successor of an element of a list
- Delete an element at a specified location of a list
- Add an element at a specified location of a list
- Retrieve an element from a list
- Update an element of a list
- Sort a list

- Print a list
- Determine the size or number of elements of a list
- Delete a list

6.5 LINKED LIST

What are the drawbacks of using sequential storage to represent stacks and queues? One major drawback is that a fixed amount of storage remains allocated to the stack or queue. Even the structure actually uses a smaller amount or possibly no storage at all. Further, no more than that the fixed amount of storage may be allocated, thus introducing the possibility of overflow.

Linked lists were developed in 1955-56 by Allen Newell, Cliff Shaw and Herbert Simon at RAND Corporation as the primary data structure for their Information Processing Language. IPL was used by the authors to develop several early artificial intelligence programs, including the Logic Theory Machine, the General Problem Solver, and a computer chess program. The problem of machine translation for natural language processing led Victor Yngve at Massachusetts Institute of Technology (MIT) to use linked lists as data structures in his COMIT programming language for computer research in the field of linguistics. A report on this language entitled "A Programming Language for Mechanical Translation" appeared in *Mechanical Translation* in 1958.

In computer science, a linked list is one of the fundamental data structures used in computer programming. It is an example of a linear data structure. A linked list or single-way list is a linear collection of data elements, called nodes. The logical ordering is represented by having each element pointing to the next element.

A linked list is a set of nodes where each node has two fields – an information or data and link or next address field. The 'data' field stores the actual piece of information, which may be an integer, a character, a string or even a large record, and 'link' field is used to point to the next node. The entire linked list is accessed from an external pointer pointing to the very first node in the list. Basically, the 'link' field is nothing but address only.

Figure 6.2 Structure of node.

Hence link list of integer 20, 40, 60, 80 is

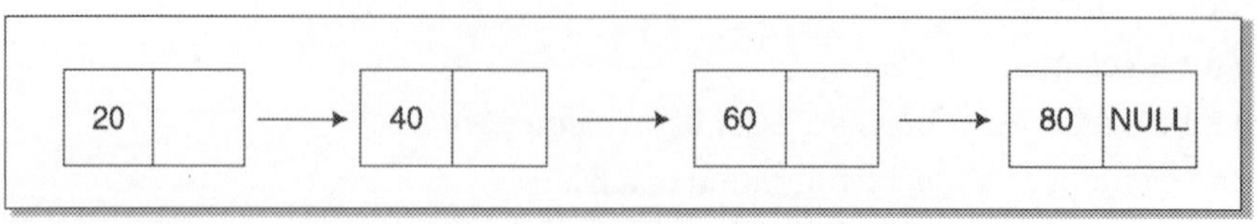

Figure 6.3 Representation of link list.

Note that the 'link' field of the last node consists of NULL which indicates the end of the list.

6.5.1 'C' Representation of Linked List

'C' structure

```
typedef struct node
 {
        int data;                /*data field */
        struct node * next;   /* link field */
 } L;
```

While declaring 'C' structure for a linked list:

- Declare a structure in which two members are there, i.e. the data member and the next pointer number
- The '**data**' member can be a character or an integer or a real kind of data depending upon the type of the information that the linked list is having.
- The '**next**' member is essentially of a pointer type. The pointer should be structure type because the 'next' field holds the address of the next node. Each node is basically a structure consisting of '**data**' and '**next**'.

Let us get introduced with concept of linked list by creating it. Here is a 'C' program for that –

```
/* Implementation of Linked List */
#include <stdio.h>
#include <conio.h>
typedef struct node
{
int data;
struct NODE *next;
} node;
node n1, n2, n3, n4;
node *one, *temp;
void main ( )
[
clrscr ( );
n1. data = 20; // Filling data in each node and attaching the nodes to each other
n1.next = &n2;
n2. data = 40;
n2.next = &n3;
n3. data = 60;
n3.next = &n4;
n4. data = 80;
n4.next = null; // terminating the linked list
one = &n1;
temp = one;
while (temp! = NULL)
{
```

```
printf ("\n % d", temp -> data);
temp = temp →next;
}
getch ( );
}
```

Explanation of the program 'C' representation of linked list:

Step 1: We have declared the nodes n1, n2, n3, n4 of structure type. The structure is for singly linked list. So every node will look like the figure below.

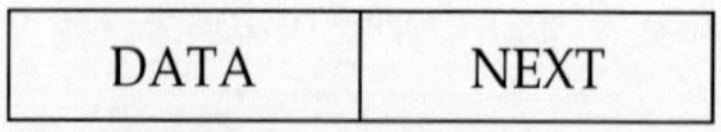

Node

Step 2: We start filling the data in each node at data field and assigning the next pointer to the next node.

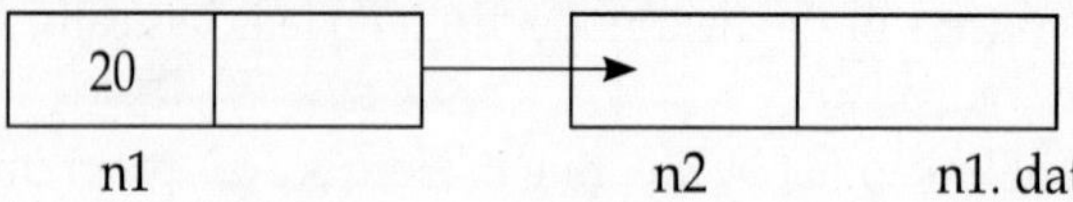

n1. data = 20; n1.next = &n2;

Here '&' is the address of the symbol. So the above figure can be interpreted as – the next pointer of n1 is pointing to the node n2. Then we will start filling the data in each node and fill again the next pointer to the next node. Continuing this we will get:

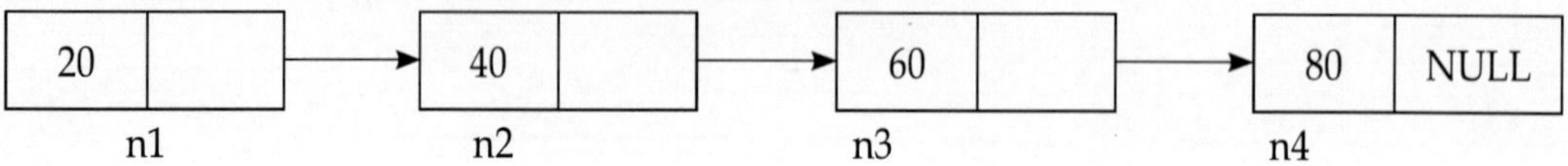

Step 3: To terminate the link list we will set

n5.next = NULL

Now we will store the starting node's address in some variable

one = &n1;

temp = one;

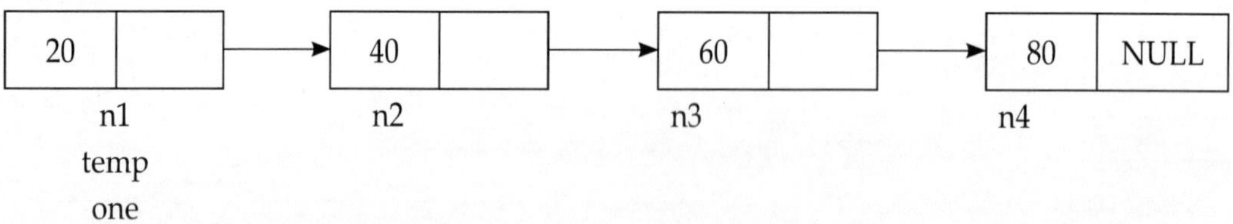

Step 4: Now to print the data in a linked list we will use - printf ("\n % d", temp → data);

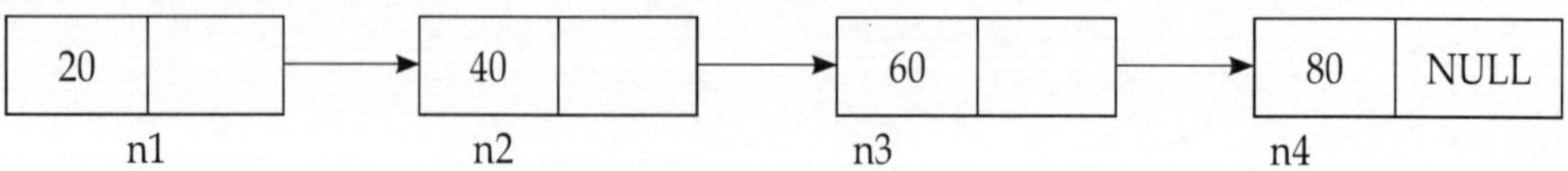

6.5.2 Advantages of Linked List

1. Linked lists are dynamic data structure which means that they can grow or shrink during the execution of program.
2. Efficient memory utilization – Memory is allocated whenever it is required and is deallocated when it is no longer needed.
3. Insertion and deletion operations are easier and efficient.
4. Many complex applications can be easily carried out with linked lists.

6.5.3 Disadvantages of Linked List

1. Linked organization does not support random or direct access.
2. If the numbers of fields are more then more memory space is needed.
3. Each data field should be supported by a link field to point to the next node.

6.5.4 Linked List and Dynamic Memory Management

Let us first understand the memory model; how memory gets allocated dynamically as shown in Figure 6.4. 'C' program uses the memory which is divided into three parts: static area, local data and heap. The static area stores the global data. The stack is for the local data area for global variables and the heap area is used to allocate and deallocate memory under the program's control. Thus, the stack and heap areas are the parts of dynamic memory management. The stack and heap grow towards each other. There areas are flexible.

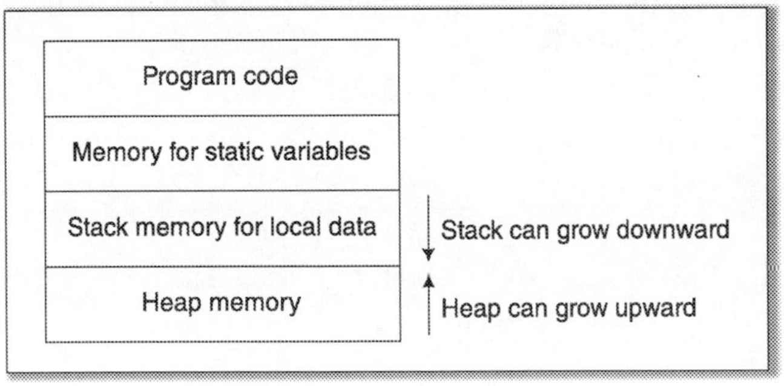

Figure 6.4 Memory model.

6.5.5 Dynamic Memory Management

In the computer world the two words 'static' and 'dynamic' have great importance. Static refers to an activity which is carried out at the time of compilation of a program and before the execution of the program whereas dynamic means the activity is carried out while the program is executed. Static memory management means allocating/de-allocating memory at the compilation time while the word dynamic refers to allocating/de-allocating memory while the program is running (after compilation). The advantage of dynamic memory management in handling linked list is that we can create as many nodes as we desire and if some nodes are not required we can de-allocate them.

6.5.6 Dynamic Memory Allocation in 'C'

In 'C' language for allocating memory dynamically the 'malloc' function is used. We should include **alloc.h** file in our program to support malloc. Similarly for de-allocating the memory the 'free' function is used.

Examples of 'malloc' and 'free' functions:

Consider a piece of 'C' code to understand how malloc works.

```
int *i;                    // pointer to integer variable
float *f;                  // pointer to float variable
char *c;                   // pointer to character variable
typedef struct student
{
 int enroll_no;
 char name [20];
 } s;
 s *s1;
 i = (int *) malloc (size of (int)); // type casting is done
 f = (float *) malloc (size of (float));
 c = (char *) malloc (size of (char));
 s1 = (s *) malloc (size of (s));
free (i);                              // memory is free or deallocated
```

In the above example s1 is the pointer to the structure s. In the malloc function one parameter is passed because the syntax of malloc is

malloc (size)

where size means how many bytes have to be allocated. The size can be obtained by the function 'sizeof' where syntax of size of is

sizeof (datatype)

When we finish using the memory, we must return it back. The function **free** in 'C' is used to free storage of a dynamically allocated variable.

The format for **free** is

free (pointer variable).

For example, the statement

```
free (i); // deallocated memory
```

6.6 ARRAY REPRESENTATION OF LINKED LIST

We know that the list can be represented using arrays. In this section we will discuss in detail how exactly a list can be represented using arrays. Basically, list is a collection of elements. To show the list using arrays we will have data and link fields in the array. The array can be created as shown in Figure 6.5.

```
struct node
{
     int data;
     int next;
}a[10];
```

Consider a list of 10, 20, 30, 40, and 50. We can store it in arrays as:

	Array a [5]	
Array index	Data	Next
a [0]	20	4
a [1]	40	3
a [2]	10	0
a [3]	50	–1
a [4]	30	1

Figure 6.5 Representation of linked list using arrays.

The next field in first node gives the index as 0. The next field in the last node gives the index as -1. - 1 is taken as end of the list.

With this concept various operations that can be performed on the list using array:

1. Creation of list
2. Insertion of any element in the list
3. Deletion of any element in the list
4. Display of list
5. Searching of particular element in the list

Let us see a 'C' program based on it.

/* Implementation of various List operations using arrays */

```
#include <stdio.h>
#include <conio.h>
#include <stdlib.h>
#include <string.h>
struct node
{
int data;
int next;
} a[10];
void main ( )
{
```

```
char ans;
int i, head, choice;
int Create ( );
void Display ( );
void Insert ( );
void Delete ( );
void Search ( );
do
{
clrscr ( );
printf("\n Main Menu");
printf("\n1 Creation ");
printf("\n2 Display");
printf("\n3 insertion of element in the list");
printf("\n4 Deletion of element from the list");
printf("\n5 Searching of element from the list");
printf("\n6 Exit");
printf("\n Enter your choice");
scanf("\n %d", &choice );
switch (choice)
{
case 1:
    for (i = 0; i <10; i++)
    {
    a[i]. data = -1;        // this for loop initialize the data field of list to -1
    }
    head = Create ( );
    break;
case 2:
    Display (head);
    break;
case 3:
    Insert ( );
    break;
case 4:
    Delete ( );
    break;
case 5:
    Search ( );
    break;
case 6:
    exit (0);
}
```

```
printf("\n Do you wish to go main menu? ");
ans = getch ( );
}
while (ans = = 'Y' !! ans = =. 'y');
getch ( );
}
int Create ( )                  // function for create a node
{
int head, i;
printf("\n Enter the index for first node ");
scanf ("%d" , &i);
head = i;
while ( i != -1)
{
 printf("\n Enter the data and index of the first element ");
 scanf ("%d %d", &a[i].data, &a[i].next);
 i = a[i].next;
 }
return head;
}
void Display (int i)            // function for display a node

{
 printf("(");
while (i != -1)
{
 if (a[i].data = = -1)
 printf ( " ");
 else
 {
 printf (" % d. " ,a[i].data);
}
i= a[i].next;
}
printf( " NULL");
}
void Insert ( )
{
int i, new_data, temp;
printf("\n Enter the new data which is to be inserted ");
scanf("%d",&new_data);
printf("\n Enter the data after which you want to insert ");
scanf("%d", &temp);
```

```
for (i =0; i < 10; i++)
{
 if (a[i].data= =temp)
 break;
}
if (a[i + 1].data = = -1)  // next location is empty
{
 a[i+1].next = a[i].next;
 a[i].next = i +1;
 a[[i+1].data = new_data;
}
}
void Delete ( )                // function for delete a node
{
int i, temp, current, new_next;
printf("\n Enter the node to be deleted");
scanf("%d", &temp);
for (i =0; i <10; i++)
{
if(a[i].data = =temp)
{
if(a[i].next = =-1)
{
 a[i].data = -1;
}
current = i;
new_next = a[i].next;
}
}
for (i =0; i <10; i++)
{
if(a[i].next = =current)
{
a[i].next = =new_next;
a[current].data = = -1;
}
}
}
void Search ( )                // function for search a node

{
int i, temp, flag = 0;
printf("\n Enter the node to be searched");
```

```
scanf("%d", &temp);
for (i =0; i <10; i++)
{
if(a[i].data = = temp)
{
flag =1;
break;
}
}
if(flag = =1)
printf("\n the %d node present in the list ", temp);
else
printf("\n the node is not present");
}
```

Output of Program

```
1. Main Menu
2. Creation
3. Display
4. Insertion of element in the list
5. Deletion of element from the list
6. Searching of element from the list
7. Exit
   Enter your choice 1
   Enter the index for first node 4
   Enter the data and index of the first element 10 1
   Enter the data and index of the first element 20 6
   Enter the data and index of the first element 30 7
   Enter the data and index of the first element 40 -1
   Do you wish to go to main menu?
   Main Menu
1. Creation
2. Display
3. Insertion of element in the list
4. Deletion of element from the list
5. Searching of element from the list
6. Exit
   Enter your choice 2
   (10, 20, 30, 40, NULL)
   Do you wish to go main menu?
```

```
   Main Menu
1. Creation
2. Display
3. Insertion of element in the list
4. Deletion of element from the list
5. Searching of element from the list
6. Exit
   Enter your choice 3
   Enter the new data which is to be inserted 21
   Enter the data after which you want to insert 20
   Do you wish to go to main menu?
   Main Menu
1. Creation
2. Display
3. Insertion of element in the list
4. Deletion of element from the list
5. Searching of element from the list
6. Exit
   Enter your choice 2
   (10, 20, 21, 30, 40. NULL)
   Do you wish to go to main menu?
   Main Menu
1. Creation
2. Display
3. Insertion of element in the list
4. Deletion of element from the list
5. Searching of element from the list
6. Exit
   Enter your choice 4
   Enter the node to be deleted 21
   Do you wish to go to main menu?
   Main Menu
1. Creation
2. Display
3. Insertion of element in the list
4. Deletion of element from the list
5. Searching of element from the list
6. Exit
```

```
    Enter your choice 2
    (10, 20, 30, 40, NULL)
    Do you wish to go to main menu?
    Main Menu
1.  Creation
2.  Display
3.  Insertion of element in the list
4.  Deletion of element from the list
5.  Searching of element from the list
6.  Exit
    Enter your choice 5
    Enter the node to be searched 40
    The 40 node is present in the list
    Do you wish to go to main menu?
    Main Menu
1.  Creation
2.  Display
3.  Insertion of element in the list
4.  Deletion of element from the list
5.  Searching of element from the list
6.  Exit
    Enter your choice 6
```

It is usually not preferred to do list implementation using arrays because of two main reasons:

1. There is a limitation on the number of nodes in the list because of the fixed size of array. Memory may get wasted because of less elements in the list or there may be large number of nodes in the list and we will not be able to store some elements in the array.
2. Insertion and deletion of elements in array is complicated.

6.7 SINGLY-LINKED LIST

The simplest kind of linked list is a singly-linked list (slist for short), which has one link per node. This link points to the nest node in the list, or to a null value or empty list if it is the final node.

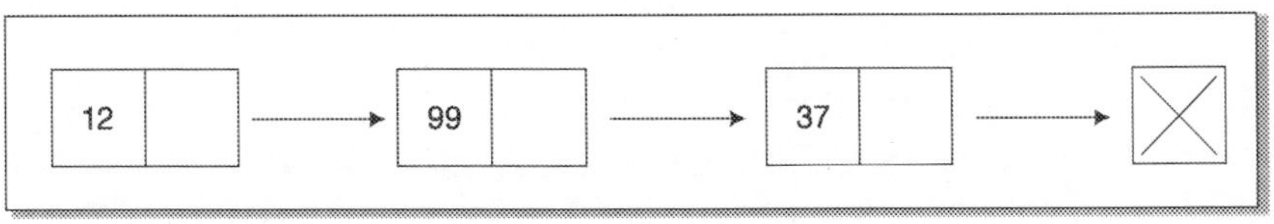

Figure 6.6 A singly-linked list containing three integer values.

6.7.1 Operation of Link List

A linked list is created using dynamic memory allocation. That means while the creating the list we are not using array at all. Hence, the main advantage of this kind of implementation is that we can create a list of nodes as per our needs. Hence, there won't be any wastage or lack of memory. Various operations of linked list are:

1. Creation of linked list
2. Display of linked list
3. Insertion of any element in the linked list
4. Deletion of any element from the linked list
5. Searching of the desired element in the linked list

6.7.1.1 *Creation of linked list*

Initially one variable flag is taken whose value is initialized to TRUE (i.e. 1). The purpose of the flag is for making a check on the creation of the first node. That means if the flag is TRUE then we have to create the head node or first node of the linked list. After creation of the first node we will reset flag (i.e. assign FALSE to the flag). Consider that we have entered the element value 20 initially then:

Step 1:

```
New = get_node ();        // memory gets allocated for new node
New → data = value;       // value 20 will be put in data field of New
```

Data	Next
20	NULL

New

Step 2:

```
if (flag = = TRUE)
{
head = new;
temp = head;  /* this node as temp because head's address will be preserved in
                 'head' and we can change 'temp' node as per requirement */
flag = FALSE;
}
```

Data	Next
20	NULL

New/head/temp

Step 3: If the head node of a linked list is created we can further create the linked list by attaching the subsequent nodes. Suppose we want to insert a node with value 20 then:

Gets created after invoking get_node ( );

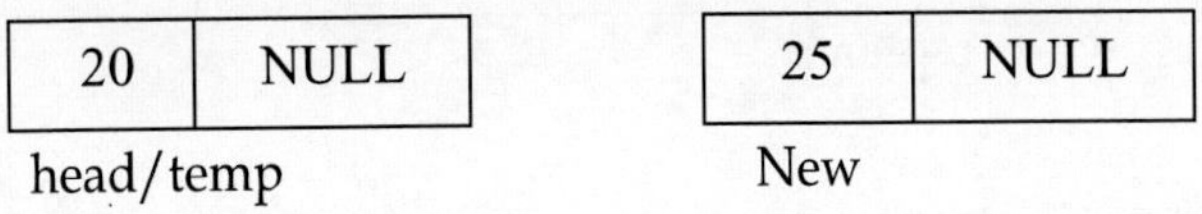

temp → next = New;

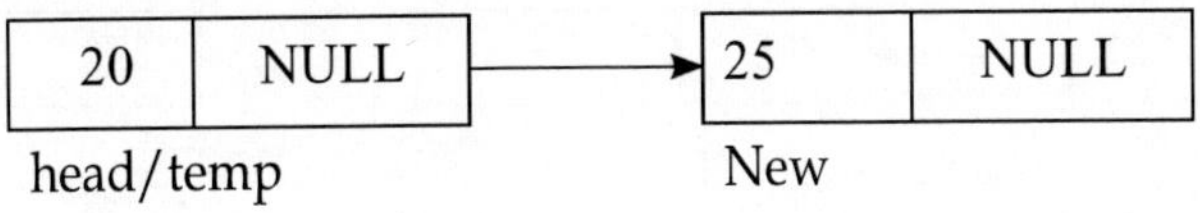

temp = new; // now temp is moved ahead

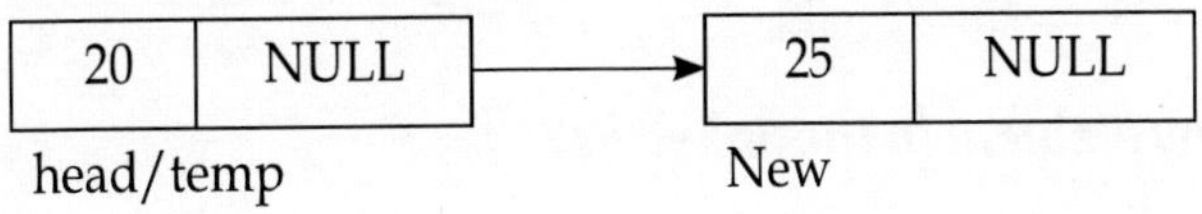

Step 4: If a user wants to enter more elements then let us say for value 30 the scenario will be:

Gets created after invoking `get_node ( );`

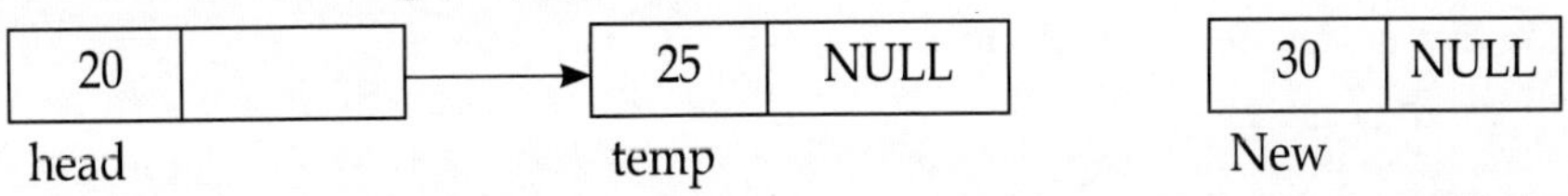

temp → next = New;

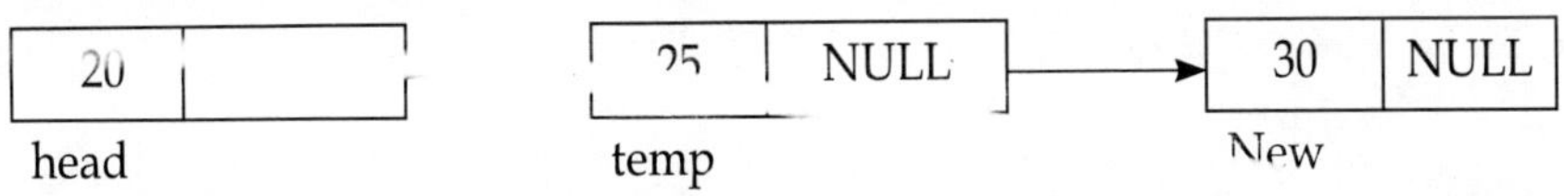

temp = new; // now temp is moved ahead

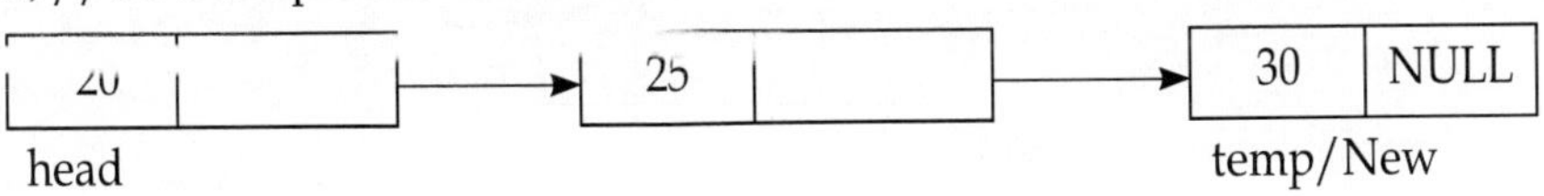

is the final linked list.

6.7.1.2 Display of linked list

We are passing the address of the head node to the display routine and calling the head as the 'temp' node. If the linked list is not created then head = temp node will be NULL. Therefore the message "the list is empty" will be displayed.

If we have created some linked list like this then:

temp → data i.e. 20 will be displayed as temp! = NULL

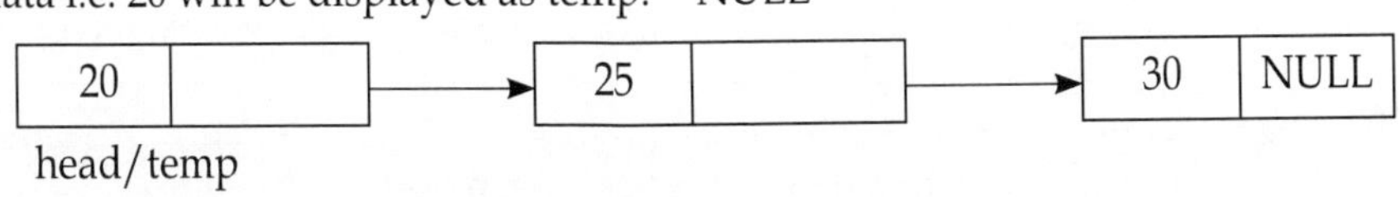

set temp = temp → next

temp → data i.e. 25 will be displayed as temp! = NULL temp

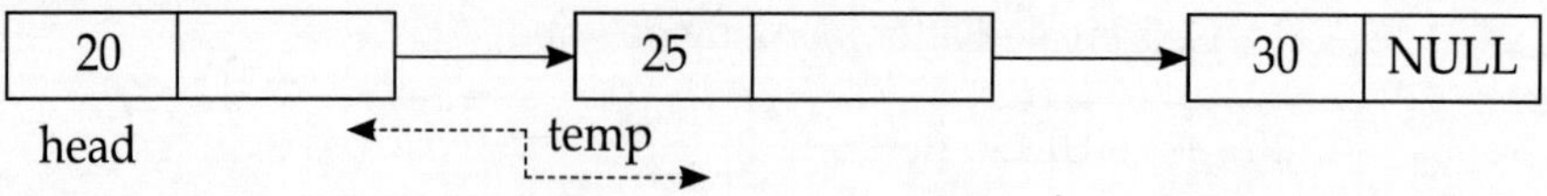

set temp = temp → next

temp → data i.e. 25 will be displayed as temp = NULL temp we will come out loop.

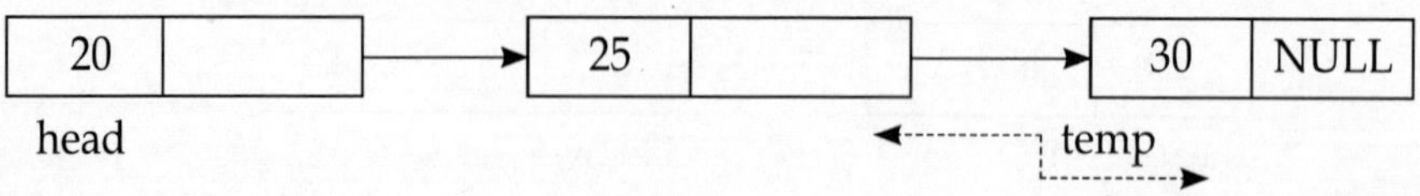

as result display on console.

20 → 25 → 30 → NULL.

6.7.1.3 *Insertion of any element in the linked list*

There are three possible cases when we want to insert an element in a linked list:

1. Insertion of a node as a head node
2. Insertion of a node as a last node
3. Insertion of a node after some node.
4. We will see the **case 1:**

Insertion of a node as head node: If there is no node in the linked list then value of a head is NULL. At that time if we want to insert 18 then

```
scanf ("%d", &New → data)
if (head = = NULL)
head = New;
```

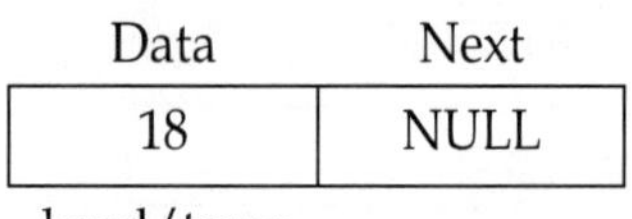

Otherwise suppose a linked list is already created like this:

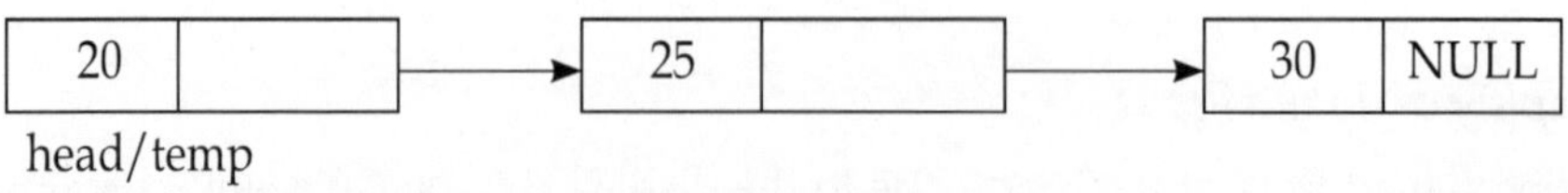

If we want to insert this node as a head node then:

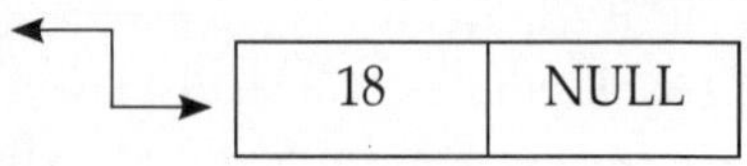

New

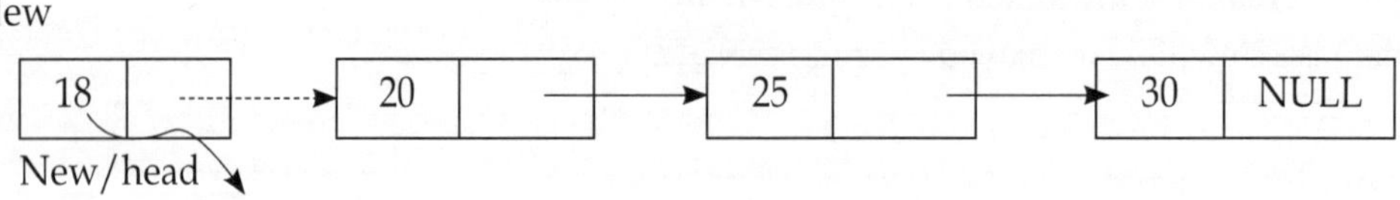

Node is attached to the linked list as a head node

New → next = temp

head = New

Now we will **insert a node at the end case 2:**

To attach a node at the end of a linked list assume that we have already created a linked list like this:

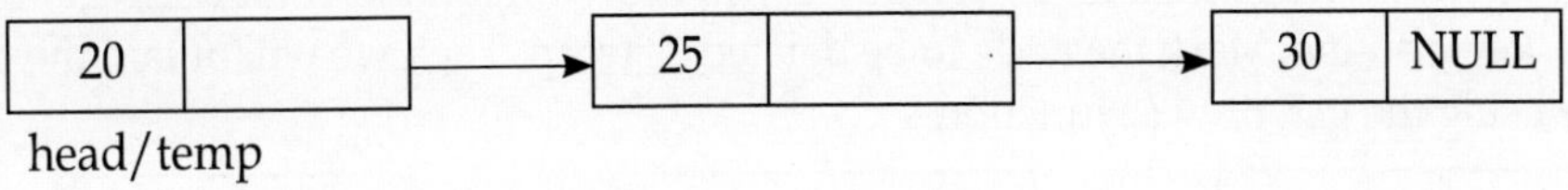

If we insert this node at the last node then:

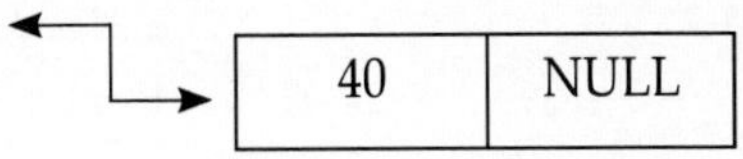

while (temp → next! = NULL)

temp = temp → next; // traversing linked list

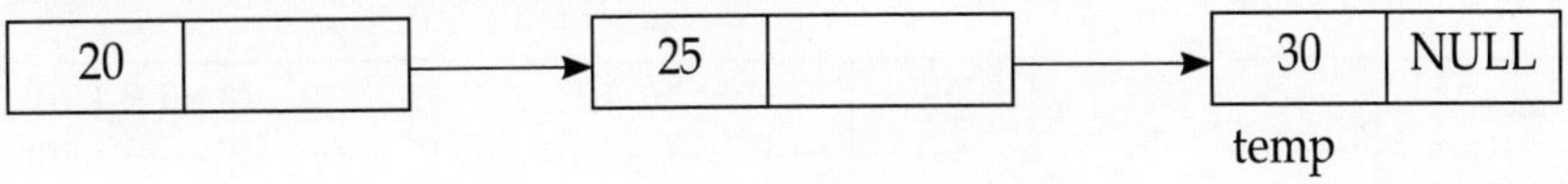

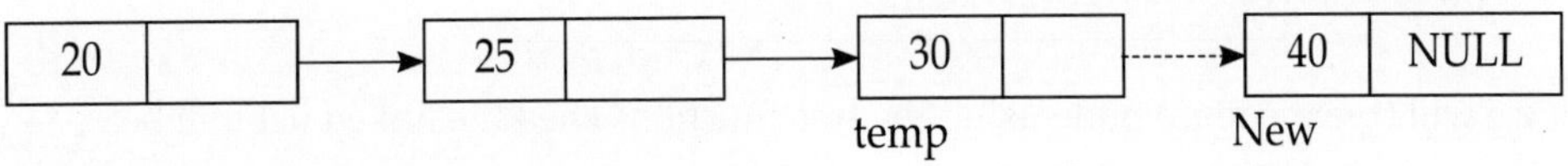

temp → next = New

New →next = NULL

Now we will **insert a node after a node case 3:**

Suppose we want to insert node 28 after containing 25 then:

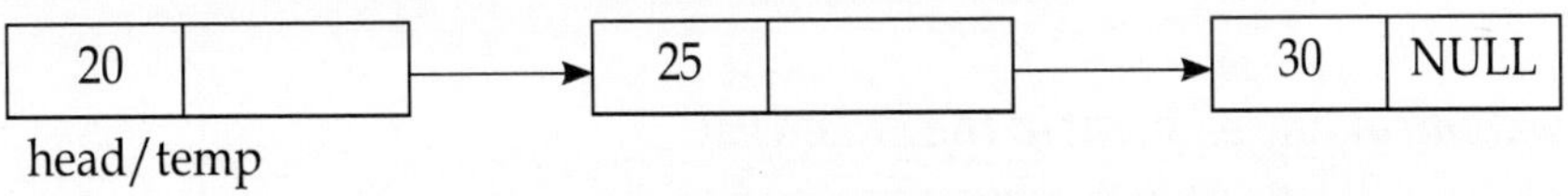

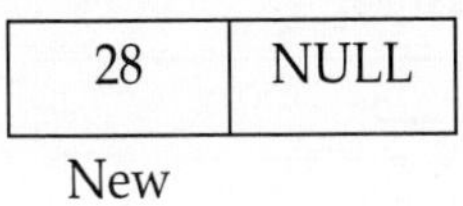

Then:

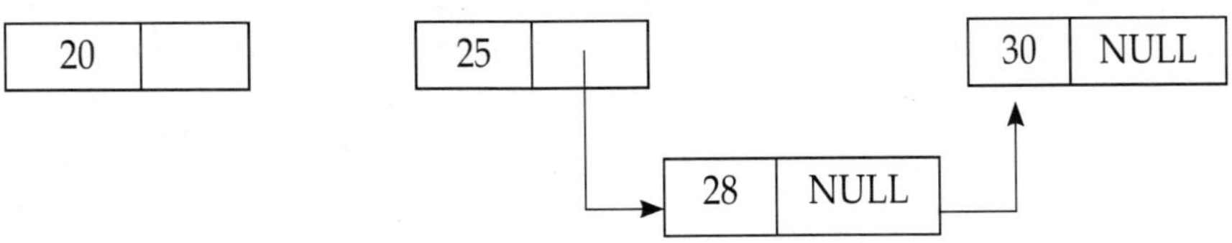


```
If (temp → data = key)
{
New → next = temp → next;
temp → next = New;
return
}
```

6.7.1.4 Deletion of any element in the linked list

Suppose we have:

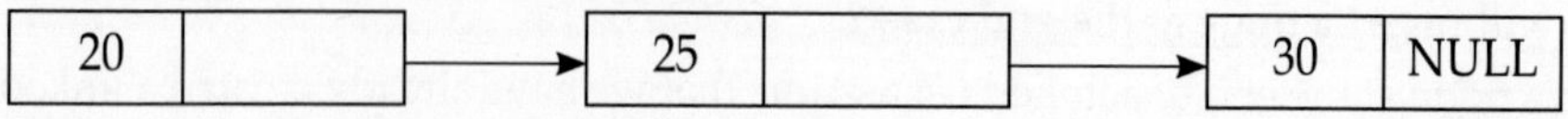

Suppose we want to delete node 25. Then we will search the node containing 25, using the search (*head, key) routine. Mark the node to be deleted as **temp**. Then we will obtain the previous node of **temp** using the get_prev ( ) function.

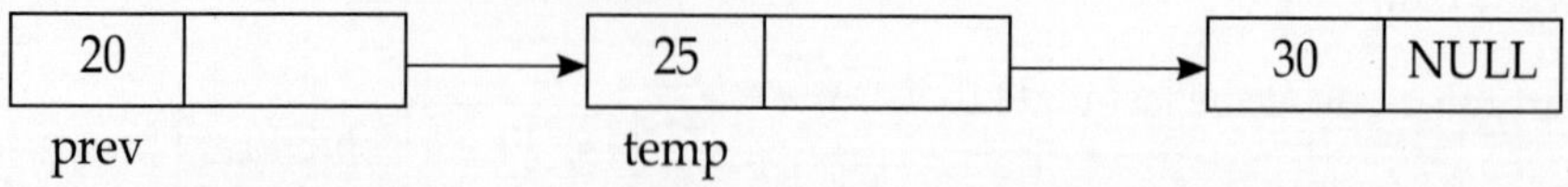

Then:

prev → next = temp → next

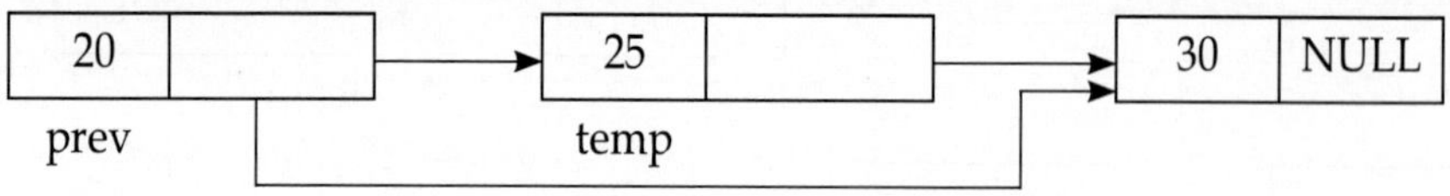

Now we will **free** the **temp** node using the free function. Then the linked list will be:

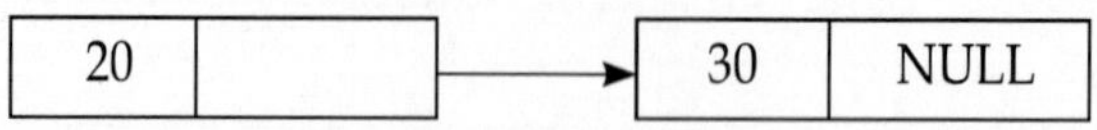

This can be done using following statements

```
*head = temp → next;
free (temp);
```

6.7.1.5 Searching of any element in the linked list

Consider that we have created a linked list as:

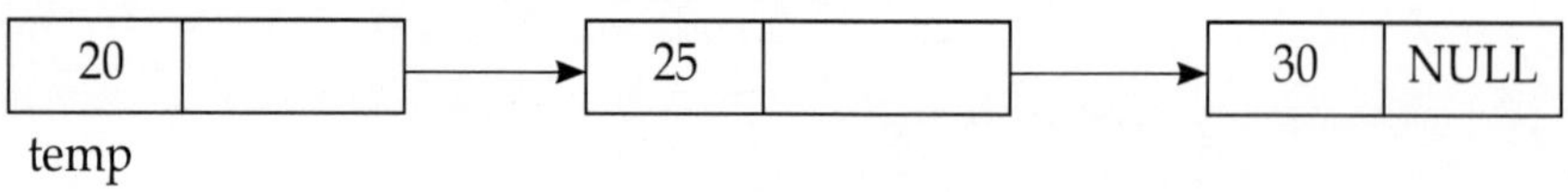

Suppose key = 30. We want a node containing value 30 then compare temp → data and key value. If there is no match then we will mark the next node as temp.

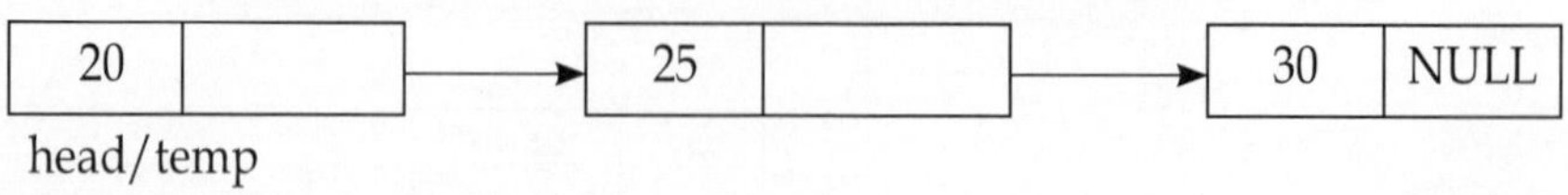

Is temp → data? Key ——→ NO

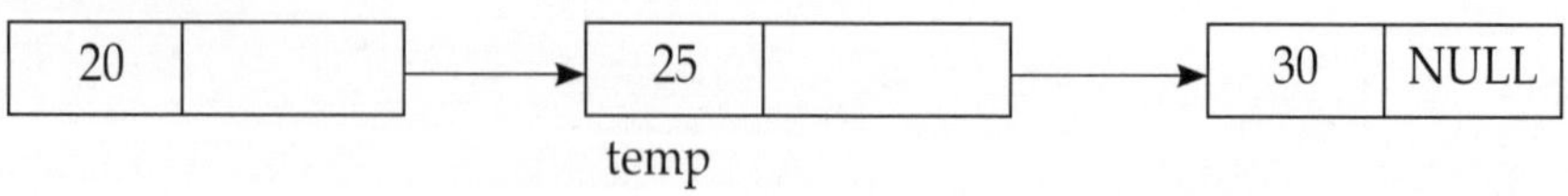

Is temp →data? Key ——→ Yes

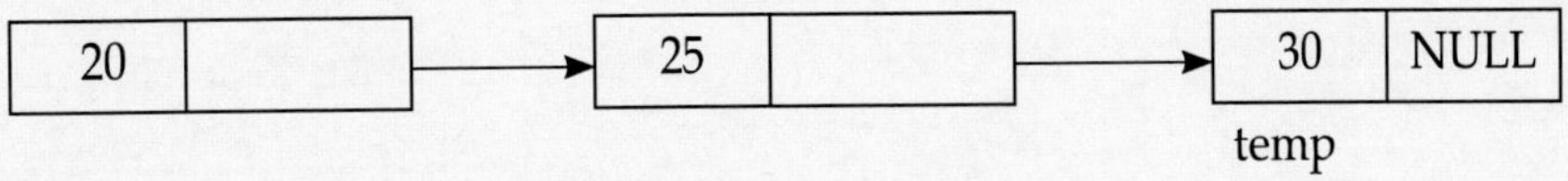

Hence print the message "the element is present in the list".

Program

To perform various operations such as creation, insertion, deletion, search and display on single link list.

```
# include <stdio.h>
# include <conio.h>
# include <stdlib.h>
# define TRUE 1
# define FALSE 0
typedef struct SLL
{   int data;
    struct SLL *next;
} node;
 node *create( );
{
 int choice, val;
 char ans;
 node *head;
 void display (node *);
 node*search (node*int);
 node *insert (node*);
 void dele(node**);
 head = null;
do
{
 clrscr ( );
 printf ("\n program to perform various operations on linked list");
 printf ("\n1.create");
 printf ("\n2.display");
 printf ("\n3.search for an item ");
 printf ("\n4.insert an element in a list");
 printf ("\n5.delete an element in from list");
 printf ('\n6.quit");
 printf ("\nenter your choice(1-6)");
 scanf ("%d",&choice);
switch (choice)
{
 case1: head = create ( );
```

```
        break;
 case2: display (head);
        break;
 case3: printf ("enter the element you want to search");
        scanf ("%d", &val);
        break;
 case4: head = insert (head);
        break;
 case5: dele (&head);
        break;
 case6: exit (0);
default: clrscr (0);
printf ("invalid choice, try again");
getch ( );
}
}
while (choice!=6);
}
node* create( )
{
node *temp,*new,*head;
int val, flag;
char ans = 'y';
node *get_node ( );
temp = null;
flag = true;
do
{
printf ("\nEnter the element:");
scanf ("%d", &val);
new = get_node)():
if (new = = null)
printf ("\n memory is not allocated");
new → data = val;
if(flag= = true)
{
head = new;
flag = flase;
}
else
{
temp →next=New;
}
```

```
printf ("\DO you want to entermore elements?(y/n)");
ans = getch ( );
}
while (ans = = 'y');
printf ("\n The singly linked list is created\n");
getch ( );
clrscr ( );
return head;
}
node*get_node( )
{
node *temp;
temp = ( node*) malloc ( sizeof (node));
temp → next=NULL;
return temp;
}
{
node *temp;
temp = head;
if(temp = = NULL)
{
printf ("\nThe list is empty\n");
getch ( );
clrscr ( );
return;
}
while (temp!=NULL)
{
printf("%d→",temp->data);
temp = temp → next:
}
printf ("NULL");
getch ( );
clrscr ( );
}
node*search(node *head, int key)
{
node*temp;
int found;
temp = head;
if ( temp = = NULL)
{
printf("The Linked list is empty\n");
```

```
getch ( );
clrscr ( );
return NULL;
}
found = FALSE;
while(temp!=NULL && found= =FALSE)
{
if(temp → data!=key)
tamp=teamp → next;
else
found=TRUE;
}
if(found= =TRUE)
{
printf("\nThe element is present in the list\n");
getch( );
return temp;
}
else
{
printf("\nThe element is not present in the list\n");
getch( );
return NULL;
}
}
node *insert(node *head)
{
int choice;
node *insert_head(note *);
void insert _after(node *);
void insert_last(node *);
printf ("\n 1.Insert a node as a head node");
printf ("\n 2.Insert a node as a last node");
printf ("\n 3. Insert a node as intermediate position in the link list");
printf ("\n Enter your choice for insertion of node");
scanf ("%d",&choice);
switch(choice)
{
case 1:head = insert_head(head);
break;
case 2:insert_last(head);
break;
case 3;insert_after(head);
```

```
break;
}
return head;
}
{
node*New,*temp;
New = get_node();
printf ("\nEnter The element which you want to insert");
scanf("%d",New→data);
if(head = =null)
head = new;
else
{
temp = head;
new → next=temp;
head = new;
}
return head;
}
void insert_last(node*head)
{
node*New,*temp;
new = get_node ( );
printf("\nenter the element which you want to insert");
scanf("%d",%new→data);
if(head= = NULL)
head = new;
else
{
temp = head;
while(temp-.next!=null)
Temp = temp→next;
temp→next=new;
new→next=null;
}
}
{
int key;
node*new,*temp;
new=get_node();
printf ("\nenter the element which you want to insert");
scanf("%d"&new→data);
if (head = = NULL)
```

```
{
head = new;
}
else
{
printf ("\n Enter the element after which you want to insert the node");
scanf ("%d", &key);
temp = head;
do
{
 if (temp → data = = key)
 {
 New → next = temp → next;
 temp → next = new;
 return;
 }
 else
 temp = temp → next;
}
while ( temp != NUUL);
}
}
node * get_pre (node * head, int val)
{
 node *temp, *prev;
 int flag;
 temp = head;
if ( temp = = NULL)
 returen NULL;
flag = FALSE;
prev = NULL;
while (temp != NULL && !flag)
{
 if ( temp → data != val)
 {
 prev = temp;
 temp = temp → next;
 }
 else
 flag = TRUE;
}
 if ( flaq)
 return prev;
```

```
 else
 return NULL;
}

void dele (node **head)
{
 node *temp, *prev;
 int key;
 temp = *head;
 if ( temp = = NULL)
{
 printf ( "\n The list is empty\n");
 getch ( );
 clrscr ();
 return;
}
clrscr ( );
printf ( "\n Enter the element you want to delete: ");
scanf ("%d", &key);
temp = search (*head, key);
if (temp != NULL)
 {
 prev = get_prev( *head, key);
 if ( prev != NULL)
 {
 prev → next = temp → next;
 free (temp);
}
else
{
 *head = temp → next;
 free (temp);
}
 printf ( "\n The element is deleted\n");
 getch ( );
 clrscr ( );
}
}
```

Output

```
Program to perform various operations on linked list
  1. Create
  2. Display
```

```
   3. Search for an item
   4. Insert an element in a list
   5. Delete an element from list
   6. Quit
      Enter your Choice ( 1-6) 1
      Enter the element: 10
      Do you want to enter more elements?(y/n) y
      Enter the element: 20
      Do you want to enter more elements?(y/n) y
      Enter the element: 30
      Do you want to enter more elements?(y/n) y
      Enter the element: 40
      Do you want to enter more elements?(y/n) n
      The Singly linked list is created
Program to perform various operations on linked list
   1. Create
   2. Display
   3. Search for an item
   4. Insert an element in a list
   5. Delete an element from list
   6. Quit
      Enter your Choice ( 1-6) 2
      10 → 20 → 30 → 40 → NULL
Program to perform various operations on linked list
   1. Create
   2. Display
   3. Search for an item
   4. Insert an element in a list
   5. Delete an element from list
   6. Quit
      Enter your Choice ( 1-6) 3
      Enter the element you want to search 30
      The element is present in the list
Program to perform various operations on linked list
   1. Create
   2. Display
   3. Search for an item
   4. Insert an element in a list
```

```
 5. Delete an element from list
 6. Quit
    Enter your Choice ( 1-6) 4
 1. Insert a node as a head node
 2. Insert a node as a last node
 3. Insert a node at intermediate position in the linked list
    Enter the your choice for insertion of node 1
    Enter the element which you want to insert 9
Program to perform various operations on linked list
 1. Create
 2. Display
 3. Search for an item
 4. Insert an element in a list
 5. Delete an element from list
 6. Quit
   Enter your Choice ( 1-6) 2
   9 →10 → 20 → 30 → 40 → NULL
```

6.8 ARRAY AND LINKED LIST COMPARISON

Sr. No.	Array	Linked List
1.	Any element can be accessed randomly with the help of the index of the array.	Any element can be accessed by sequential access only.
2.	Only logical deletion of data is possible.	The data can be deleted physically.
3.	Insertion and deletion of data is difficult.	Insertion and deletion of data is easy.
4.	The memory allocation is static.	The memory allocation is dynamic.

6.9 TYPES OF LINKED LIST

There are various types of linked list such as:

- Singly linked list
- Singly circular linked list
- Doubly linear linked list
- Doubly circular linked list

Singly linked list

It is called singly linked list because this list consists of only one link, to point to the next node or element. This is also called linear list because the last element points to nothing and it is linear in nature. The last field of last node is NULL. This means that there is no further list. The very first node is called head or first node.

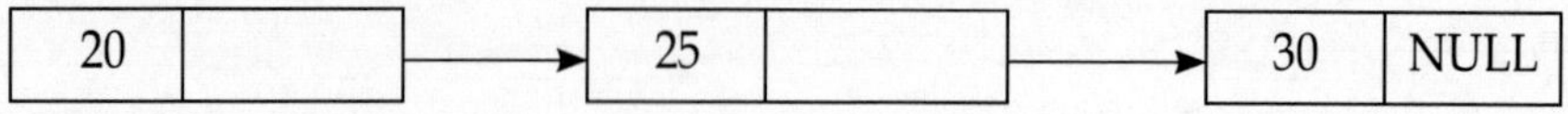

Singly circular linked list

In this type of linked list only one link is used to point to the next element and this list is circular which means that the last node's link field points to the first or head node. That means that according to the example given below after 40 the number will be 10. So the list is circular in nature.

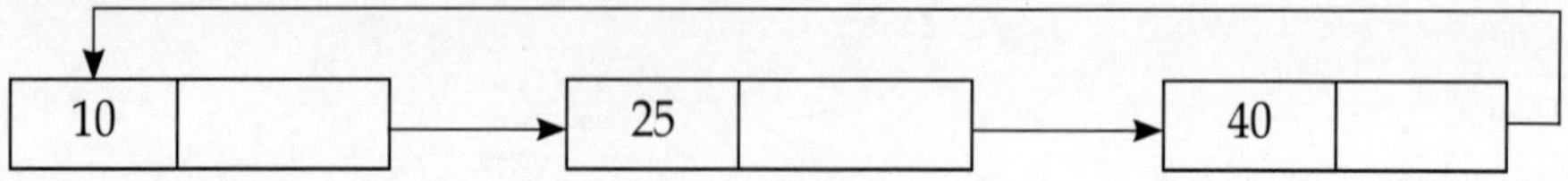

Doubly linked list

This list is called doubly linked list because each node has two pointers, previous and next pointers. The previous pointer points to the previous node and next pointer points to the next node. In case of the head node the previous pointer is obviously NULL, and last node's next pointer points to NULL.

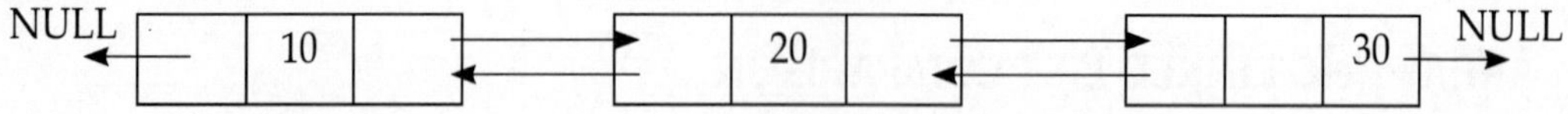

Doubly circular linked list

In doubly circular linked list the previous pointer of the first node and the next pointer of the last node is pointed to the head. The head node is a special node which may have any dummy data or it may have some useful information such as total number of nodes in the list which may be used to simplify the algorithms carrying various operations on the list.

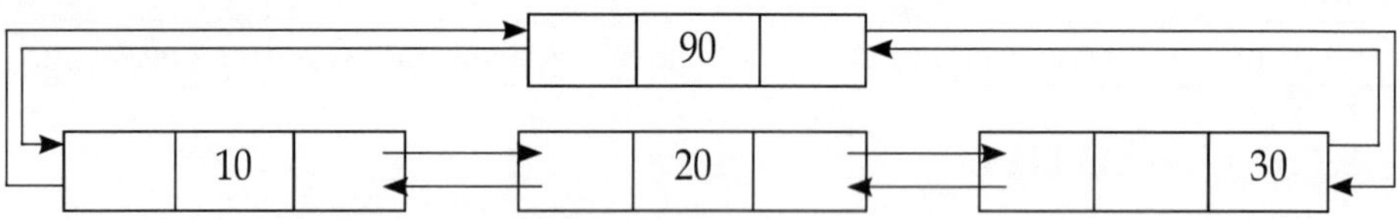

6.10 CIRCULAR LINKED LIST (CLL)

A circular linked list (CLL) is similar to a singly linked list except that the last node's next pointer points to the first node. In a singly linked list, the last node of such a list contains the null pointer. We can improve this by replacing the null pointer in the last node of a list with the address of its first node. Such a list is called a **circularly linked list** or a **circular list**.

A circular linked list is shown below:

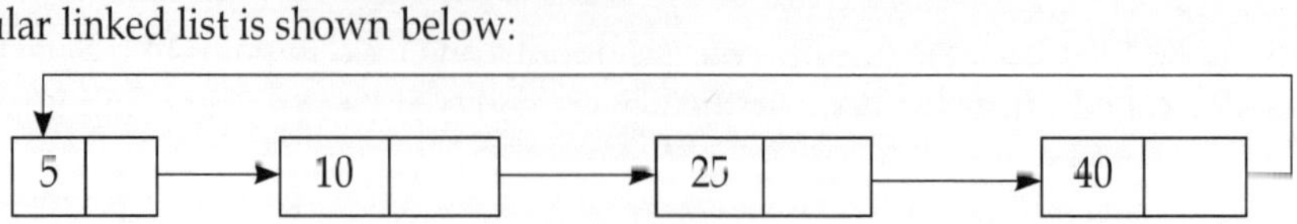

When we traverse a circular list, we must be careful as there is a possibility to get into an infinite loop, if we are not able to detect the end of the list. To do that we must look for the starting node. We can keep an external pointer at the starting node and look for this external pointer as a stop sign. An alternative method is to place the header node at the first node of a circular list. This header node may contain a special value in its **info** field that cannot be the valid contents of a list in the context of the problem. If a circular list is empty then the external pointer will point to null.

Various operations that can be performed on circular linked list are:

1. Creation of a circular linked list.
2. Insertion of a node in a circular linked list
3. Deletion of any node from a linked list
4. Display of a circular linked list

1. Creation of circular linked list

First we will allocate memory for **New** node using a function **get_node ( ).** There is one variable flag whose purpose is to check whether the first node is created or not. That means that when the flag is 1 (set) then the first node is not created. Therefore, after creation of the first node we have to reset the flag (set to 0).

Initially, the variable **head** indicates the starting node. Suppose we have taken element '10' and the flag =1, head = New;

New → next = head;

flag = 0;

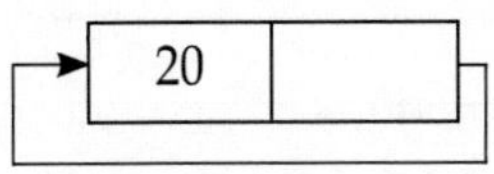

Now as flag = 0, we can further create the nodes and attach them as follows. When we have taken element '10'

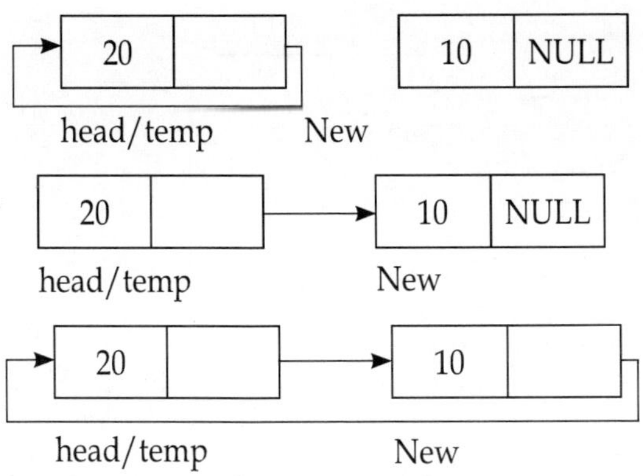

temp = head;

temp → next = head;

temp → next = New;

New → next = head;

2. Insertion of a node in circular linked list

For inserting a new node in the circular linked list, there are 3 cases:

(i) Inserting a node as a head node

(ii) Inserting a node as a last node

(iii) Inserting a node at an intermediate position

(i) If we want to insert a **New** node as a head node then,

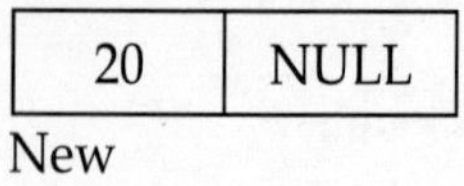

Then

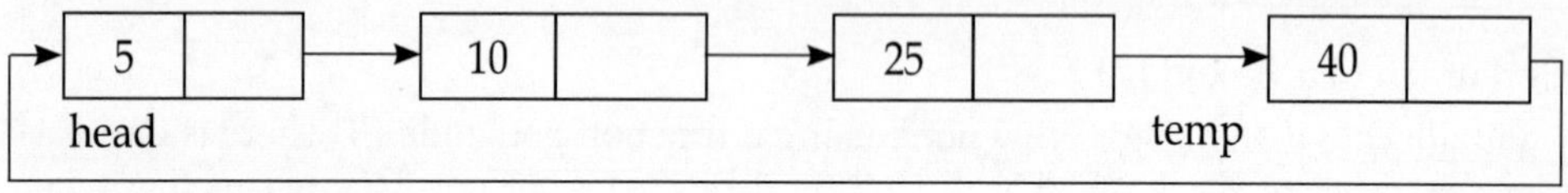

temp → next = New;

New → next = head;

head = New;

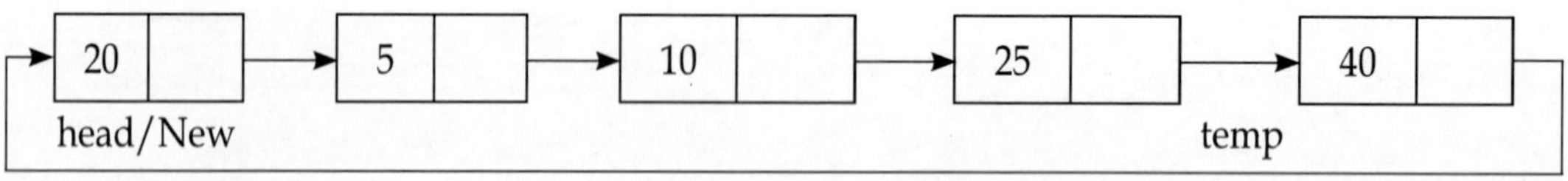

(ii) If you want to insert a New node as a last node consider a circular linked list given below:

A **New** node as a last node then,

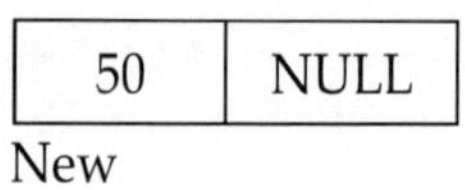

Then,

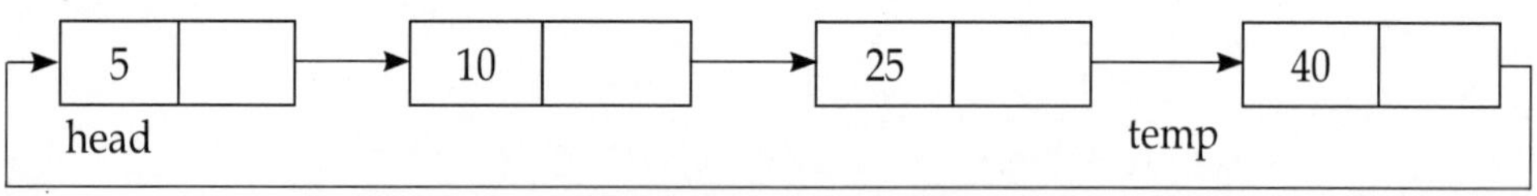

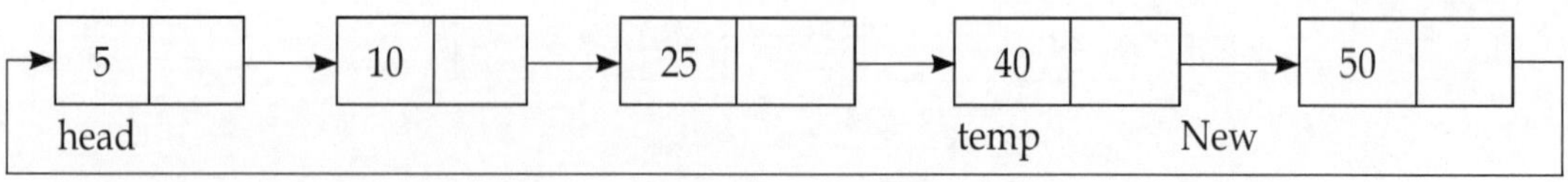

(iii) If we want to insert an element 30 after node 25 then

A **New** node 30 then,

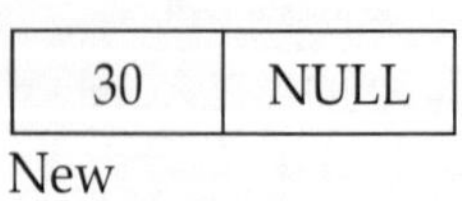

Then,

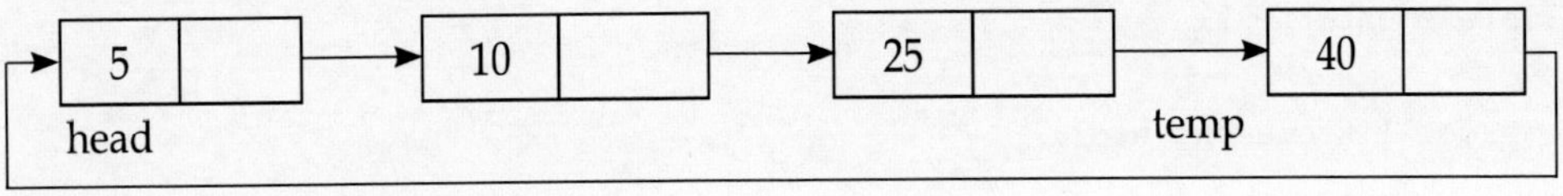

as key = 30 and temp → data = 30

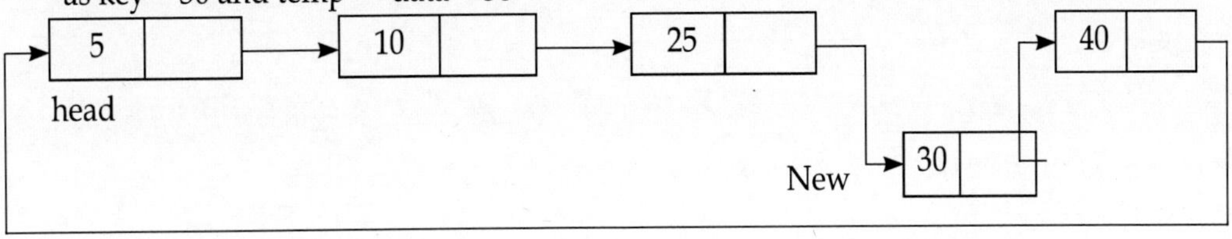

New → next = temp → next;

temp → next = New;

3. Deletion of any node in circular linked list

Suppose we have created a linked list as below, then:

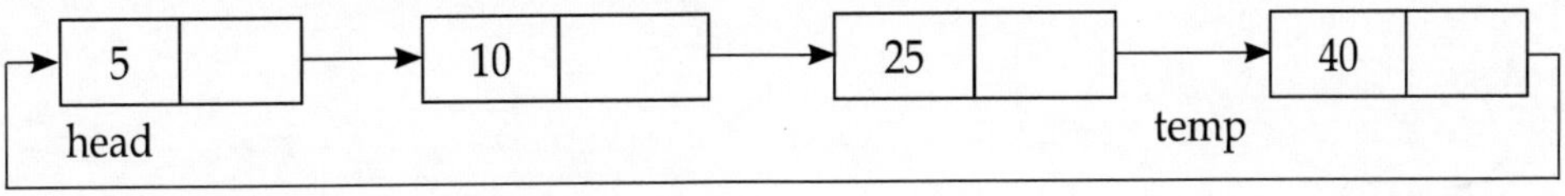

if we want to delete temp → data node 5 then

temp = temp1 → New;

while (temp → next ! head)

temp = temp → next;

temp → next = temp1;

head = temp1;

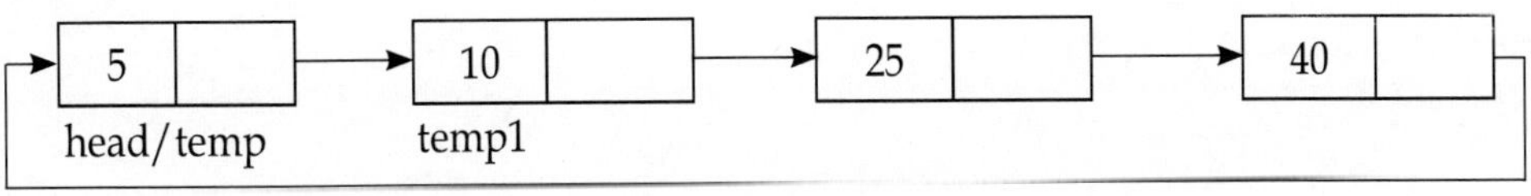

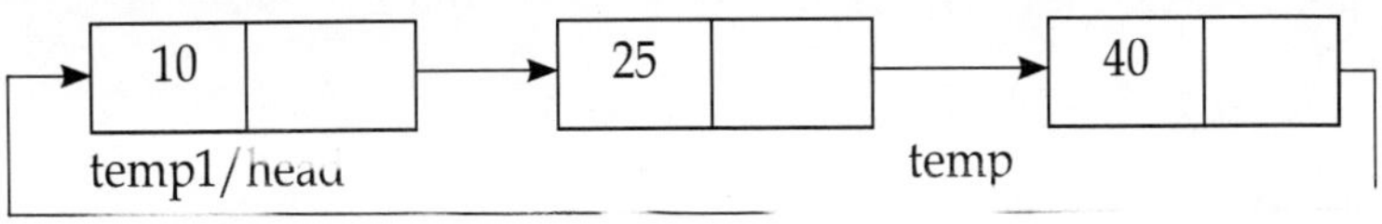

Program of Circular Linked List Operation in 'C'

Circular Linked list

```
#include <stdio.h>
#include <conio.h>
#include <alloc.h>
#define NULL 0
struct listelement
{
int item;
```

```
struct listelement *next;
};
typedef struct listelement node;
int menu( )
{
int choice;
do
{
printf("\n\n MAIN MENU");
printf("\n ---------");
printf("\n 1.CREATE \n 2.INSERT \n 3.DELETE \n 4.Exit");
printf("\n Enter your choice:");
scanf("%d",&choice);
if(choice<1||choice>4)
printf("\n Wrong choice");
}while(choice<1||choice>4);
return (choice);
}

node *create(node **lastnode)
{
node *temp,*firstnode;
int info;
*lastnode = NULL;
firstnode = NULL;
printf("\n Enter the data:");
scanf("%d",&info);
while(info!=-999)
{
temp = (node *)malloc(sizeof(node));
temp→ item=info;
temp→next=NULL;
if(firstnode = =NULL)
firstnode = temp;
else
(*lastnode) →next=temp;
(*lastnode) = temp;
scanf("%d",&info);
}
if(firstnode! = NULL)
temp→next=firstnode;
return(firstnode);
}
```

```
void display (node *first, node *last)
{
do
{
printf("\t %d", first→item);
first = first→next;
}while(last->next!=first);
return;
}
void insert(node **first, node **last)
{
node *new node;
node *temp;
int newitem, pos, i;
printf("\n Enter the new item:");
scanf("%d",&newitem);
printf("\n Position of insertion:");
scanf("%d",&pos);
if(((*first) = =NULL)||(pos = =1))
{
newnode = (node *)malloc(sizeof(node));
newnode→item=newitem;
newnode→next=*first;
*first = newnode;
if((*last)!=NULL)
(*last) →next=*first;
}
else
{
i=1;
temp=*first;
while((i < (pos-1)) && ((temp→next)!=(*first)))
{
i++;
temp = temp→next;
}
newnode = (node *)malloc(sizeof(node));
if(temp→next==(*first))
*last = newnode;
newnode→item = newitem;
newnode→next=temp→next;
temp→next = newnode;
}
```

```
}
void delet(node **first,node **last)
{
node *temp;
node *prev;
int target;
printf("\n Data to be deleted:");
scanf("%d",&target);
if(*first= =NULL)
printf("\n List is empty");
else if((*first) →item= =target)
{
if((*first) →next= =*first)
*first=*last=NULL;
else
{
*first=(*first) →next;
(*last) →next=*first;
printf("\n Circular list\n");
display(*first,*last);
}
}
else
{
temp=*first;
prev=NULL;
while((temp→next!=(*first))&&((temp→item)!=target))
{
prev = temp;
temp=temp→next;
}
if(temp→item!=target)
{
printf("\n Element not found");
}
else
{
if(temp= =*last)
*last=prev;
prev→next=temp→next;
printf("\n CIRCULAR LIST");
display(*first,*last);
}
```

```
}
}

void main()
{
node *start,*end;
int choice;
clrscr();
printf("\n CIRCULAR LINKED LIST");
printf("\n --------------------");
do
{
choice = menu();
switch(choice)
{
case 1:
printf("\n Type -999 to stop");
start=create(&end);
printf("\n Circular list\n");
display(start,end);
continue;
case 2:
insert(&start,&end);
printf("\n Circular list \n");
display(start,end);
continue;
case 3:
delet(&start,&end);
continue;
default:
printf("\n End");
}
}while(choice!=4);
}
```

Sample Input and Output

```
MAIN MENU
1.CREATE
2.INSERT
3.DELETE
4.EXIT
```

```
Enter your choice: 1
Type -999 to stop
Enter the data: 10
20
30
-999
Circular list
10 20 30
MAIN MENU
1.CREATE
2.INSERT
3.DELETE
4.EXIT
Enter your choice: 2
Enter the new item: 40
Position of insertion: 2
Circular list
10 40 20 30
MAIN MENU
1.CREATE
2.INSERT
3.DELETE
4.EXIT
Enter your choice: 3
Data to be deleted: 20
Circular List
10 40 30
MAIN MENU
1.CREATE
2.INSERT
3.DELETE
4.EXIT
Enter your choice:3
Data to be deleted: 60
Element not found
```

Advantages of circular linked list over singly linked list

In a circular linked list the next pointer of the last node points to the head node. Hence we can move from the last node to the head node of the list very efficiently. Hence accessing of any node is much faster than that of a singly linked list.

6.11 CONCEPT OF HEADER NODE

A header node is a linked list which always contains a special node, called the header node. The head node is a node which resides at the beginning of the linked list. Sometimes such an extra node needs to be kept at the front of the list. This node basically does not represent any data of the linked list. But it may contain some useful information about a linked list such as the total number of nodes in the list, address of the last or some specific unique information.

The following are two kinds of header list:

- A **grounded header list** is a header list where the last node contains the null pointer.
- A **circular head list** is a header list where the list node points back to the header node.

For example:

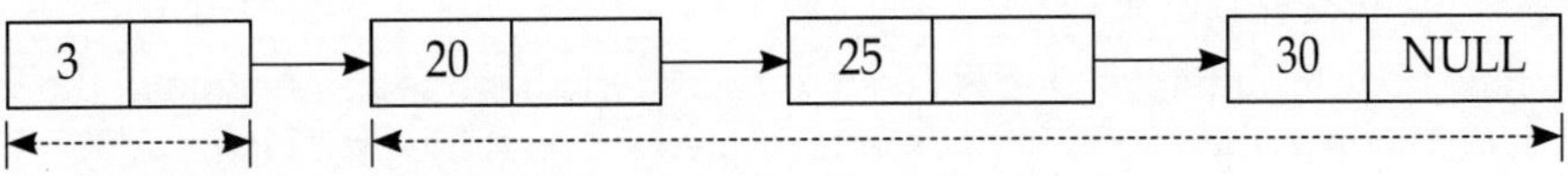

Head node contains The linked list is considered from 20 to 30

Total number of nodes in the list

The importance of the head node is that we get the starting address of the linked list, and using next pointers from the head node subsequent nodes in the linked list can be accessed.

6.12 DOUBLY LINKED LIST (DLL)

A circular linked list has advantages over a linear list. But it still has several drawbacks. One cannot traverse such a list backward, nor can a node be deleted from a circular linked list, given only pointer to that node.

A doubly linked list is one in which nodes are linked together by multiple number of links. Each node in a doubly linked list contains two pointers, one link field is the previous pointer and the other linked field is the next pointer. Thus, each node in a doubly linked list contains three fields – an info field that contains the data in the node, and prev and next fields. A doubly linked list can traverse in both the directions, forward as well as backward.

It may be either linear or circular and may not contain a header node as shown in Figure 6.7.

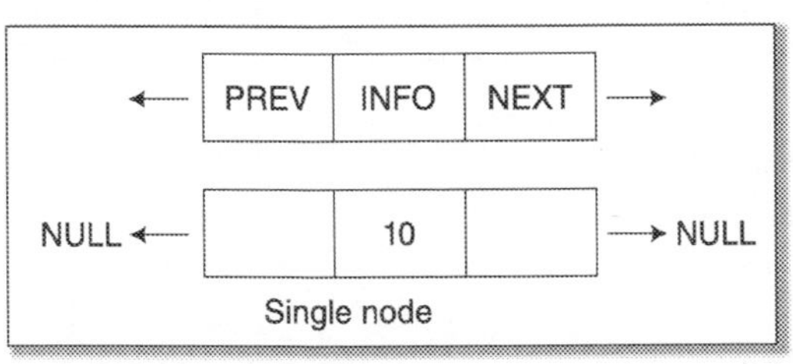

Figure 6.7

'C' Structure of doubly linked list:

```
typedef struct node
{
    int data;
    struct node *prev;
    struct node * next;
}dnode;
```

The linked representation of a doubly linked list is

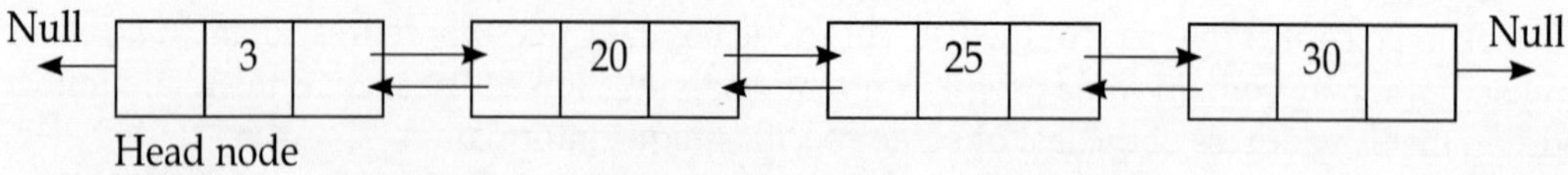

Various operations that can be performed on a doubly linked list are:

1. Insertion of a node in a doubly linked list
2. Deletion of any node from a linked list

Insertion of a node in doubly linked list:

Step 1: Set a new node as initially a flag is taken to check whether it is a first node in the variable first, as first = 0; as soon as the very first node gets created we reset the first. First = 1;

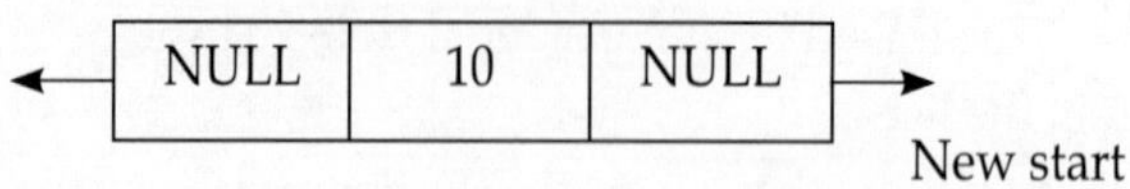

Step 2: For further addition of the nodes the New node is created.

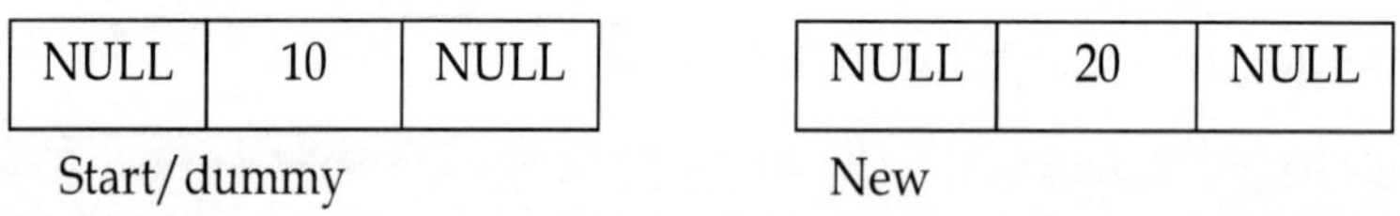

dummy → next = New;

New → prev = dummy;

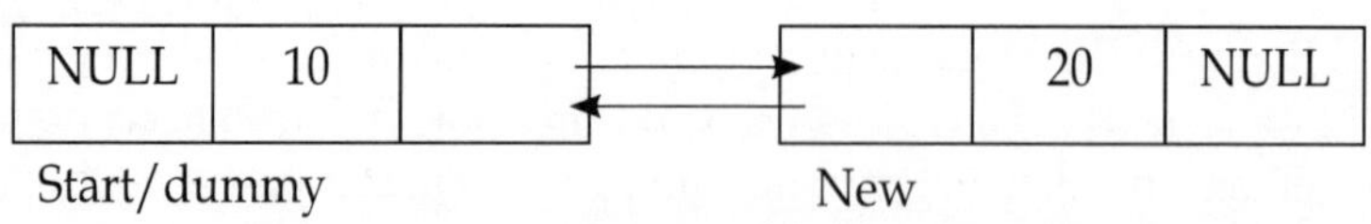

Step 3: For further addition of the nodes the New node is created.

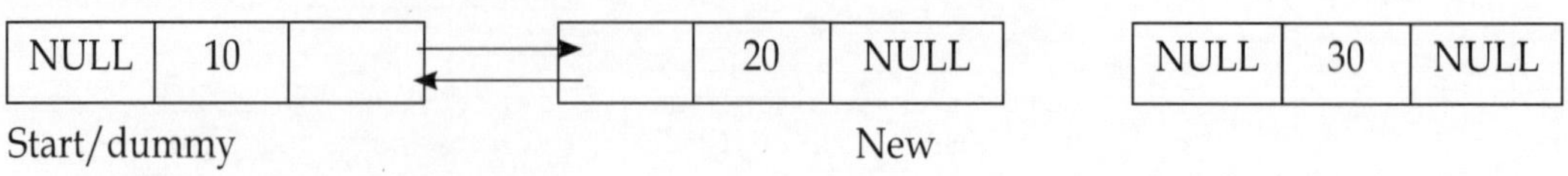

When dummy → next! = NULL;

dummy = dummy → next;

then attach new node in the linked list.

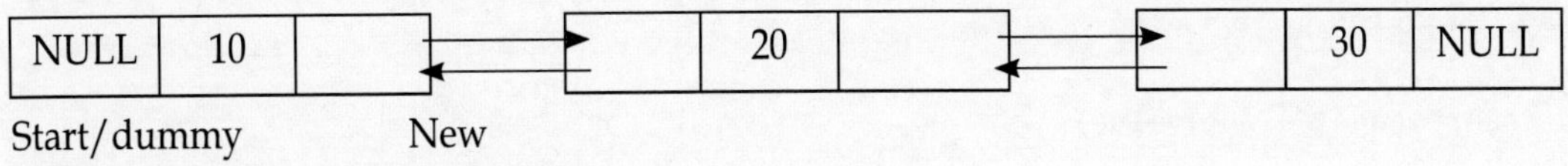

Deletion of any node from linked list

Step 1: We assume the linked list as.

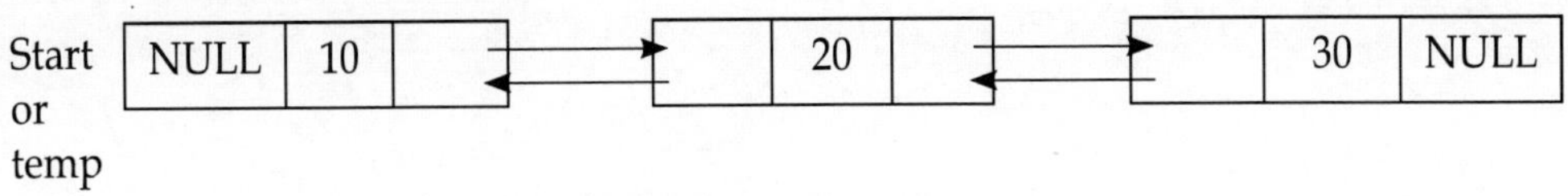

If the very first node has to be deleted, then:

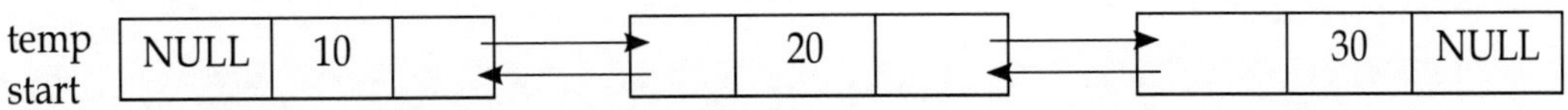

start = start→ next

start → prev = NULL

temp → next = NULL

Step 2: If we want to delete any node other than the first node then, we want to delete the node other than 20 and call it as temp node.

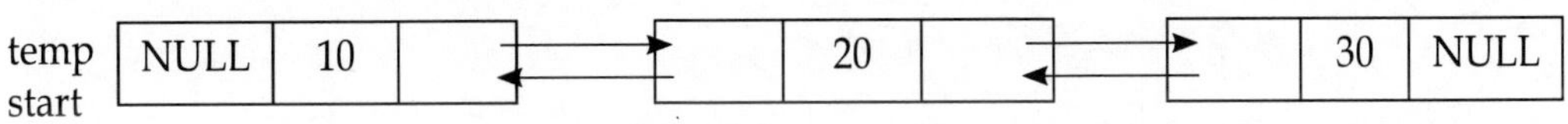

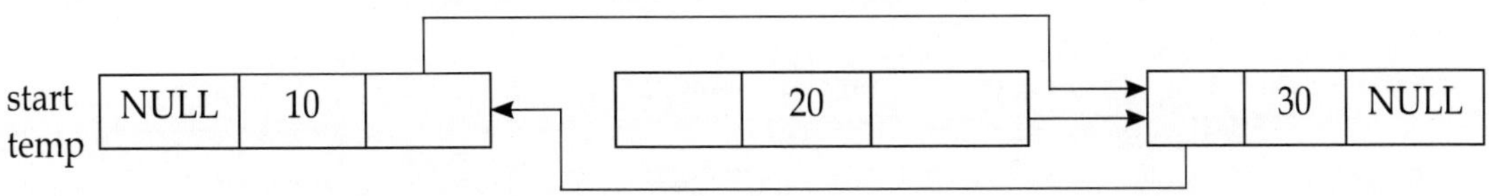

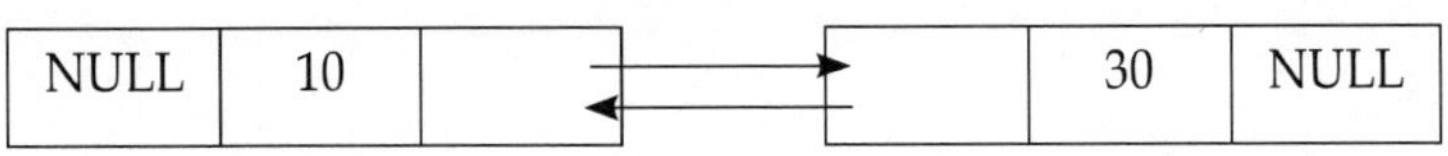

Thus the node 20 gets deleted.

Program

```
#include <stdio.h>
#include <conio.h>
#include <stdlib.h>
struct node
{
     struct node *previous;
     int data;
     struct node *next;
```

```
}*head, *last;

void insert_begning(int value)
{
    struct node *var,*temp;
    var = (struct node *)malloc(sizeof(struct node));
    var→data=value;
    if(head= =NULL)
    {
        head = var;
        head→previous=NULL;
        head→next=NULL;
        last = head;
    }
    else
    {
        temp = var;
        temp→previous=NULL;
        temp→ next=head;
        head→previous=temp;
        head= temp;
    }
}
void insert_end(int value)
{
    struct node *var,*temp;
    var=(struct node *)malloc(sizeof(struct node));
            var→data = value;
    if(head= =NULL)
    {
        head= var;
        head→previous=NULL;
        head→next=NULL;
        last= head;
    }
    else
    {
        last= head;
        while(last!=NULL)
        {
            temp= last;
            last= last→next;
        }
```

```
    last= var;
    temp→next=last;
    last→previous=temp;
    last→next=NULL;
    }
}
int insert_after(int value, int loc)
{
    struct node *temp,*var,*temp1;
    var= (struct node *)malloc(sizeof(struct node));
    var→data=value;
        if(head==NULL)
    {
         head= var;
         head→previous=NULL;
         head→next=NULL;
    }
    else
    {
         temp= head;
         while(temp!=NULL && temp→data!=loc)
         {
              temp=temp→next;
         }
         if(temp = =NULL)
         {
             printf(«\n%d is not present in list «,loc);
         }
         else
         {
         temp1=temp→next;
         temp→next = var;
         var→previous = temp;
        var→ next=temp1;
         temp1→previous = var;
         }
    }
    last= head;
    while(last→next!=NULL)
    {
         last= last→next;
    }
}
```

```
int delete_from_end( )
{
      struct node *temp;
      temp= last;
      if(temp→ previous= =NULL)
      {
           free(temp);
           head= NULL;
           last= NULL;
           return 0;
      }
      printf(«\nData deleted from list is %d \n»,last->data);
      last= temp→previous;
      last→next= NULL;
      free(temp);
      return 0;
}

int delete_from_middle(int value)
{
    struct node *temp,*var,*t, *temp1;
    temp= head;
    while(temp!= NULL)
    {
        if(temp→data = = value)
        {
             if(temp→ previous= =NULL)
             {
                  free(temp);
                  head=NULL;
                  last=NULL;
                  return 0;
             }
             else
             {
                  var→next= temp1;
                  temp1→previous = var;
                  free(temp);
                  return 0;
             }
        }
        else
        {
```

```
                var= temp;
                temp= temp→next;
                temp1=temp→next;
            }
        }
        printf(«data deleted from list is %d»,value);
}

void display( )
{
     struct node *temp;
     temp= head;
     if(temp= =NULL)
      {
         printf(«List is Empty»);
      }
     while(temp!=NULL)
     {
          printf(«→ %d ",temp→data);
          temp=temp→next;
     }
}
int main()
{
     int value, i, loc;
     head=NULL;
     printf(«Select the choice of operation on link list»);
     printf(«\n1.) insert at begning\n2.) insert at at\n3.) insert at middle»);
      printf(«\n4.) delete from end\n5.) reverse the link list\n6.) display list\n7.)
exit»);
     while(1)
     {
          printf(«\n\nenter the choice of operation you want to do «);
          scanf(«%d»,&i);
          switch(i)
          {
                 case 1:
                 {
                  printf(«enter the value you want to insert in node «);
                  scanf(«%d»,&value);
                  insert_begning(value);
                  display();
                  break;
```

```
 }
case 2:
 {
 printf(«enter the value you want to insert in node at last «);
 scanf(«%d»,&value);
 insert_end(value);
 display();
 break;
 }
 case 3:
 {
 printf(«after which data you want to insert data «);
 scanf(«%d»,&loc);
 printf(«enter the data you want to insert in list «);
 scanf(«%d»,&value);
 insert_after(value,loc);
 display();
 break;
 }
 case 4:
 {
 delete_from_end( );
 display( );
 break;
 }
 case 5:
 {
 printf(«enter the value you want to delete»);
 scanf(«%d»,value);
 delete_from_middle(value);
 display( );
 break;
 }
case 6 :
 {
 display( );
 break;
 }
 case 7 :
 {
      exit(0);
      break;
 }
```

```
        }
    }
    printf("\n\n%d",last->data);
    display( );
    getch( );
}
```

6.12.1 Difference between Singly and Doubly Linked Lists

<table>
<tr><th>S.No.</th><th>Singly Linked List</th><th>Doubly Linked List</th></tr>
<tr><td>1.</td><td>Singly linked list is a collection of nodes and each node has one data field and next link field.
For example:<table><tr><td>Data</td><td>Next</td></tr></table></td><td>Doubly linked list is a collection of nodes and each node has one data field, one previous link field and one next link field.
For example:<table><tr><td>Previous</td><td>Data</td><td>Next</td></tr></table></td></tr>
<tr><td>2.</td><td>Less efficient access to elements.</td><td>More efficient access to elements.</td></tr>
<tr><td>3.</td><td>The elements can be accessed using the next link.</td><td>The elements can be accessed using both the previous link as well as the next link.</td></tr>
<tr><td>4.</td><td>No extra field is required; hence a node takes less memory in SLL.</td><td>One field is required to store the previous link: hence a node takes more memory in DLL.</td></tr>
</table>

6.13 GENERALIZED LINKED LIST

A generalized linked list A, is defined as a finite sequence of $n \geq 0$ elements, $a_1, a_2, a_3, \ldots, a_n$ such that a_i are either atoms or the list of atoms. Thus $A = (a_1, a_2, a_3, \ldots, a_n)$
where n is the total number of nodes in the list.

Now to represent such a list of atoms we will have certain assumptions about the node structure

Flag	Data	Down Pointer	Next Pointer

Flag = 1 means down pointer exists.
= 0 means next pointer exists.

Data means the element. **Down pointer** is the address of the node which is down of the current node. **Next pointer** is the address of the node which is attached as the next node.

6.13.1 Polynomial Representation of Linked List

Linked lists are used to represent and manipulate polynomials. In the linked representation of polynomials, each term is represented as a node. Each node contains three fields, one representing the coefficient, second representing the exponent and the third is a pointer to the next term. The polynomial node structure is shown in Figure 6.8.

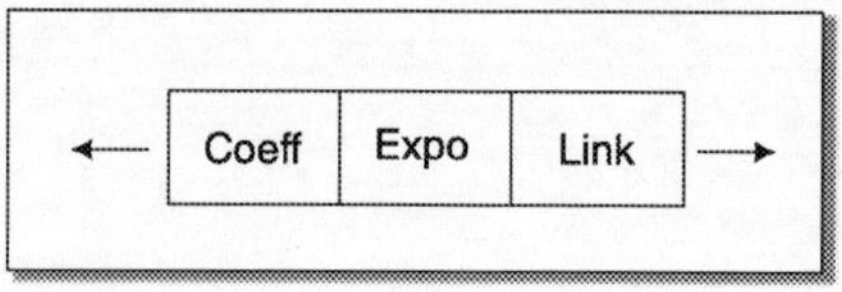

Figure 6.8 Structure of a polynomial node.

The important information about a polynomial is contained in the coefficient and exponents of x. The variable x are dropped. The variable x itself is just a place holder variable. Thus, each node will be a structure which contains a non-zero coefficient, an exponent and a pointer to the next of the polynomial. So the polynomial,

$$4x^4 + 2x^3 - x^2 + 3$$

is represented as a list of structures as shown in Figure 6.9.

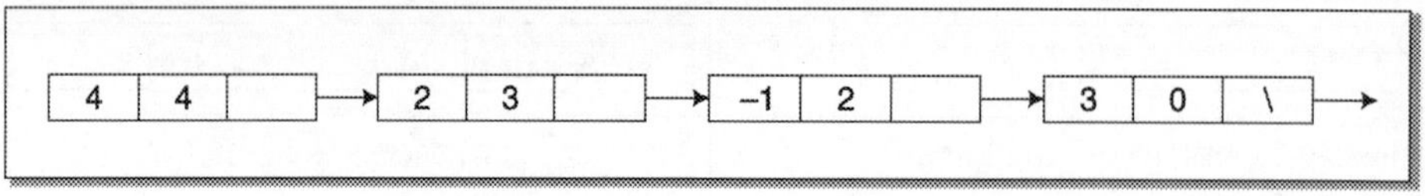

Figure 6.9 List structure of a polynomial.

To represent a term a polynomial in the variables x and y, each node consists of four sequentially allocated fields. The first two fields represent the power of the variables x and y respectively. The third and fourth field represent the coefficient of the term in the polynomial and the address of the next term in the polynomial. For example:

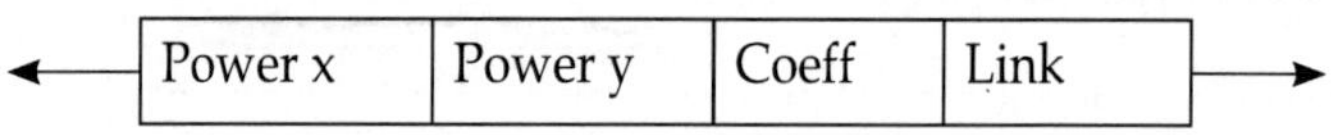

The polynomial $4x^4y^2 + 2x^3y - x^2 + 3$ is represented as linked list by Figure 6.10.

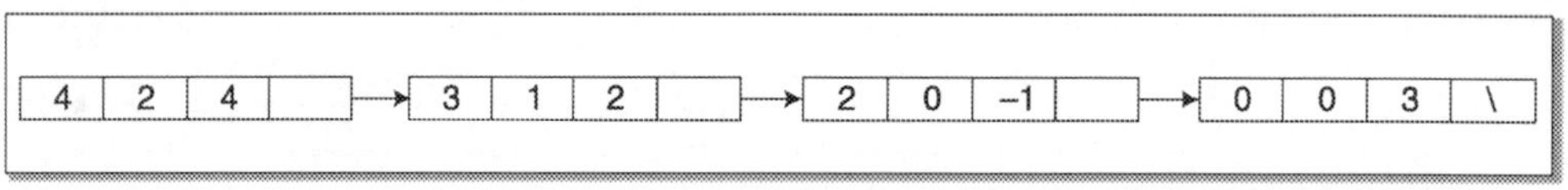

Figure 6.10 Linked representation of a polynomial two variable.

Polynomial Arithmetic

- Addition of two polynomial
- Multiplication of two polynomial
- Evaluation of polynomial

6.14 GARBAGE COLLECTION AND COMPACTION

Garbage collection is the method of detecting and reclaiming free memory. The memory allocation for the objects is done from the heap. If some objects are created and which are not used for a long time then such an object is called garbage. The garbage collection is a technique in which all such garbage is collected and recycled. The garbage collector cleans up the heap so that the memory occupied by unused objects can be freed and can be used for allocating the new objects.

The garbage collection algorithm works in two steps as follows:

1. **Mark:** In the marking process all the live objects are located and marked as non-collected objects, or all nodes that are accessible from an external pointer are marked.
2. **Collection or Sweep:** The collection phase involves proceeding sequentially through the memory and freeing all nodes that have not been marked. In this step, all the unmarked objects are swept from the heap and the space that has been allocated by these objects can be used for allocating new objects.

But the drawback of this mark and collection algorithm is that multiple fragments of memory get created hence the technique called compaction is used.

Compaction: The process of moving all used (marked) objects to one end of memory and all the available memory to the other end is called compaction. In this technique the allocated space is moved in the heap and the free space is moved up to from the contiguous block of free space in the heap.

Garbage collection is also called **automatic memory management**.

Advantages

1. The manual memory management done by a programmer (after malloc use of free or delete at the end of the function) is time consuming and error prone. Hence automatic memory management is done.
2. Reusability of the memory can be achieved with the help of garbage collection.

Disadvantage

1. The execution of the program is paused or stopped during the process of garbage collection.
2. Thus we have learned a dynamic data structure represented by a linear organization.

6.15 APPLICATIONS OF LINKED LIST

Various applications of linked list are:

1. Representing the polynomials.
2. Linked list is used in symbol tables. Symbol tables are the data structures used in compilers for keeping a track of variables and constants that are used in application programs.
3. Linked lists are used to represent a sparse matrix. A sparse matrix is a kind of matrix which contains very few non-zero elements.

7

TREE

7.1 INTRODUCTION

In the previous chapters we have studied some linear data structures such as arrays, stacks, queues, linked lists. Now we will study some non-linear data structures such as trees and graphs. Trees are one of the most important data structures in computer science. Trees are basically used to represent the data objects in a hierarchical manner.

7.2 DEFINITION OF TREES

A tree is a non-linear data structure in which data or items are arranged in a sorted sequence. It is used to represent the hierarchical relationship exiting amongst several data items. It is one of the most important data structures in computer science and is widely used in many application.

A tree 'T' can be defined as a finite set of one or more nodes, in such a manner that:

- There exists a unique node known as **root** node of the tree
- The remaining nodes of a tree are divided into n ≥ disjoint subsets, $T_1, T_2, T_3 ...... T_n$, where each of these sets belongs to a tree.

The disjoint sets $T_1, T_2, T_3 ..... T_n$ are called the sub-trees of tree. The definition of a tree is recursive as its subtrees can also be treated as trees. Figure 7.1 shows a tree with 12 nodes.

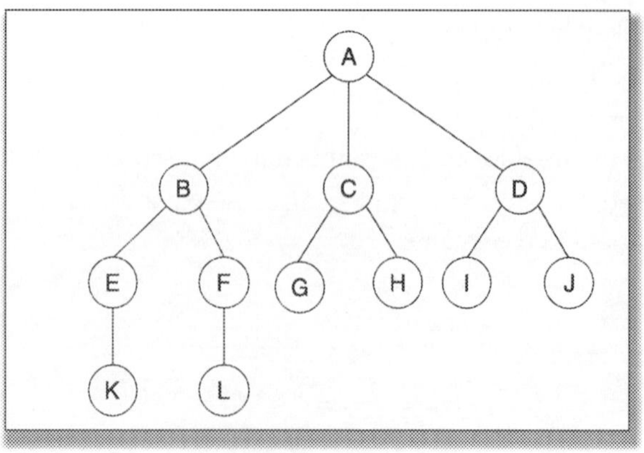

Figure 7.1 Tree

A **forest** can be defined as a set of n ≥ 0 disjoint trees. A forest can be generalized if we remove a root node from the given tree. One such tree and the respective forest are shown in Figures 7.1 and 7.2.

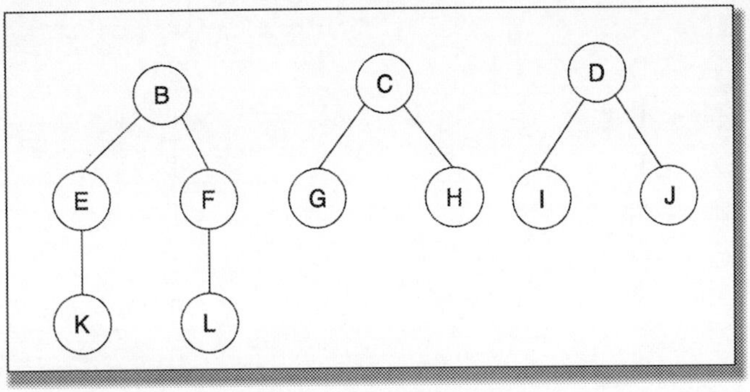

Figure 7.2 Forests.

7.3 TERMINOLOGIES

Consider a tree as shown in Figure 7.3. The tree has 14 nodes. Node 'A' is a **root** node. The number of sub-trees of a node is referred to its **degree**. Thus the degree of a node 'A' is 3. Similarly the degree of node 'E' is 1, and 'L' is 0. The degree of a tree is the maximum degree of any nodes in the tree. The degrees of various nodes are given below:

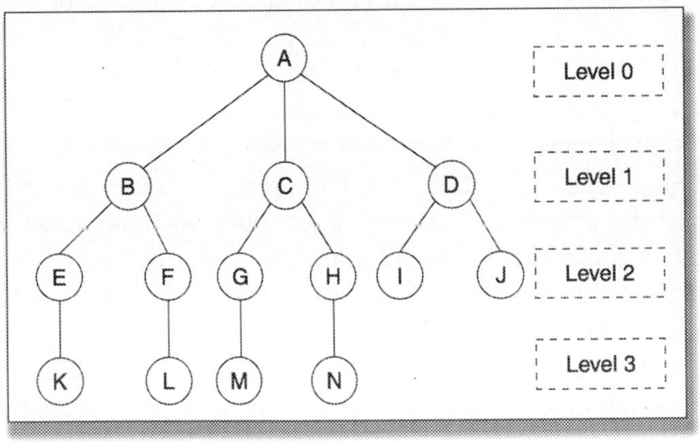

Figure 7.3 A sample tree.

Nodes having the degree zero are known as **terminal nodes** or **leaf nodes** and the nodes other than these nodes are known as **non-terminal nodes** or **non-leaf nodes.**

The degree of tree shown in Figure 7.3 is 3.

NODES	DEGREES
A	3
B	2
C	2
D	2
E	1
F	1
G	1
H	1
I	0
J	0
K	0
L	0
M	0
N	0

Terminal Nodes {I, J, K, L, M, N}

Non-terminal nodes {A, B, C, D, E, F, G, H}

The node 'A' is the root node of a tree, and that ; 'A' is the **parent** of nodes labeled 'B', 'C' and 'D'. Nodes labeled 'B', 'C' and 'D' are the **children** of node 'A'. Children of the same parent are called siblings. 'A' is the parent of nodes labeled 'B', 'C' and 'D' hence 'B', 'C' and 'D' are siblings. The **ancestors** of a node are all the nodes along the path from the root node to that node. The ancestors of node 'K' are 'E', 'B' and 'A'. The **descendents** of a node are all the nodes along the path from the node to the terminal node. The descendents of 'A' are 'B', 'E' and 'K'.

A **path** is referred to as a linear subset of a tree. For instance A-B-E-K, and A-D-J are paths. It is to be noted that there exists a unique path between a root node any other node. The **length** of the path is either calculated by the number of the intermediary nodes or the number of edges on the path. The **level** of a node is determined by setting the root node level at zero. If any node has level 'l' then its children are at level $l + 1$, (see Figure 7.3).

The **depth** of root node is zero, and the depth of any node is one plus the depth of its parent. The **height** (or sometimes depth) of a tree is the maximum level of any node in the tree.

7.4 COMMON OPERATIONS ON TREES

- Enumerating all the items
- Searching for an item
- Adding a new item at a certain position on the tree
- Deleting an item
- Removing a whole section of a tree (pruning)

- Adding a whole section to a tree (grafting)
- Fining the root of any node

7.5 COMMON USES FOR TREES

- Manipulate hierarchical data
- Make information easy to search
- Manipulate sorted lists of data

7.6 BINARY TREE

Binary tree is a special class of data structure in which the number of children of any node is restricted to almost two. A binary tree is a finite set of element that is either empty or is partitioned into three disjoint subsets. The first subset contains a single element called the root of the tree. The other two subsets are themselves binary trees, called the left and right sub-trees of the original tree. A left or right sub-tree can be empty. The distinction between a binary tree and tree is that, there is no tree having zero nodes, but there is an empty binary tree.

The binary tree 'BT' may also have zero nodes, and can be defined recursively as:

- An empty tree is binary tree.
- A distinguished node (unique node) known as root node.
- The remaining nodes are divided into two disjoint sets 'L' and 'R', where 'L' is a left sub-tree and 'R' is right sub-tree such that these are binary tree once again. Some binary trees are shown in Figure 7.4.

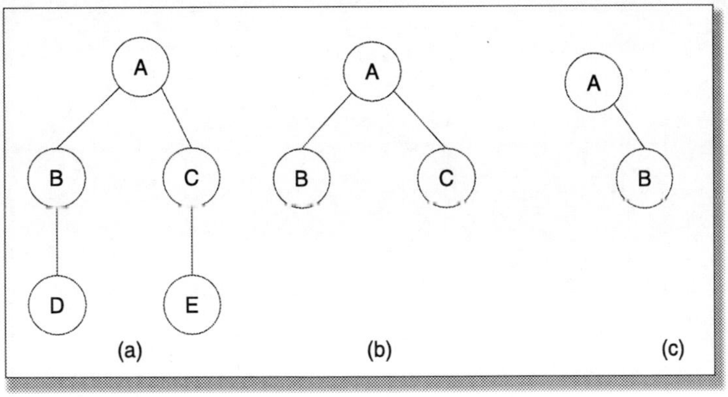

Figure 7.4 Binary tree.

7.6.1 Strictly Binary Tree

A binary tree is called a strictly binary tree if every non-leaf or terminal node in the binary tree has non-empty left and right subtree. It means that each node in a tree will have either 0 or 2 children. Figure 7.5 shows strictly binary tree.

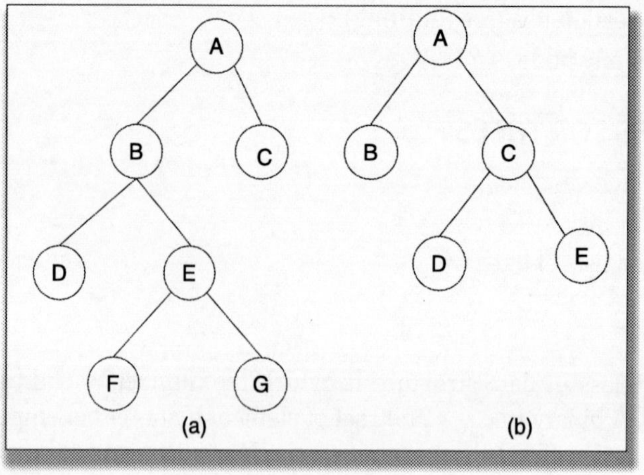

Figure 7.5 Strictly binary tree.

7.6.2 Almost Complete Binary Tree

A binary tree of depth d is an almost complete binary tree if:

- Any node at level less than d - 1 has two sons.
- For any node in the tree with a right descendent at level d, the node must have a left son and every left descendent of the node is either a leaf at level d or has two sons.

Figure 7.6 shows almost complete binary tree.

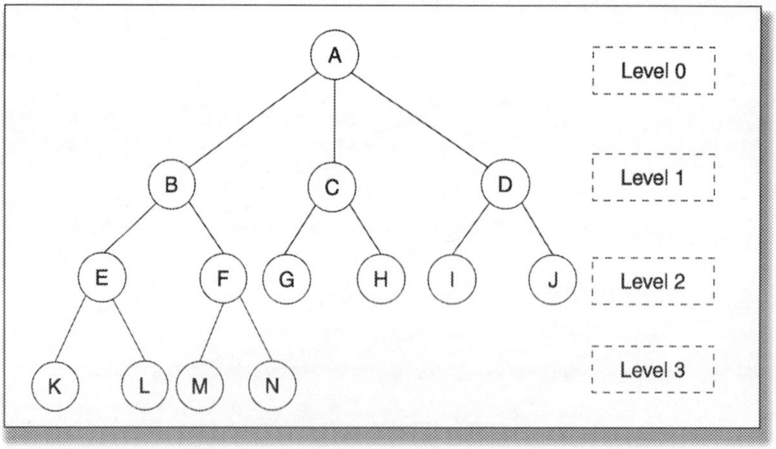

Figure 7.6 Almost complete binary tree.

7.6.3 Complete Binary Tree

A complete binary or full binary tree is a tree in which all non-terminal nodes have degree 2 and all terminal nodes are at the same depth.

A binary tree with n nodes and of depth k is complete if its nodes correspond to the nodes which are numbered one to n in the full binary tree of depth k. If there are m nodes at level l then a binary tree contains at most 2m nodes at level $l + 1$. Figure 7.7 shows a complete binary tree.

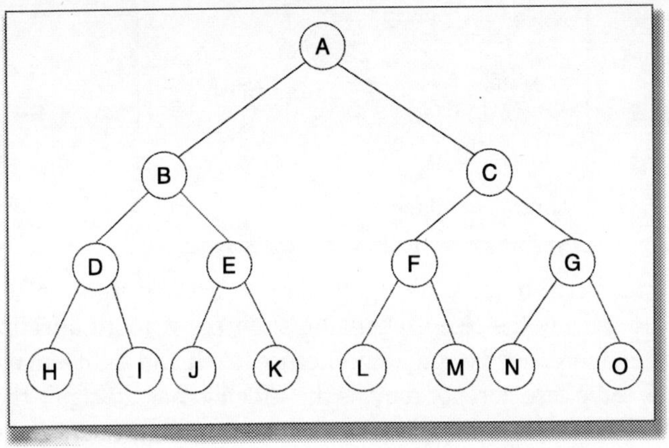

Figure 7.7 Complete binary tree.

7.6.4 Extended Binary Tree

A binary tree is called extended or 2-tree if each node N has either 0 or 2 children. In this case, the nodes with degree 2 are called internal and the nodes with degree 0 are called external nodes. Figure 7.8 shows an extended binary tree using circles for internal nodes and squares for external nodes.

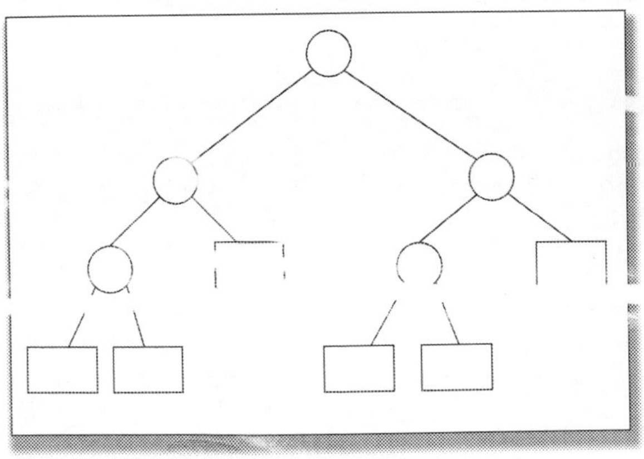

Figure 7.8 An extended binary tree.

7.6.5 Ordered Trees

There are two basic types of tree. In an unordered tree, there is no distinction between the various children of a node – none is the 'first child' or 'last child'. A tree, in which such distinctions are made, is called an ordered tree, and data structures built on them are called ordered tree data structures.

An ordered tree is a rooted tree in which the children of each vertex are assigned an order. For example, consider this tree:

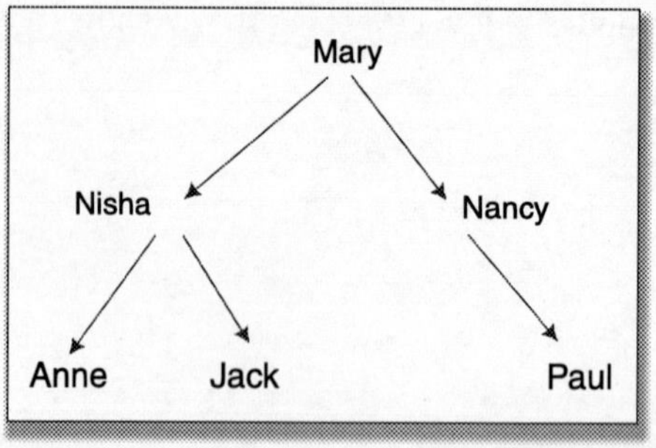

If this is a family tree, there could be no significance to left and right. In this case, the tree is unordered, and we could redraw the tree exchanging sub-trees without affecting the meaning of the tree. On the other hand, there may be some significance to left and right - may be the left child is younger than right or (as is the case here) or may be the left child has the name that occurs earlier in the alphabet system. Then the tree is ordered and we are not free to move around the sub-trees.

7.6.6 Skewed Trees

Two special binary trees, **left-skewed binary tree** in which each node has only left child, and **right-skewed binary tree** in which each node has only right child are shown in Figure 7.9.

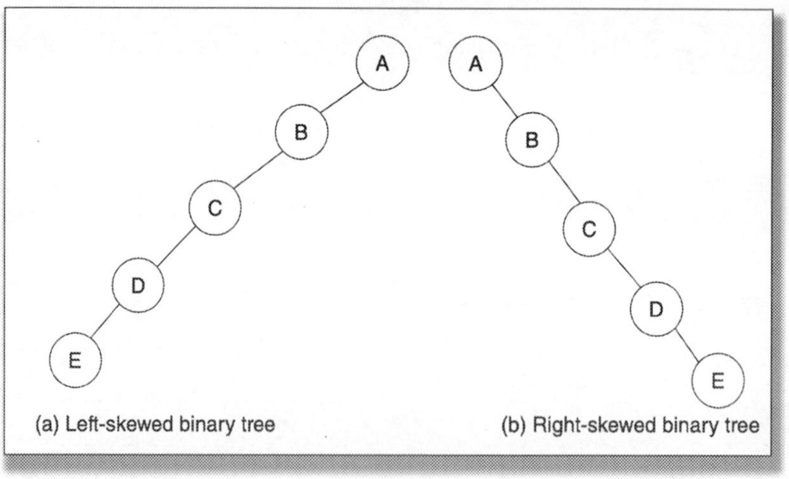

Figure 7.9

Lemma 1: A tree having 'n' nodes has exactly (n-1) edges or branches.

Proof: The proof is by induction on 'n'.

Induction Base

If n = 1 that means that the tree has only 1 node and hence 0 edge.

Induction Hypothesis

A tree having 'n' nodes must have a unique node called a root node, and 'C' children, C > 0. If 'n_i' $0 \le i \le j - 1$, thus,

$$n = 1 + \sum_{i=0}^{j-1} (n_i)$$

Induction step

It can be observed that the number of edges in the *i* th child of the root is (n_i -1).

Total number of edges in all the children of the root is

$$\sum_{i=0}^{j-1}(n_i - 1)$$

Also, the original tree contains 'C' edges from the root to its 'C' children. Thus, the total number of edges in the tree is:

$$\sum_{i=0}^{j-1} (n_i) - j + 1 \rightarrow n - 1$$

Thus, the above lemma is proved for any tree.

Lemma 2: The maximum number of nodes on level '*l*' of a binary tree is 2^l, $l \ge 0$

Proof: The proof is by induction on '*l*'

Induction base

On level $l = 0$, the root node is the only node, hence, the maximum number of nodes present at level $l = 0$, $2^l = 2^0$, which is 1.

Induction Hypothesis

It can be seen that the maximum number of nodes on level '*l*', $0 \le i \le l$, is 2^i.

Induction step

By the induction hypothesis, it can be observed that the maximum number of nodes at the level $k - 1$ is 2^{k-1}. Also, a binary tree has a property that each node can have a of maximum two degrees. Thus the maximum number of nodes on level '*l*' is twice the maximum number on level $l - 1$, which is 2^{l-1}. So, for the '*l*' level we have 2. 2^{l-1},which results to 2^l.

Thus, the above lemma is proved.

Lemma 3: The maximum number of nodes in a binary tree of height 'h' is $2^{h+1} - 1$, $h \ge 0$.

Proof: The proof is by induction on 'h'

Induction base

On level $l = 0$, the root node is the only node. Hence, the height 'h' of the tree is zero.

Induction Hypothesis

Let us assume a tree with height h = m for all k, $0 \le k \le h$, and the maximum number of nodes on level k is 2^{k+1}.

Induction step

By induction hypothesis, it can be seen that the maximum number of nodes on level j – 1 is 2^{j-1}. Thus, the maximum number of nodes in a binary tree of height 'h':

$$= \sum_{l=0}^{h} (\text{maximum number of nodes on level } 1)$$

$$= \sum_{l=0}^{h} 2^{l+1} - 1$$

$$= 2h^{+1} - 1$$

Thus, the above lemma is proved.

7.7 BINARY TREE REPRESENTATION

A binary tree can be represented by two popular traditional methods that are used to maintain tree in the memory. These are sequential allocation method and using linked lists.

1. **Sequential Allocation:** A binary tree can be represented by means of a linear array. An array can be used to store the nodes of a binary tree. The nodes stored in an array are accessible sequentially. In C, arrays start with index 0 to MAXSIZE – 1. Hence, numbering of binary tree nodes start from 0 rather than 1.

   Thus, the maximum number of nodes is specified by MAXSIZ. The root node is at index 0. Then, in successive memory locations the left child and the right child are stored.

   Some of the binary trees along with their sequential representations are shown in Figure 7.10.

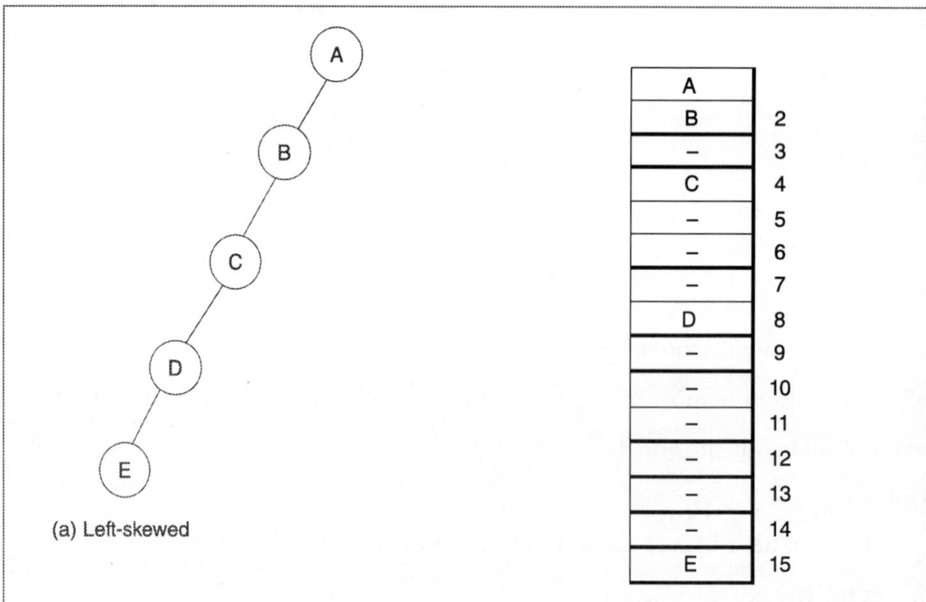

(a) Left-skewed

(b) Sequential representation of tree (a)

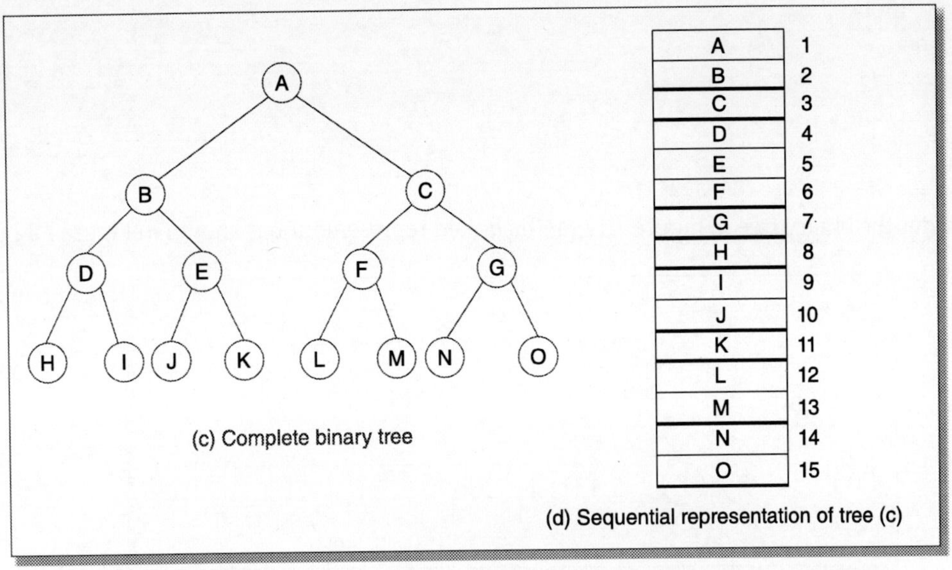

Figure 7.10 Sequential representation of binary tree.

The sequential representation consumes more space for representing a binary tree. But for representing a complete binary tree proved to be efficient as no space is wasted.

2. **Linked List Representation:** In this representation each node of a binary tree consists of three parts where:
   - The first part contains data
   - The second and third parts contain the pointer field which points to the left child and right child.

   The structure of a node is given in Figure 7.11.

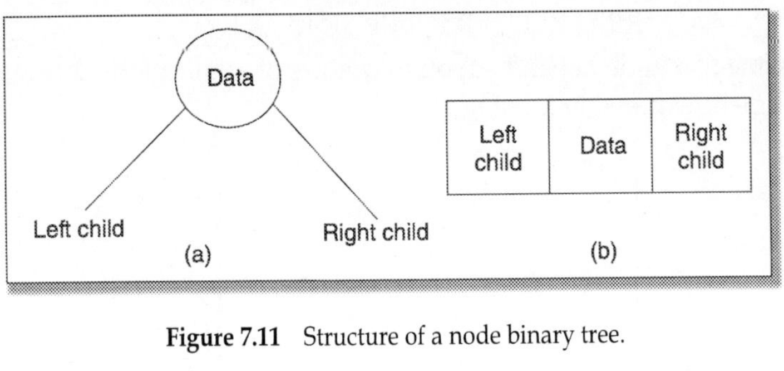

Figure 7.11 Structure of a node binary tree.

Tree nodes may be implemented as array elements or dynamically allocated variables. Each node of a tree contains data, lchild and rchild fields.

Using the array implementation, we can declare

```
# define MAXSIZE 10
struct treenode
```

```
{
    int data;
    int lchildd;
    int rchild;
};
struct treenode BTNODE [MAXSIZE];
```

Consider the binary tree in Figure 7.12 (a). Its linked representation is shown in Figure 7.12 (b).

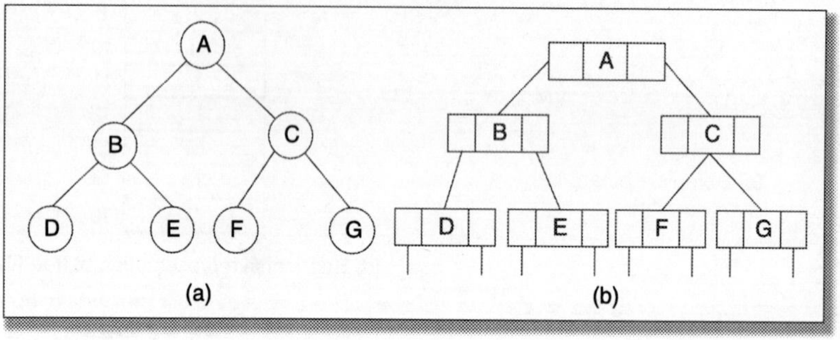

Figure 7.12 Linked list representation.

7.8 BINARY TREE TRAVERSAL

Binary tree traversing is the method of processing every node in the tree exactly once. The traversal is the most important operation performed on the tree data structures. The complete traversing of a binary tree signifies processing of nodes in some systematic manner. While traversing trees, once we start from the root, there are two ways to go, either left or right. At a given node, there are three things to do in the some order. To visit the node itself, to traverse its left sub-tree and to traverse its right sub-tree. If the root, left sub-tree and right sub-tree are designated by R′, L, R respectively then the possible traversal orders can be

RR′L, RLR′, LR′R, LRR′, R′RL, R′LR

Here the processing of a node depends upon the nature of application. Consider a binary tree representing an arithmetic expression (see Figure 7.13).

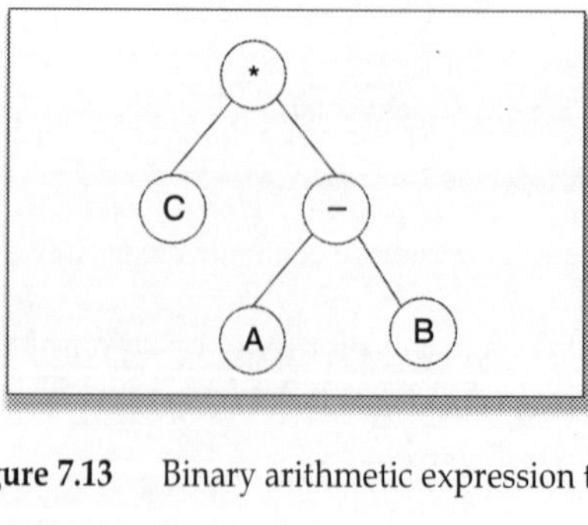

Figure 7.13 Binary arithmetic expression tree.

The three standard traversal orders are:

1. **Pre-order Traversal (R′LR):** The pre-order traversal of a binary tree is as follows:
   - First, process the root node.
   - Second, traverse the left sub-tree in pre-order.
   - Lastly, traverse the right sub-tree in pre-order.

If the tree has an empty sub-tree the traversal is performed by doing nothing. That means a tree having NULL sub-tree is considered to be completely traversed when it is encountered. The algorithm for the pre-order traversal in a binary tree is given below:

Algorithm Pre-order (Node):

The pointer variable **'Node'** stores the address of the root node.

Step 1: **Is empty?**
If (empty [Node]) then
Print "Empty tree" return

Step 2: **Process the root node**
If (Node ≠ NULL) then
Output: (Data [Node])

Step 3: **Traverse the left sub-tree**
If (Lchild [Node] ≠ NULL) then
Call preorder (Lchild [Node])

Step 4: **Traverse the right sub-tree**
If (Rchild [Node] ≠ NULL) then
Call preorder (Rchild [Node])

Step 5: **Return at the point of call**
Exit

Consider a binary tree and binary arithmetic expression tree shown in Figure 7.14 (a) and (b).

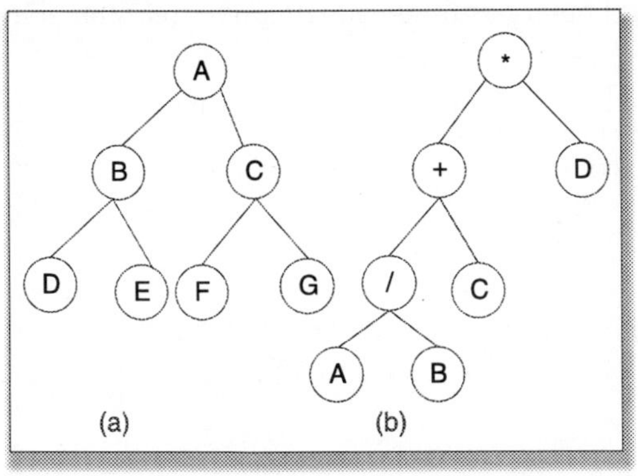

Figure 7.14 Binary tree (a) and (b).

Pre-order traversal:

Figure 7.14 (a): ABDECFG

Figure 7.14 (b): *+/ABCD

2. **In-order Traversal (LR'R):** The in-order traversal of a binary tree is as follows:
   - First, traverse the left sub-tree in in-order.
   - Second, process the root node.
   - Lastly, traverse the right sub-tree in in-order.

If the tree has an empty sub-tree the traversal is performed by doing nothing. That means a tree having NULL sub-tree is considered to be completely traversed when it is encountered. The algorithm for the in-order traversal in a binary tree is given below:

Algorithm In-order (Node): The pointer variable '**Node**' stores the address of the root node.

Step 1: **Is empty?**
If (empty [Node]) then
Print "Empty tree" return

Step 2: **Traverse the left sub-tree**
If (Lchild [Node] ≠ NULL) then
Call in-order (Lchild [Node])

Step 3: **Process the root node**
If (Node ≠ NULL) then
Output: (Data [Node])

Step 4: **Traverse the right sub-tree**
If (Rchild [Node] ≠ NULL) then
Call in-order (Rchild [Node])

Step 5: **Return at the point of call**
Exit

Consider a binary tree and binary arithmetic expression tree shown in Figure 7.15 (a) and (b).

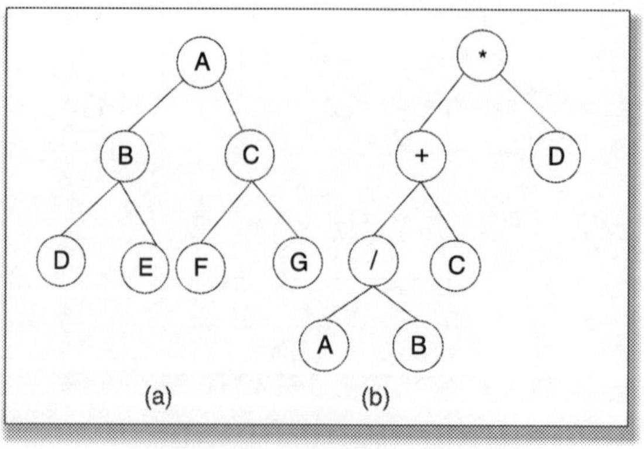

Figure 7.15 Binary tree (a) and (b).

In-order traversal:

Figure 7.15 (a): DBEAFCG

Figure 7.15 (b): A/B+C*D

3. **Post-order Traversal (LRR'):** The post-order traversal of a binary tree is as follows:
   - First, traverse the left sub-tree in post-order.
   - Second, traverse the right sub-tree in post-order.
   - Lastly, process the root node.

If the tree has an empty sub-tree the traversal is performed by doing nothing. That means a tree having NULL sub-tree is considered to be completely traversed when it is encountered. The algorithm for the post-order traversal in a binary tree is given below:

Algorithm Post-order (Node):

The pointer variable **'Node'** stores the address of the root node.

Step 1: Is empty?
If (empty [Node]) then
Print "Empty tree" return

Step 2: Traverse the left sub-tree
If (Lchild [Node] ≠ NULL) then
Call post-order (Lchild [Node])

Step 3: Traverse the right sub-tree
If (Rchild [Node] ≠ NULL) then
Call post-order (Rchild [Node])

Step 4: Process the root node
If (Node ≠ NULL) then
Output: (Data [Node])

Step 5: Return at the point of call
Exit

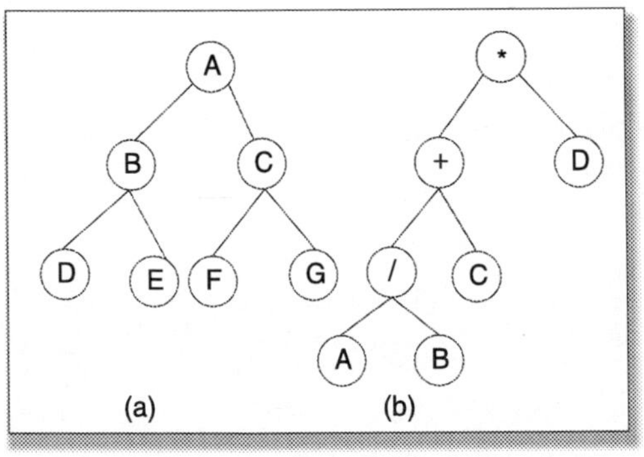

Figure 7.16 Binary tree (a) and (b).

Consider a binary tree and binary arithmetic expression tree shown in Figure 7.16 (a) and (b).

Post-order traversal:

Figure 7.16 (a): DEBFGCA

Figure 7.16 (b): AB/C+D*

7.8.1 Creation of a Binary Tree From Tree Traversals

We have already seen in-order, pre-order and post-order traversals. Now a question may come in our mind that is it possible to predict a tree from any one traversal. To predict the exact tree from the tree traversals we require at least any two traversals.

Let us see the procedure of predicting a binary tree from given traversals.

Post-order: H I D E B F G C A

In-order: H D I B E A F C G

Step 1: The last node in post-order (left, right and root) sequence is the root node. In the above example 'A' is the root node. Now the in-order sequence locates the 'A'. Left sequence to 'A' indicates the left sub-tree and right sequence to 'A' indicates the right sub-tree.

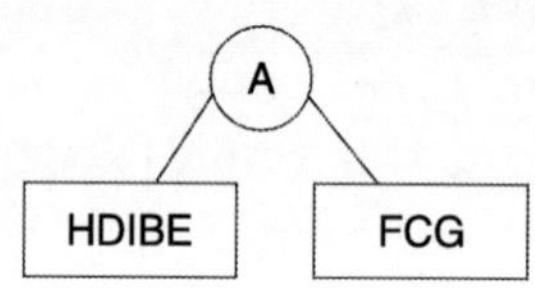

Step 2: These alphabets H, D, I, B, E observe the post-order and sequence in in-order

Post-order: H I D E **B**

In-order: H D I **B** E

Here B is parent node; therefore pictorially the tree will be as shown in the figure below.

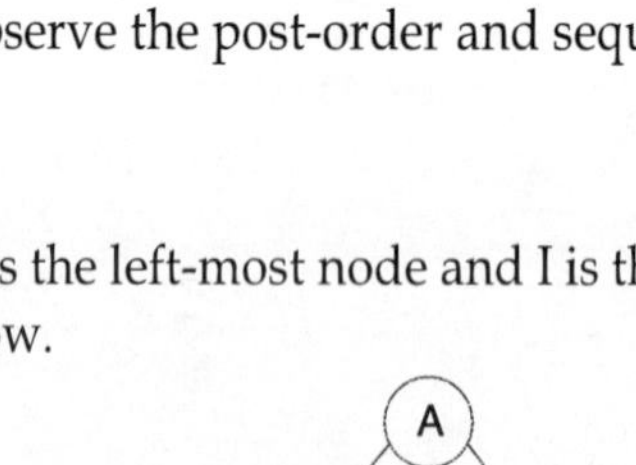

Step 3: These alphabets H, D, I observe the post-order and sequence in in-order

Post-order: H I **D**

In-order: H **D** I

Here D is the parent node; H is the left-most node and I is the right child of D node. So the tree will be as shown in the figure below.

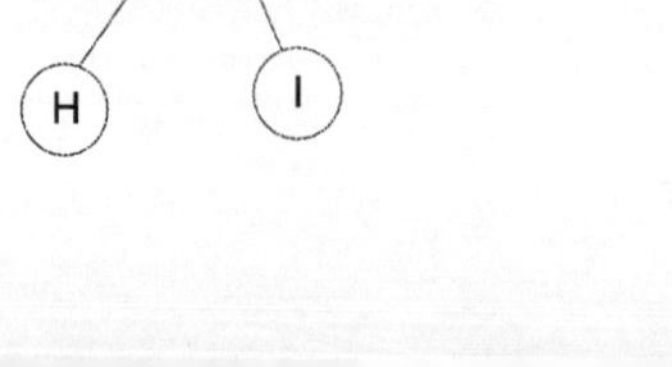

Step 4: Now we will solve for the right sub-tree of root 'A' with the alphabets F, C, G. Observe both the sequences:

Post-order: F G C

In-order: F C G

C is the parent node, F is the left child and G is the right child. So finally the tree will be as shown in the figure below.

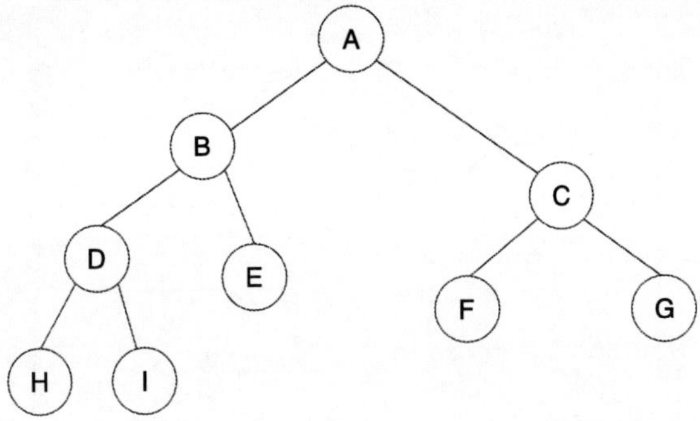

7.9 THREADED BINARY TREE

Linked representation of a binary tree produces large number of NULL pointer if nodes have either empty or one child. Thus for a node that does not have a left child (left sub-tree) then its left child pointer field is set to NULL. Similarly, if a node does not contain a right child (right sub-tree) then its right child pointer field is set to NULL. Likewise, for an empty sub-tree of a node its both left and right child pointers are set to NULL. Thus, it can be easily observed that more than that of actual pointers occurs in these. The above discussion is illustrated in Figure 7.17.

To solve these problems of wasted space for these NULL pointers the idea is to use these pointers to point some node in the tree. These NULL pointers are converted into useful links called **threads** (optimizing NULL pointers concept of thread used). Thus, the representation of a binary tree using these threads is called a threaded binary tree. To which node a NULL pointer should point is decided according to the in-order traversal.

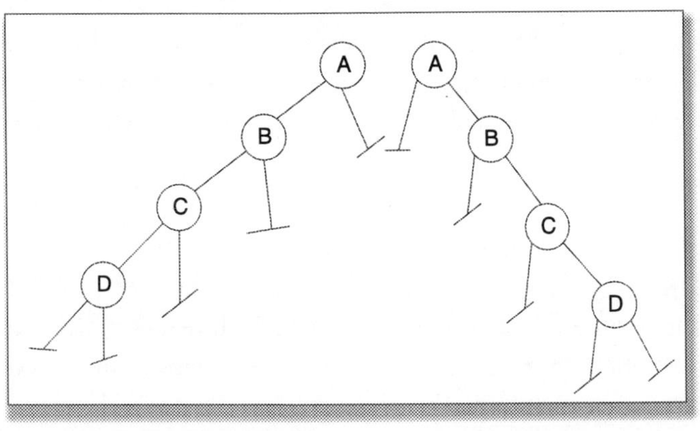

Figure 7.17 Computing pointer in a binary tree.

If the link of a node P is NULL then this link is replaced by the address of the predecessor of P. similarly, if a right link is NULL then this link is replaced by the address of the successor of the node which would come after node P. Internally, a thread and a pointer, both are addresses. These can be distinguished by the assumption that a normal pointer is represented by positive addresses and threads are represented by negative addresses. Figure 7.18 shows a threaded binary tree where normal pointers and threads are shown by solid lines and dashed lines respectively.

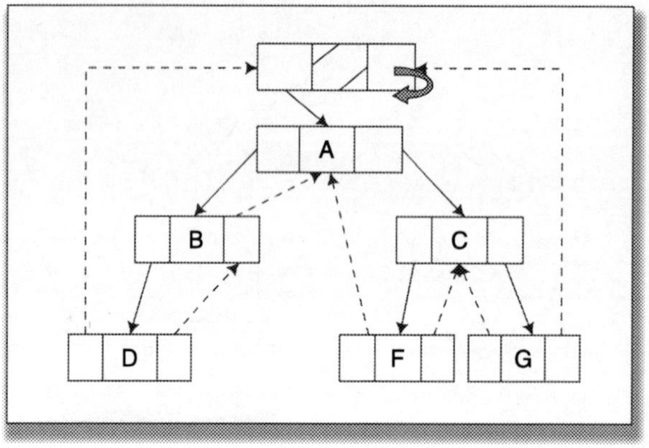

Figure 7.18 A threaded binary tree.

It is to be noted that by making little modification in the structure of a binary tree we can get the threaded tree structure, thereby distinguishing threads and normal pointer by adding two extra one-bit fields-lchildthread and rchildthread.

$$\text{lchildthread} = \begin{cases} 1, & \text{lchild (A) is a normal pointer} \\ 0, & \text{rchild (A) is a thread} \end{cases}$$

also,

$$\text{rchildthread} = \begin{cases} 1, & \text{rchild (A) is a normal pointer} \\ 0, & \text{lchild (A) is a thread} \end{cases}$$

Advantages

1. The in-order traversal of a threaded tree is faster than its unthreaded version.
2. With a threaded tree representation, it may be possible to generate the successor or predecessor of any arbitrarily selected node without having to incur the overhead of using a stack.

Disadvantages

1. Threaded trees are unable to share common sub-trees.
2. If negative addressing is not permitted in the programming language being used, two additional fields are required to distinguish between the thread and structural links.
3. Insertions and deletions from a threaded tree are time consuming, since both thread and structural links must be maintained.

7.10 BINARY SEARCH TREE (BST)

For the purpose of search we use binary search tree. It is a special sub-class of binary tree. In binary search tree, the data items are arranged in a certain order. The order may be numerical, alphabetical (or lexicographical). If the order is numerical (or lexicographical) then the left sub-tree of the binary search tree contains those nodes that have less or equal numerical (or lexical) value than those associated with the root of the tree (or sub-tree). Similarly, the right sub-tree contains those nodes that have greater or equal numerical (or lexical) values than those associated with the root of the tree (or sub-tree).

A binary search tree is a binary tree which is either empty or satisfies the following rules:

- The value of the key in the left child or left sub-tree is less than the value of the root.
- The value of key in the right child or right sub-tree is more than or equal to the value of the root.
- All the sub-trees of the left and right child observe the two rules.

Figure 7.19 shows a binary search tree.

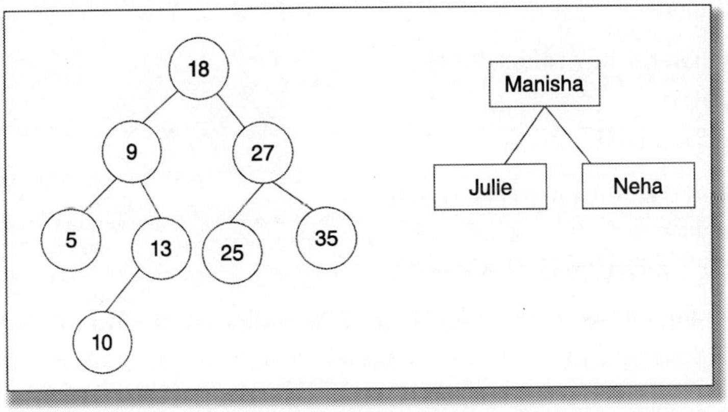

Figure 7.19 Binary search tree.

7.10.1 Operations of Binary Search Tree

7.10.1.1 Searching

In a binary search tree, the search of the desired data item can be performed by branching into the left or right-subtree until the desired data item (node) is reached. The search starts from the root node. If the tree is empty then the search is completed by doing nothing which means that the search is unsuccessful. Otherwise, we compare the key 'K' of the desired data items with the key of the root. If 'K' is less than the key of the root then only the left-subtree is to be reached, as no data item in the right sub-tree has key value 'K'. if 'K' is greater than the key in the root then only the right sub-tree need to be searched. If 'K' equals to the key in the root then the search terminates successfully. In a similar manner the sub-trees are also searched.

The time complexity for searching the desired data item in the binary search tree is O (h), where 'h' is the height of the tree being searched.

The algorithm for searching the desired data item in a binary search tree is given below.

Algorithm of BST search

The pointer 'R' stores the address of the root node and 'K' is the key of the desired data item to be searched.

Step 1: Checking, Is empty?
If (R = 0), then
Print: "Empty tree"
Return 0

Step 2: if 'K' is equal to the value of the root node
If (R[data] = K)
Print: "search is successful"
Return (R[data])

Step 3: 'K' is less than the key value at root
If (K < R[data])
Return (BST search (R[lchild], K)

Step 4: 'K' is greater than the key value at root
If (K > R[data])
Return (BST search (R[rchild], K)

Example: Given the binary search tree, see Figure 7.20. Suppose we have to search a data item having key K = 13, then searching of the data item can be done by using the searching algorithm as follows.

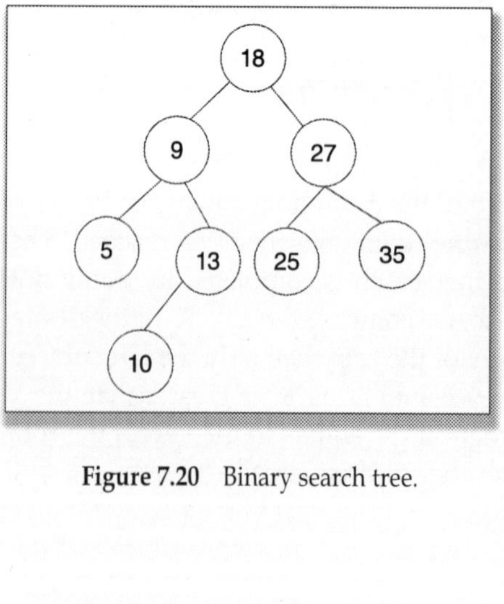

Figure 7.20 Binary search tree.

Solution

Step 1: Initially
K = 13
R[data] = 18
(K < R[data]), so,
Left sub-tree to be searched

Step 2: K = 13
R[data] = 9
(K > R[data]), so,
Right sub-tree to be searched

Step 3: K = 13
R[data] = 13
(K = R[data]), so,

Search is successful and it terminates.

7.10.1.2 Insertion

In a binary search tree we do not allow any replica of the data items. So to insert a data item having key 'K' into a binary search tree, we must check that its key is different from those of the existing data items by performing a search for the data item with the same key 'K'. If the search for 'K' is unsuccessful then the data item is inserted into a binary search tree at the point where the search is terminated.

While inserting the new data item having key 'K' three cases arise:

1. If the tree is empty then a new data item is inserted as the root node.
2. If the tree has only one node, root node, then depending upon the key value of the data item it is inserted in the tree.
3. If the tree is non-empty, has a number of nodes, then by comparing the value of the key the node is inserted. If 'K' is less than the root then it is inserted in the left sub-tree, otherwise, in the right sub-tree. The whole process is repeated until the appropriate place is obtained for the insertion.

The algorithm for the insertion of a new data item in the binary search tree is given below:

Algorithm of BST Insertion

The pointer 'R' stores the address of the root node and 'new' points to the new node which store the 'K' is the key of the desired data item to be inserted.

Step 1: Checking, Is empty?
If (R = NULL), then
Print: "Empty tree"
Set new [data] ← K
Set (rchild) ← NULL

Set new [lchild] ← NULL

Set R ← new

Step 2: Inserting node 'new' into a tree having single node

If (new [data] < R[data]) then

Set R [lchild] ← new

Set R [rchild] ← NULL

Else

Set R ← lchild ← NULL

Set R ← rchild ← new

Step 3: Inserting node 'new' into a tree having more nodes

While (R ≠ NULL)

{

If (R [data] < new [data]) then

{

If (R [lchild] = NULL) then

{

Set R [lchild] ← new

Set R ← NULL

}

Else

Set R ← R[lchild]

Else if (R [rchild] = NULL) then

{

Set R [rchild] ← new

Set R ← NULL

}

Else

Set R ← R[rchild]

Step 4: Return to the point of call

Return

The insertion of a new data item into a binary search tree is performed in O (h) time where 'h' is the height of the tree.

Example: Suppose T is an empty binary search tree. Now we have to insert following five data items into the binary search tree:

5 30 2 40 35

Solution

Step 1: Insertion 5

So, the node becomes the root node as the tree is empty.

Step 2: Insertion 30

Checking with the root node 30 > 5

So, it is inserted at right of the root node.

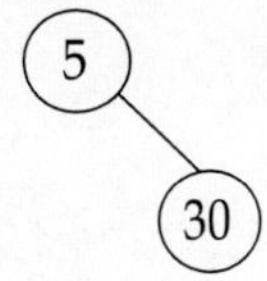

Step 3: Insertion 2

Checking with the root node 2 < 5

So, it is inserted at the left of the root node

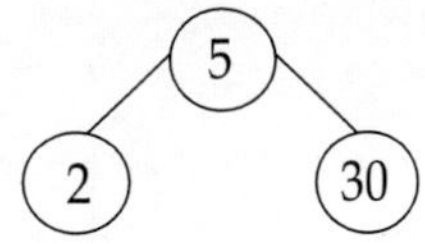

Step 4: Insertion 40

Checking with root node 40 > 5,

So, it is inserted at the right sub-tree of the root node,

Checking with the root node of the right sub-tree 40 > 30

So, it is inserted at the right.

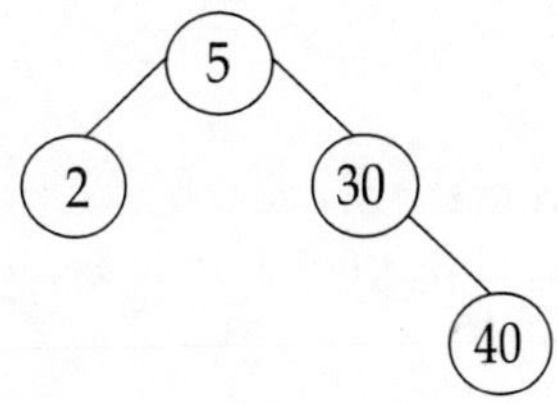

Step 5: Insertion 35

Checking with root node 35 > 5,

So, it is inserted at the right sub-tree of the root node,

Checking with the root node of the right sub-tree 35 > 30,

So, it should be in the right sub-tree, but

35 < 40

So, it is inserted in its left sub-tree.

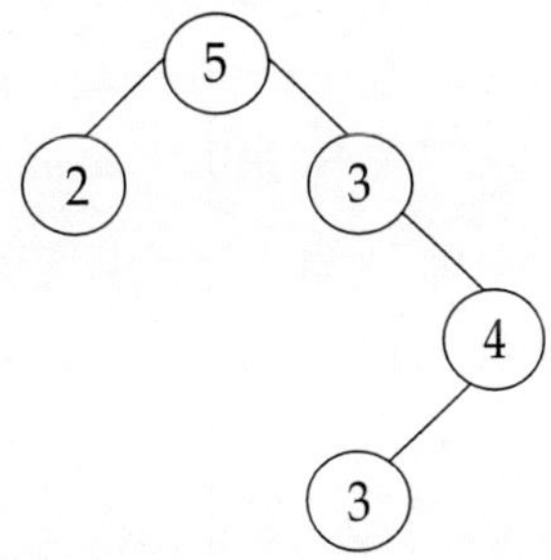

7.10.1.3 Deletion

In a binary search tree, for deleting a particular node from the binary search, it is searched first by the searching algorithm discussed previously. If the search is not successful then the algorithm is terminated. Otherwise from a binary search tree there are three cases which are possible for the node to delete those that contain the data items.

(i) Deletion of the leaf node.

(ii) Deletion of a node having one child.

(iii) Deletion of a node having two children.

Case 1: Deletion of leaf node

Consider Figure 7.21. In this 'delete' is the left leaf node which has to be deleted. The only task for the deletion of this node is by discarding the leaf node, to set its parent left child pointer to NULL.

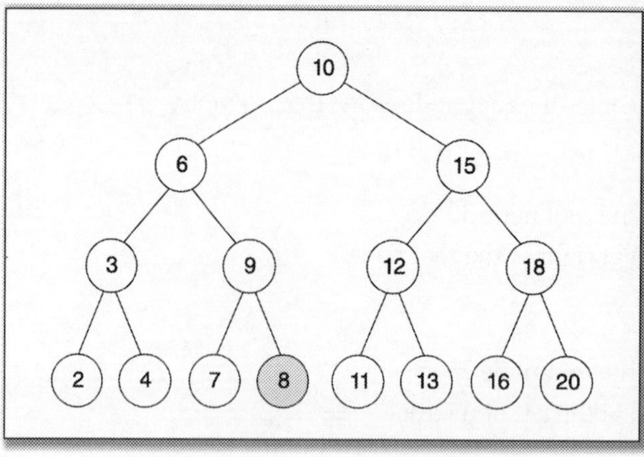

Figure 7.21 Before deletion.

From the above tree, we want to delete the node having the value 8. Then we will set the right pointer of its parent node as NULL that is the right pointer of the node having the value 9 is set to NULL.

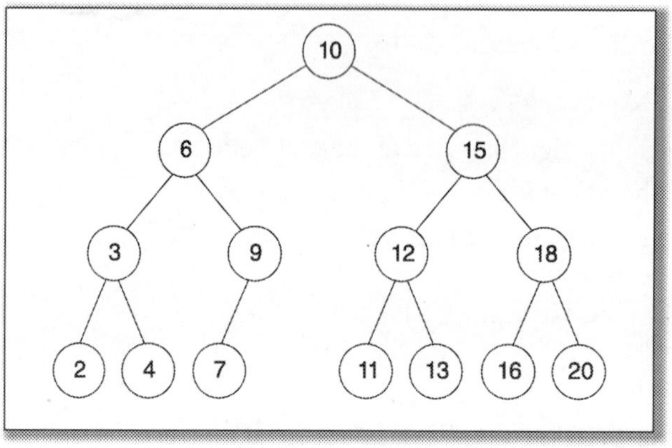

Figure 7.22 After deletion.

Algorithm of BST deletion of leaf node

The procedure deletes the node pointed by 'del' from the binary search tree.

Step 1: Searching leaf node

Call to BSTsearch (R, del)

Step 2: Deletion of leaf node

if (x (lchild) = NULL and (x (rchild) = NULL) then

{

if (parent (lchild) = x)

```
{
set parent (lchild) = NULL)
}
else
set parent (lchild) = NULL)
}
```

Step 3: Free the node

Freenode (x).

Case 2: Deletion of a node having one child

Consider Figure 7.23. In this delete the darkened point's node which has exactly one non-empty tree.

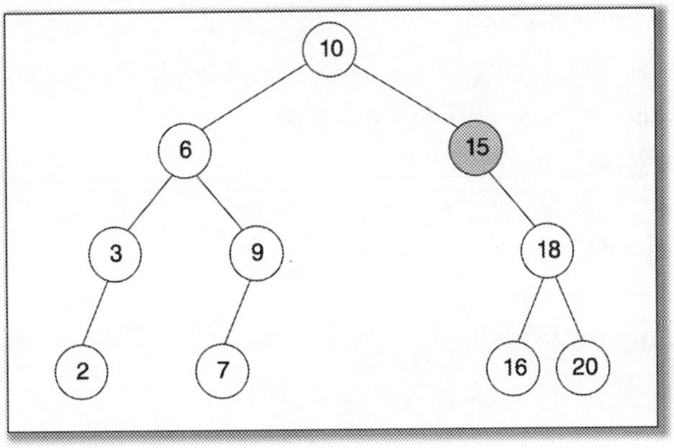

Figure 7.23 Before deletion.

If we want to delete the node 15, then we will simply copy node 18 of 15 and then set the node free. If the delete node that has a right child then the right child pointer value is assigned to the right child value of its parent, but if the delete node that has a left child then the left child pointer value is assigned to the left child value of its parent.

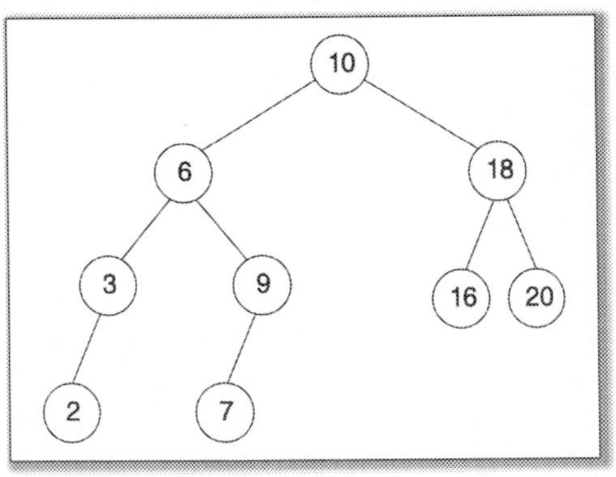

Figure 7.24 After deletion of node from tree.

Algorithm of BST Deletion of a node having one child

The procedure deletes the node pointed by 'del' from the binary search tree which has exactly one non-sub-tree.

Step 1: If node pointed by 'del' has only right sub-tree

```
if ( del (lchild) = NULL) then
{
if (parent (lchild) = del) then
{
set parent (lchild)← del (rchild)
}
else
set parent (rchild)← del (rchild)
}
```

Step 2: If node pointed by 'del' has only left sub-tree

```
if ( del (rchild) = NULL) then
{
if (parent (lchild) = del) then
{
set parent (lchild)← del (lchild)
}
else
set parent (rchild)← del (lchild)
}
```

Step 3: Free the node

Freenode (del).

Case 3: Deletion of a node having two children

Consider Figure 7.25. In this delete the darkened point's node which has exactly two non-sub-trees.

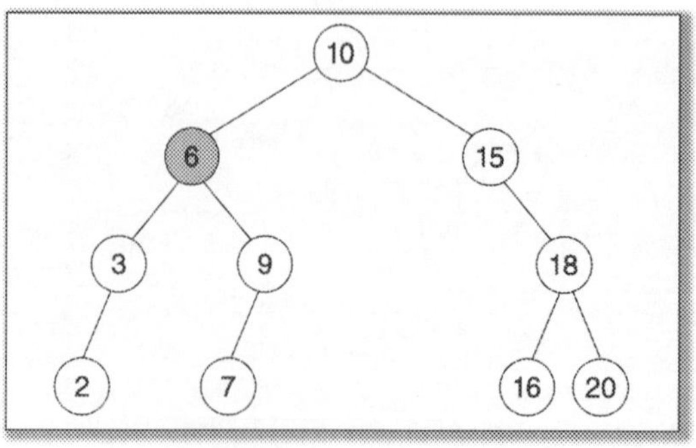

Figure 7.25 Before deletion.

We want to delete the node having the value 6. We will then find out the in-order successor of node 6. The in-order successor will be simply copied at location of node 6. That means copy 7 at the position where value of the node is 6. Set the left pointer of 9 as NULL. This completes the deletion procedure.

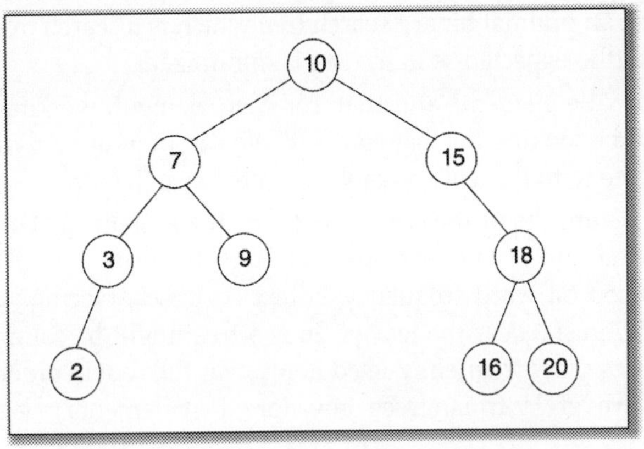

Figure 7.26 After deletion of node from tree.

Algorithm of BST Deletion of a node having two children

The procedure deletes the node pointed by 'del' from the binary search tree which has exactly two non-sub-trees.

Step 1: Initialization

set parent ← del

set inos ← del (rchild)

Step 2: Loop, finding in-order successor

while (inos (lchild) ≠ NULL

{

set parent ← inos

set inos ← inos (lchild)

}

Step 3: Substituting in-order successor to the appropriate place

set del (data) ← inos (data)

set del ← inos

Step 4: Return the node to the free storage pool

Freenode (del).

7.10.2 Types of Binary Search Tree

There are many types of binary search tree. AVL trees and red-black trees are both forms of self-balancing binary search trees. A splay tree is a binary search tree that automatically moves frequently accessed elements nearer to the root. In a treap ('tree heap'), each node also holds a priority and the parent node has a higher priority than its children.

7.10.2.1 Optimal binary search tree

If we don't plan on modifying a search tree and we know exactly how often each item will be accessed, we can construct an optimal binary search tree which is a search tree where the average cost of looking up an item (the expected search cost) is minimized.

Assume that we know the elements and that, for each element, we know the proportion of future lookups which will be looking for that element. We can then use a dynamic programming solution to construct the tree with the least possible expected search cost.

Even if we only have estimates of the search costs, such a system can considerably speed up lookups on average. For example, if you have a BST of English words used in a spell checker, you might balance the tree based on word frequency in text corpuses, placing words like 'the' near the root and words like 'agerasia' near the leaves. Such a tree might be compared with Huffman trees, which similarly seek to place frequently-used items near the root in order to produce a dense information encoding. However, Huffman trees only store data elements in leaves.

7.10.2.2 digital binary search tree

In a digital search tree, instead of key comparison, a sequence of digits or characters are made. For instance, if a key is a set of integers then each position of a digit determines one of the ten possible children of a given node. But, if a key is a set of characters, determine one of the twenty-six possible children of a given node. In this search tree, the leaf node is represented by a special symbol 'E_k', which indicates end key. The node structure of a digital search tree is as follows:

- Each node consists of three fields
- Symbol key
- Child, pointer to the first sub-tree
- Csib, child sibling which is a pointer to the next sibling.

In Figure 7.27, a forest is represented as a set of data items from the given sets:

$$S = \{111, 199, 153, 1672, 27,245, 2221, 310, 389, 3333\}$$

Binary tree representation method is not the only method to represent digital search tree. If binary tree representation is not used, then for 'n' symbols in each position of the key, each node in a tree contains 'n' pointers to the corresponding symbols. In such type of tree representation, the node pointer is associated with a symbol value based at its position in the node. This implementation of digital search tree is known as 'trie' search tree, where 'Trie' is derived from the word 'retrieval'.

7.10.2.3 Red- black tree

A red-black tree is a type of self-balancing binary search tree, a data structure used in computer science, which is typically used to implement associative arrays. The original structure was invented in 1972 by Rudolf Bayer who called them 'symmetric binary B-trees', but acquired its modern name in a paper in 1978 by Leo J. Guibas and Robert Sedgewick. It is complex, but has good worst-case running time for its operations and is efficient in practice. It can search, insert and delete in O (log n) time, where n is the number of elements in the tree.

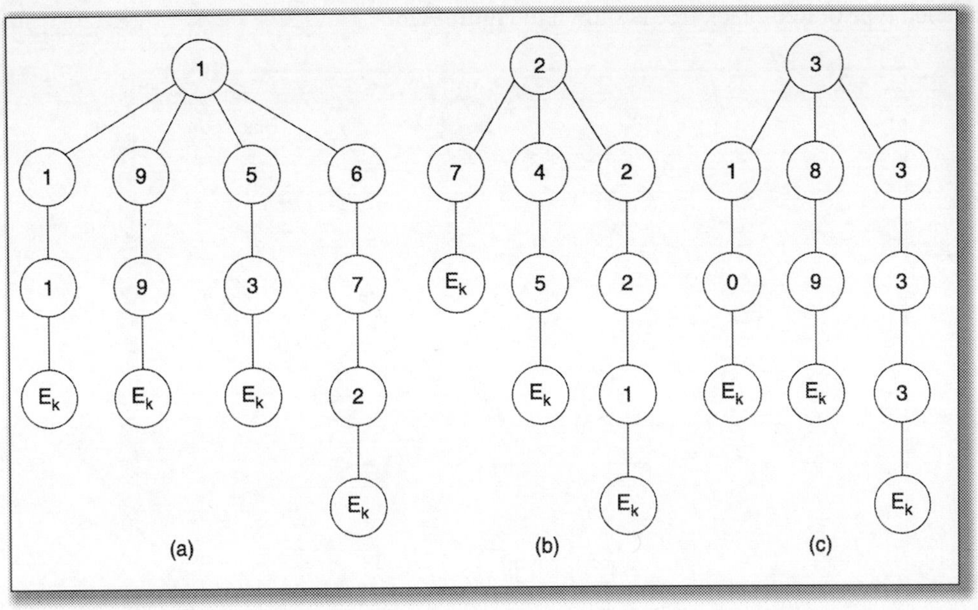

Figure 7.27 Forest representing set of data items.

A red-black tree is a special type of binary tree, which is a structure used in computer science to organize pieces of comparable data, such as numbers. Each piece of data is stored in a node. One of the nodes always functions as our starting place, and is not the child of any node. We call this the root node or root. It has up to two 'children', which are other nodes to which it connects. Each of these children can have children of its own, and so on. The root node thus has a path connecting it to any other node in the tree. If a node has no children, we call it a leaf node, since intuitively it is at the edge of the tree. A sub-tree is the portion of the tree that can be reached from a certain node, considered as a tree itself. In red-black trees, the leaves are assumed to be null or empty.

As red-black trees are also binary search trees, they must satisfy the constraint that every node contains a value greater than or equal to all the nodes in its left sub-tree, and less than or equal to all nodes in its right sub-tree. This makes it quick to search the tree for a given value.

Properties

A red-black tree is a binary search tree where each node has a color attribute the value of which is either red or black. In addition to the ordinary requirement imposed on binary search trees, we add the following conditions to any valid red-black tree:

- Every node is colored either black or red.
- The root is black.
- All leaves are black.
- Both children of every red node are black.
- Every leaf-nil node, known as external node is colored black.
- All paths from any given node to its leaf nodes contain the same number of black nodes.

One such type of Red-black tree is shown in Figure 7.28.

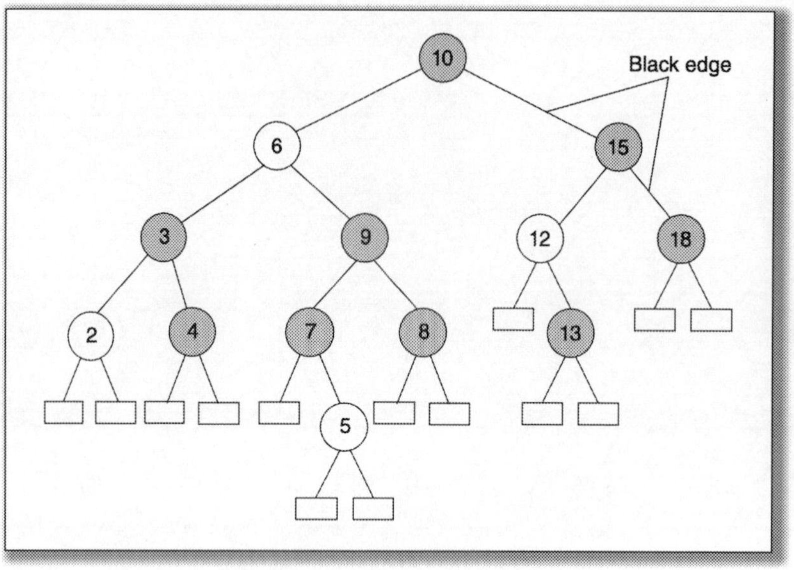

Figure 7.28 A red-black tree.

7.11 HEIGHT BALANCED (AVL) TREE

Balance trees are useful data structures that are useful to store the data at a desired location or at a specific location. The time to search an element in binary search tree is limited by the height (or depth) of the tree. Each step in the search goes down one level, so in the absolute worst case we will have to go all the way from the root to the deepest leaf in order to find element (X), or to find out that X is not in the tree. So we can say with certainty that search is O (Height). Height balanced tree solve the depth problem in searching skewed binary tree.

As compared to simple binary tree, the balanced search trees are more efficient because the insertion or deletion of nodes in this data structure requires O (log n) time. These balanced structures allow performing various dictionary operations such as insertions and deletions. In balanced tree, as items are inserted and deleted, the tree is restricted to keep the nodes balanced and the search paths uniform.

AVL TREE

Adelsion Velski and Lendis in 1962 introduced a binary tree structure that is balanced with respect to height of sub-trees. The tree can be made balanced and because of this retrieval of any node can be done in O (log n) times, where n is total number of nodes. From the name of these scientists the tree is called AVL tree.

An empty tree is height balanced if T is a non-empty binary tree with T_L and T_R as its left and right sub-trees. The T is height balanced if and only if

- T_L and T_R are height balanced.
- Height of left h_L – h_R height of right < = 1 where h_L and h_R are height of T_L and T_R.

The idea of balancing a tree is obtained by calculating the balanced factor of a tree.

Balanced Factor

The balanced factor BF (T) of a node in binary tree is defined to $\mathbf{h_L - h_R}$ where h_L and h_R are height of left and right sub-trees of T.

For any node in AVL tree the balanced factor i.e. BF (T) is **– 1, 0, 1.**

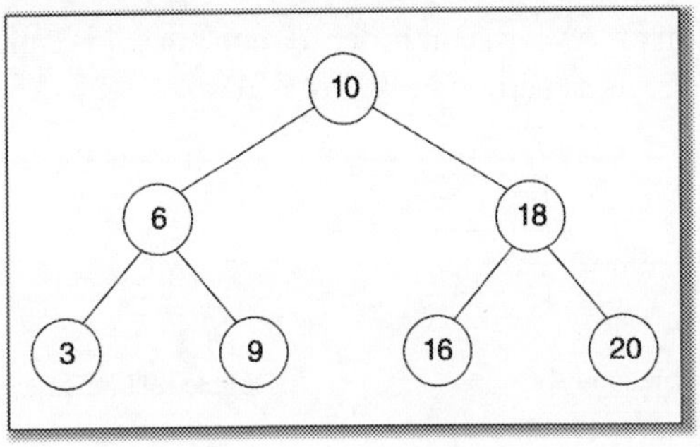

Figure 7.29 An AVL tree.

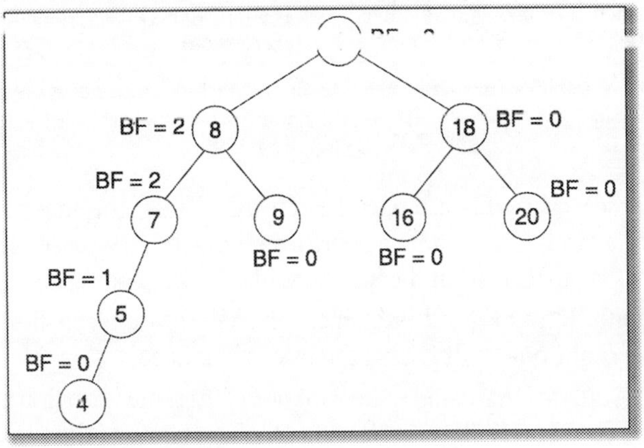

Figure 7.30 Not an AVL tree.

7.11.1 Operation of AVL Tree

- Insertion
- Deletion
- Searching

The AVL tree follows the property of binary search tree. In fact AVL trees are basically binary search trees with balanced factor as -1, 0, 1. After insertion of any tree if the balanced factor of any node becomes other than -1, 0, 1 then it is said that the AVL property is violated.

Insertion

There are four different cases when rebalancing is required after insertion of a new element or node.

1. An insertion of a new node into the left sub-tree of left child (LL).
2. An insertion of a new node into the right sub-tree of left child (LR).
3. An insertion of a new node into the left sub-tree of right child (RL).
4. An insertion of a new node into the right sub-tree of right child (RR).

Some modification done on an AVL tree in order to rebalance it is called **rotations** of AVL tree. These are classification of rotations as shown in Figure 7.31.

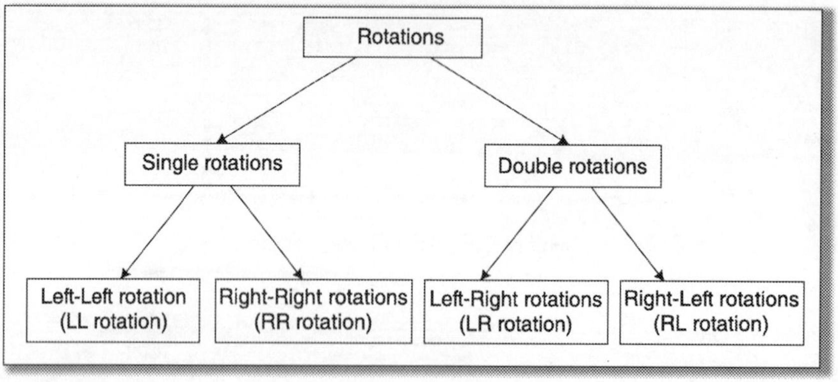

Figure 7.31 Types of rotation.

Insertion in an AVL search tree is a binary search tree. Thus, the insertion of the data item having key 'K' in an AVL search tree is same as performed in a binary search tree. The insertion of the data item with key 'K' is performed at the leaf, in which three cases arise.

- If the data item with 'K' is inserted into an empty AVL search tree, then the node with key 'K' is set to be the root node. In this case the tree is balanced.
- If the tree contains only a single node, the root node, then the insertion of node with key 'K' depends upon the value of 'K'. If 'K' is less than the key value of the root then it is appended to the left of the root. Otherwise, for a greater value of 'K' it is appended to right of the root. In this case the tree is height balanced.
- If an AVL search tree contains number of nodes (which are height balanced), then in that case it has to be taken from inserting a data item with the key 'K' so that after the insertion the tree is height balanced.

We have noticed that insertion may cause unbalancing the tree. So, rebalancing of the tree is performed for making it balanced. The rebalancing is accomplished by performing four kinds of rotations. The rotations for balancing the tree are characterized by the nearest ancestor of inserted node whose balance factor becomes ± 2.

(1) Left-Left (L-L) Rotation: Given an AVL search tree as shown in Figure 7.32. After inserting the node with the value 15 the tree becomes unbalanced. So, by performing an LL rotation the tree becomes balanced. After inserting the new node 15 the tree as in Figure 7.32 it becomes unbalanced. So by performing an LL rotation the tree becomes balanced as shown in Figure 7.33.

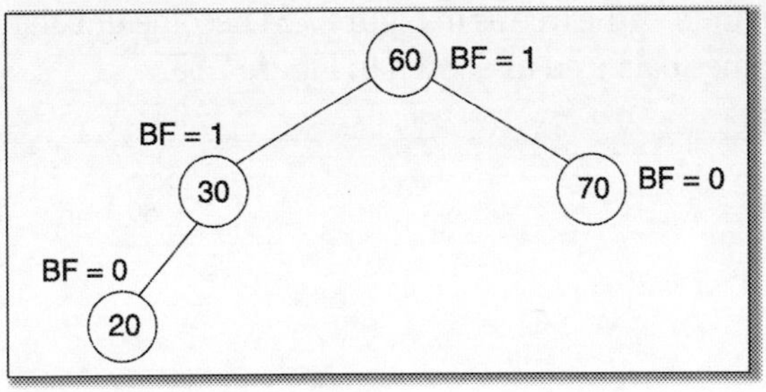

Figure 7.32 Balanced AVL search tree.

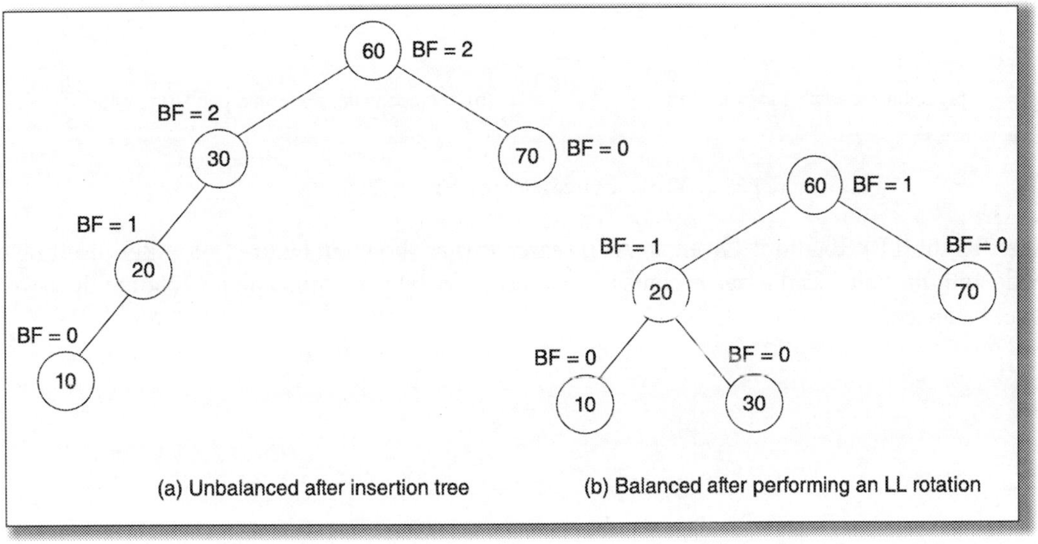

Figure 7.33 AVL search tree after performing LL rotation.

(2) Right-Right (RR) Rotation: Given an AVL search tree as shown in Figure 7.34. After inserting the node with the value 75 the tree becomes unbalanced. So, by performing an RR rotation the tree become balanced.

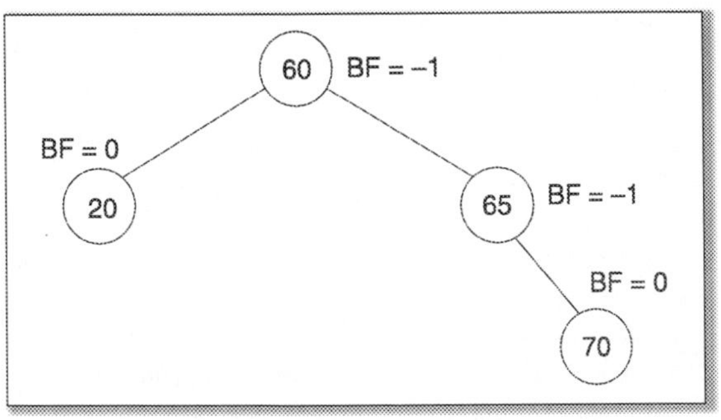

Figure 7.34 Balanced AVL search tree.

After inserting the new node 75 the tree as in Figure 7.34 become unbalanced. So by performing an RR rotation the tree becomes balanced as shown in Figure 7.35.

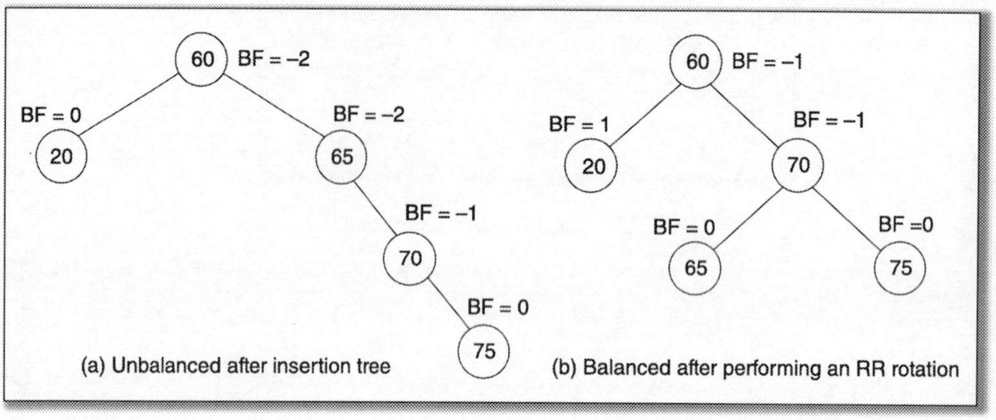

Figure 7.35 AVL search tree after performing RR rotation.

(3) Left-Right (LR) Rotation: Given an AVL search tree as shown in Figure 7.36. After inserting the node with the value 25 the tree becomes unbalanced. So, by performing an LR rotation the tree becomes balanced.

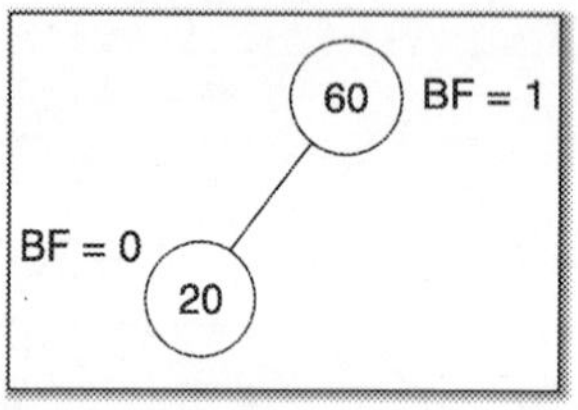

Figure 7.36 Balanced AVL search tree.

After inserting the new node 25 the tree as in Figure 7.36 becomes unbalanced. So by performing an LR rotation the tree becomes balanced as shown in Figure 7.37.

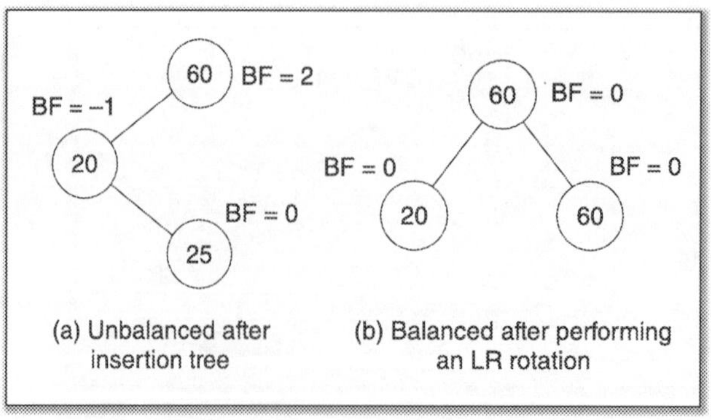

Figure 7.37 AVL search tree after performing an LR rotation.

(4) Right-Left (RL) Rotation: Given an AVL search tree as shown in Figure 7.38. After inserting the node with the value 25 the tree becomes unbalanced. So, by performing an RL rotation the tree becomes balanced.

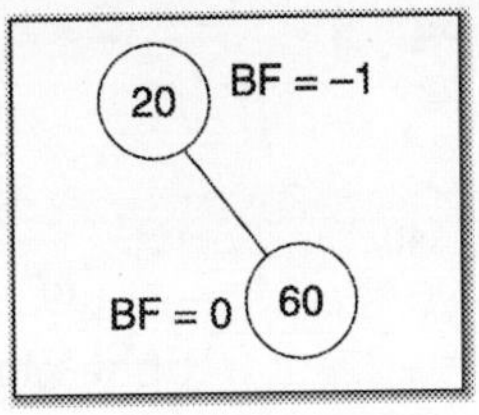

Figure 7.38 Balanced AVL search tree.

After inserting the new node 25 the tree as in Figure 7.38 becomes unbalanced. So by performing an LR rotation the tree becomes balanced as shown in Figure 7.39.

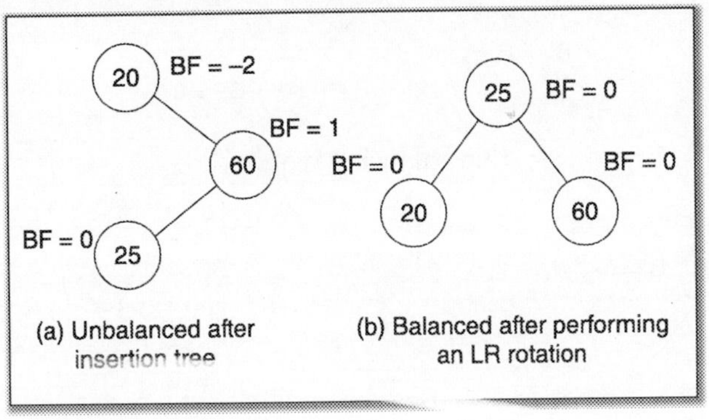

Figure 7.39 AVL search tree after performing RL rotation.

Example: Creation of an AVL search tree is illustrated from the given set of values:

20, 30, 10, 50, 60, 57, 56, 55.

Solution Insertion – 20

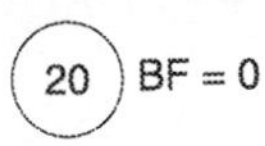

No balancing required because BF = 0

Insertion – 30

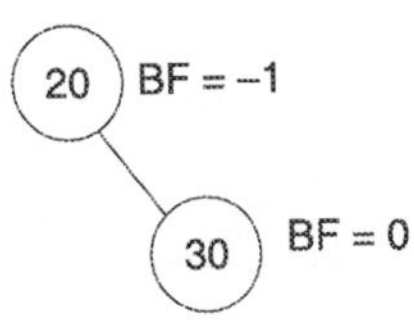

No balancing required because BF = – 1, 0

Insertion - 40

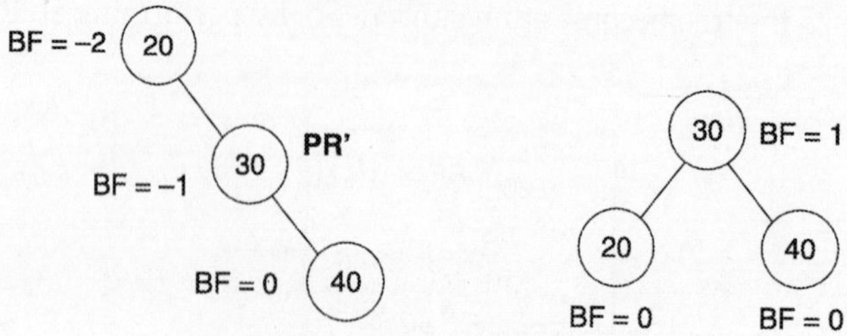

Balancing required because BF = - 2, - 1, 0 **Right-Right rotation** for a balanced tree

Insertion - 50

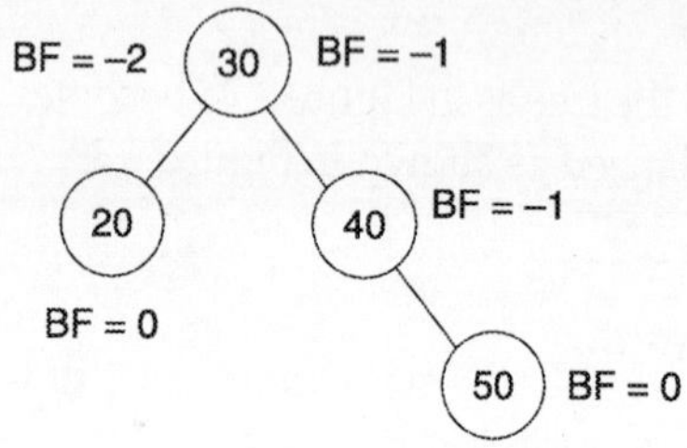

No balancing required

Insertion - 60

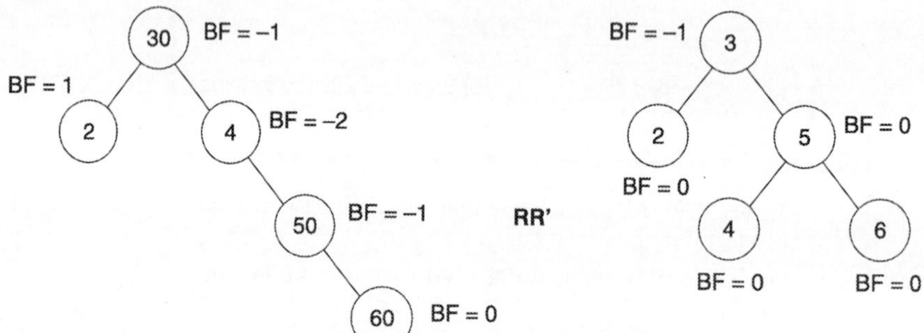

Balancing required **Right–Right rotation** tree

Insertion - 57

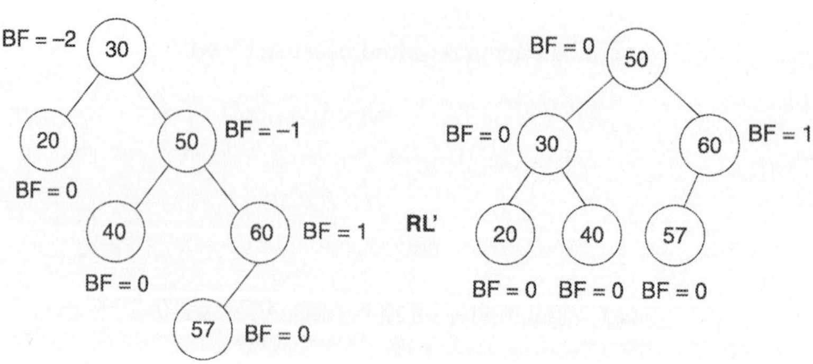

Balancing required **Right Left rotation** tree

Inserting - 56

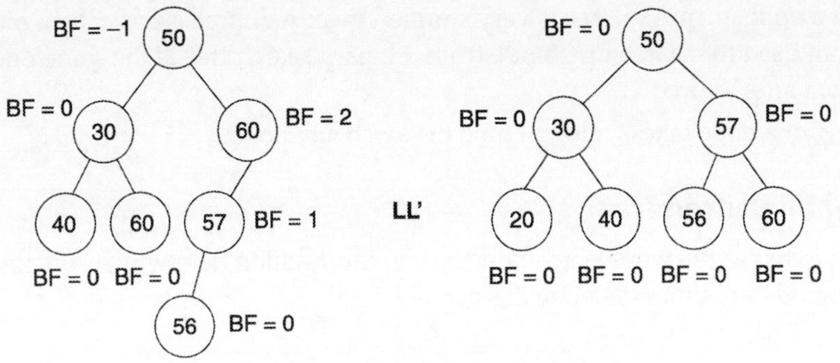

Balancing required **Left–Left rotation** tree

Insert - 55

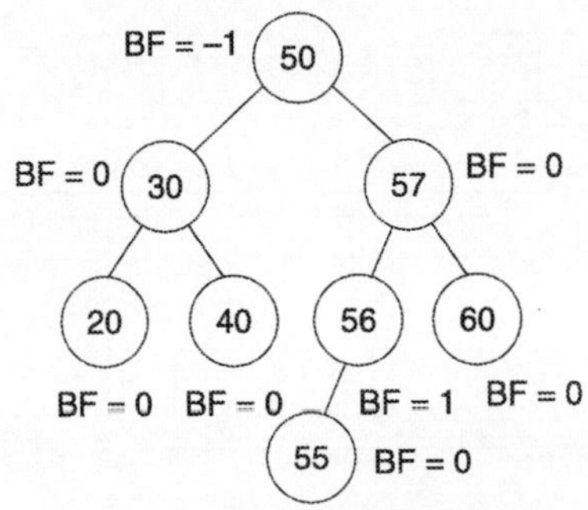

No balancing required

Deletion

For deletion of any particular node from an AVL tree, the tree has to be reconstructed in order to preserve the AVL property, and various rotations are needed to be applied for balancing the tree.

Algorithm for deletion

The deletion algorithm is more complex than insertion algorithm.

1. Search the node which is to be deleted.
2. (A) If the node to be deleted is a leaf node then simply make it NULL to remove it.

   (B) If the node to be deleted is not a leaf node i.e. the node has one or two children, then the node must be swapped with its in-order successor. Once the node is swapped, we can remove the node.
3. Now we have to traverse back up the path towards the root, checking the balance factor of every node along the path. If we encounter unbalancing in some sub-tree then balance that sub-tree using an appropriate single or double rotation.

The deletion algorithm takes O (log n) time to delete any node.

Searching

The searching of a node in an AVL tree is very simple. As an AVL tree is basically a binary search tree, the algorithm used for searching a node from a binary search tree is the same one is used to search a node from an AVL tree.

The searching of a node takes O (log n) time to search any node.

7.11.2 Weight Balanced Tree

Weight balanced tree is a tree whose each node has an information field which contains the name of the node and number of times the node has been visited.

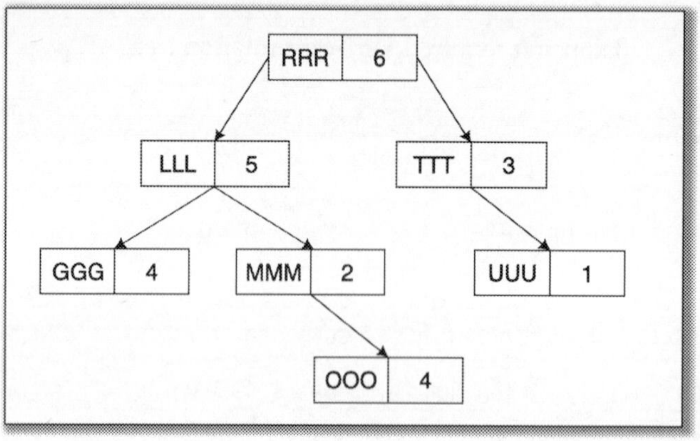

Figure 7.40

For example, consider the tree given in Figure 7.40. This is a balanced tree, which is organized according to the number of accesses.

The rules for putting a node in a weight balanced tree are expressed recursively as follows:

1. The first node of tree or sub-tree is the node with the highest count of number of times it has been accessed.
2. The left sub-tree of the tree is composed of nodes with values lexically less than the first node.
3. The right sub-tree of the tree is composed of nodes with value lexically higher the first node.

7.12 B-TREES

The working with large amount of data elements is inconvenient when considering primary storage (RAM). Instead, for large data elements, only a small portion is maintained in the primary storage and the rest of them reside in the secondary storage. If required it can be accessed from the secondary storage. Secondary storage, such as a magnetic disk, is slower in accessing data then the primary storage.

B-Trees are balanced trees and a specialized multiway (m-way) tree is used to store the records in a disk. There are a number of sub-trees to each node. The height of the tree is relatively small so that only small number of nodes must be read from the disk to retrieve an item. The goal of B-trees is to get a fast access to the data. B-trees try to minimize the disk accesses, as disk accesses are expensive.

Multiway search tree

A multiway search tree of order m is an ordered tree where each node has at the most m children. If there are n number of children in a node then (n-1) is the number of keys in the node.

The **B-tree** is of order 'm' if it satisfies following conditions:

1. The root node should have at least two children.
2. Except the root node, each node has at most **m** children and at least m/2 children.
3. The entire leaf node must be at the same level. There should be no empty sub-tree above the level of the leaf nodes.
4. If order of tree **m,** it means that **m-1** keys are allowed.

7.12.1 Operation on B-Trees

1. Insertion

First search the place where the element or record must be put. If the node can accommodate the new record, the insertion is simple. The record is added to the node with an appropriate pointer so that number of points remain one more that the number of records. If the node overflows because there is an upper bound on the size of a node, splitting is required.

The node is split into three parts. The middle record is passed upward and inserted into the parent, leaving two children behind where there was one before. The splitting may propagate up the tree because the parent into which a record to be split in its child node, may overflow. Therefore, it may also split. If the root is required to be split, a new root is created with just two children, and the tree grows taller by one level.

For example of a B-tree, we will construct of order 5 using the following numbers.

3, 14, 7, 1, 8, 5, 11, 17, 13, 6, 23, 12, 20.

The order 5 means at the most 4 keys are allowed. The internal node should have at least 3 non-empty children and each leaf node must contain at least 2 keys.

Step 1: Insert 3, 14, 7, 1 as follows.

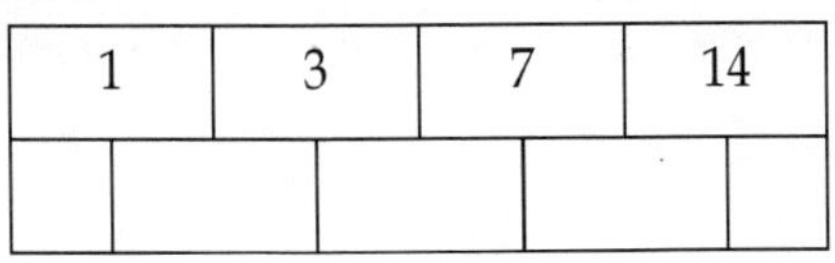

Step 2: Insert the next element 8. Then we need to split the node 1, 3, 7, 14 at medium. Hence,

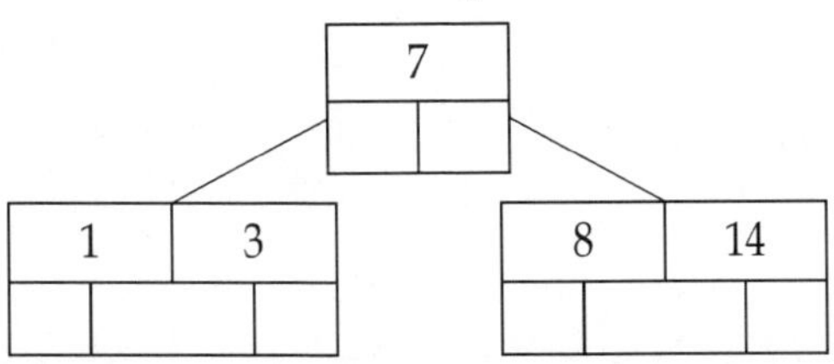

Here 1 and 3 are < 7 so these are at left branch, node 8 and 14 > 7 so these are at right branch.

Step 3: Insert 5, 11, 17 which can be easily inserted in a B-tree.

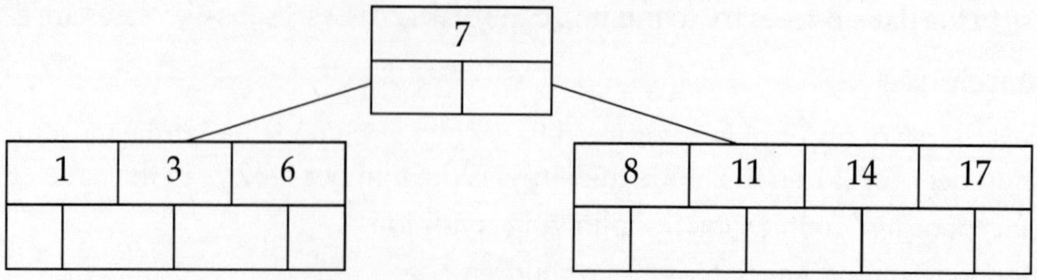

Step 4: Insert next element 13. But if we insert 13 then the leaf node will have 5 keys which are not allowed. Hence 8, 11, 13, 14, 17 is split and the medium node 13 is moved up.

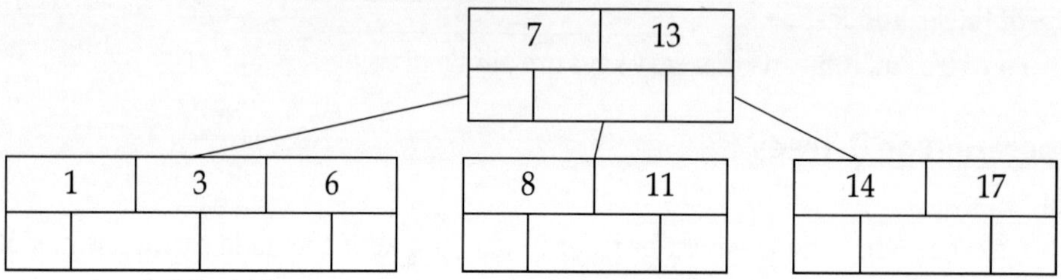

Step 5: Insert 6, 23, 12, 20 without any split.

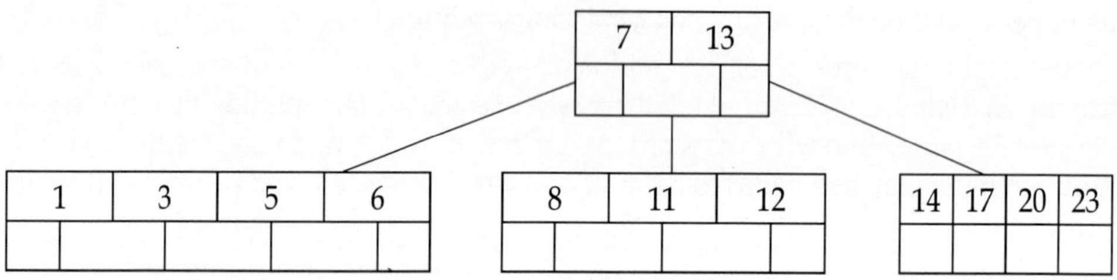

2. Deletion

As in the insertion method, the record to be deleted is first searched for. If the record is in the terminal node, the deletion is simple. The record along with an appropriate pointer is deleted. If the record is not in the terminal node, it is replaced by a copy of its successor, which is a record with the next higher value.

Consider a B- Tree,

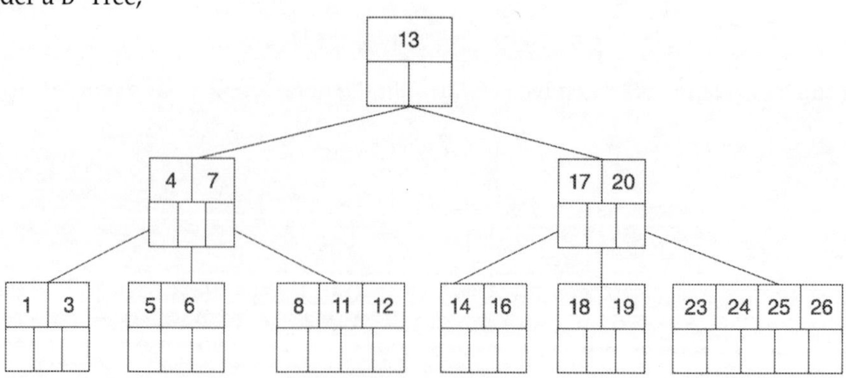

If we want to delete 8 then,

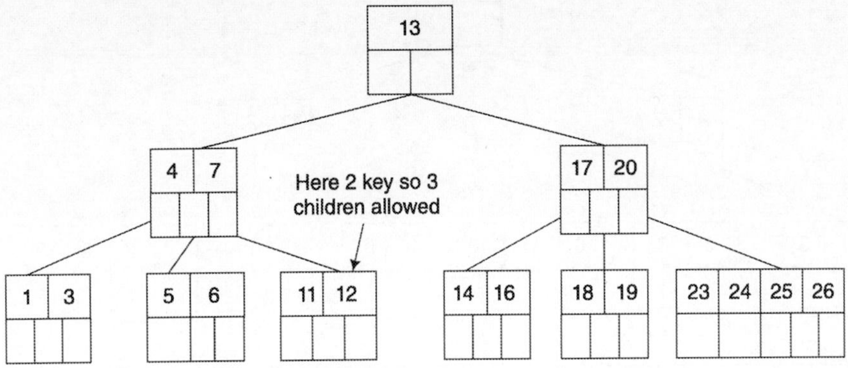

Now we want delete 20, the 20 is not in a leaf node so we will find its successor which is 23. Hence 23 will be moved up to replace 20.

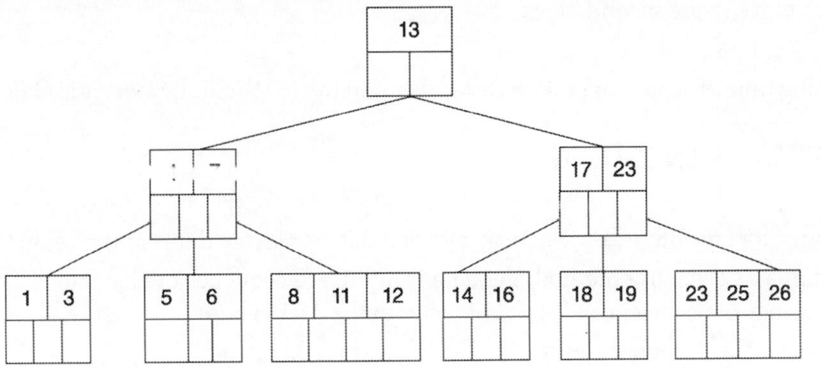

Next we will delete 18; Deletion of 18 from the corresponding node causes the node with only one key, which is not desired in B-tree of order 5. The sibling node to immediate right has an extra key. In such a case we can borrow a key from parent and move spare key of sibling to up.

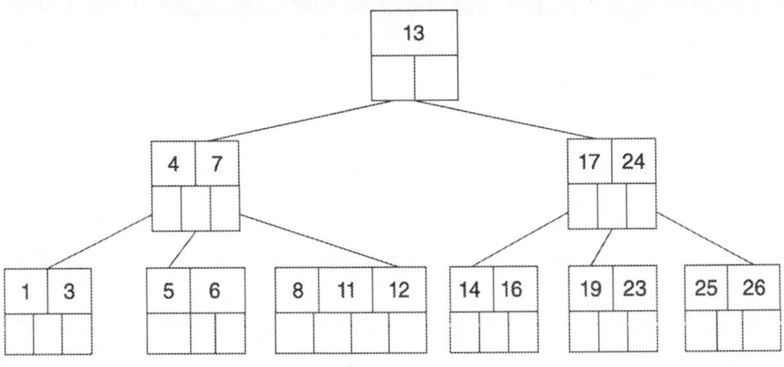

3. Searching

The search operation on a B-tree is similar to a search on binary search tree. Instead of choosing between a left and right child as in binary tree, B-tree makes an m-way choice. Consider a B-tree as given below:

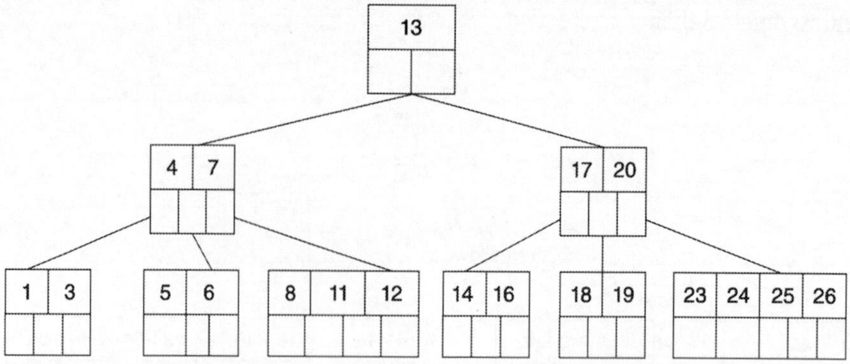

If we want to search node 11 then

1. 11 < 13 : Hence search left node
2. 11 > 7 : Hence right most node
3. 11 > 8 , move in the second block
4. Node 11 is found.

The running time of search operation depends upon the height of the tree. It is O (log n).

7.13 HUFFMAN'S ENCODING

The Huffman's algorithm was developed by David Huffman at MIT. This algorithm is basically a coding technique for encoding data. Such an encoded data is used in data compression techniques.

- In Huffman's encoding method, the data is input as a sequence of characters. Then a table of frequency of occurrence of each character in the data is built.
- From the table of frequencies the Huffman's tree is constructed.
- The Huffman's tree is further used for encoding each character, so that the binary encoding is obtained for the given data.
- In Huffman coding there is a specific method of representing each symbol. This method produces a code in such a manner that no code word is a prefix of some other code word. Such codes are called Prefix codes or Prefix Free code. Thus this method is useful for obtaining optimal data compression.

The technique of Huffman's coding with the help of some examples are given below.

Example: Obtain Huffman's encoding for following data:

A : 40 B : 12 C : 10 D : 30 E : 8 F : 5

Solution There are two types of coding - variable length coding and fixed length coding. If we used fixed length coding we will need fixed number of bits to represent any character from a to h. we use 3-bits to represent any character. Hence we will arrange the given symbols along with their frequencies as follows:

Step 1: The symbols are arranged in ascending order of frequencies

| F : 3 | F : 8 | C : 10 | B : 12 | D : 30 | A : 40 |

Step 2:

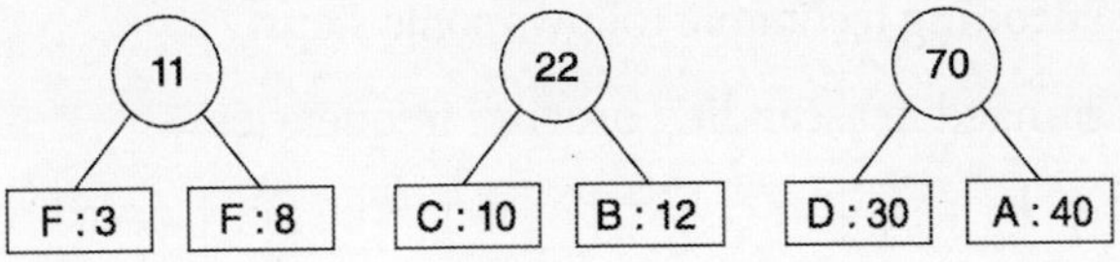

We will encode each of the above branches. The encoding should start from top to down. If we follow the **left branch** then we should encode it as '0' and if we follow the **right branch** then we should encode it as '1'. Hence, we get

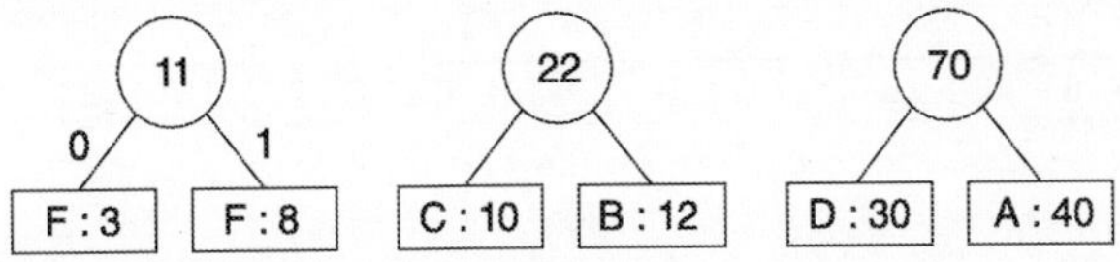

Step 3:

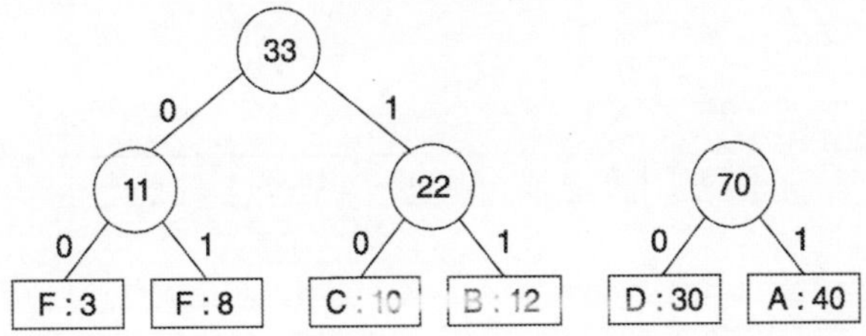

Step 4:

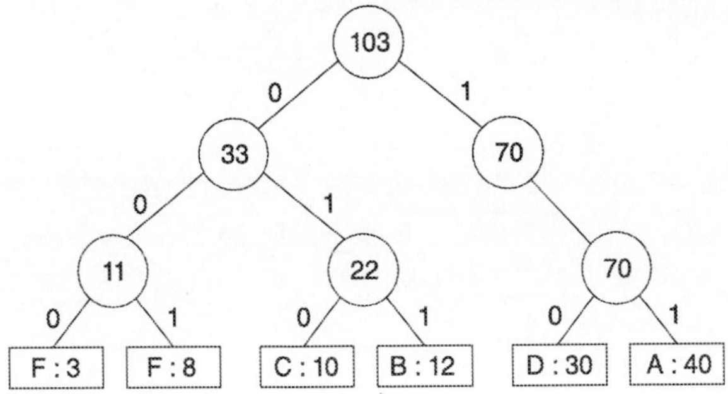

Hence the Huffman's coding with the fixed length code will be

Symbol	Code word
A	111
B	011
C	010
D	110
E	001
F	000

If we want to encode a string 'BCCD' then we get **011010010110** as a code word.

Now **variable length encoding** technique follows some steps:

Step 1: The symbols are arranged in ascending order of frequencies.

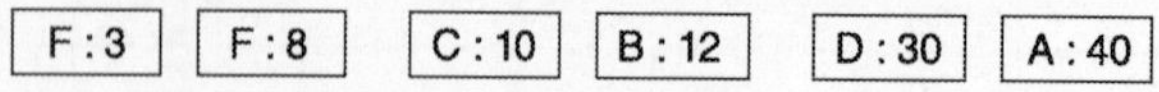

Step 2:

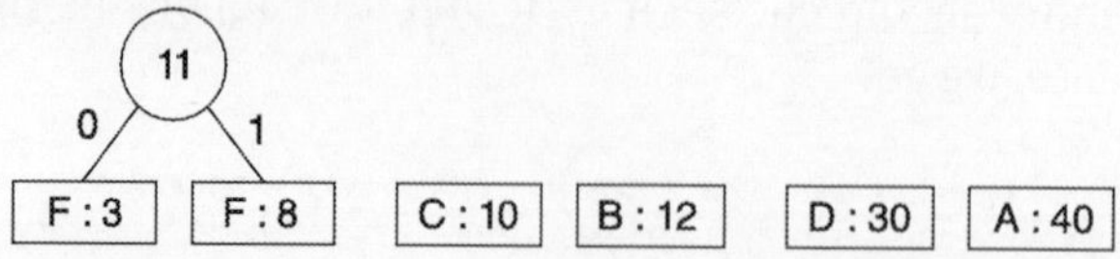

Step 3:

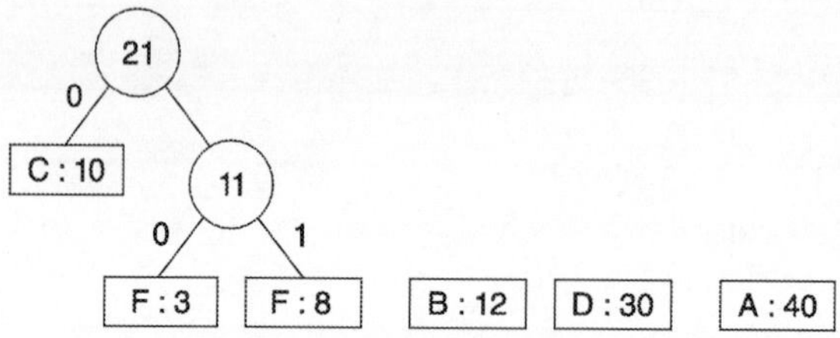

Step 4:

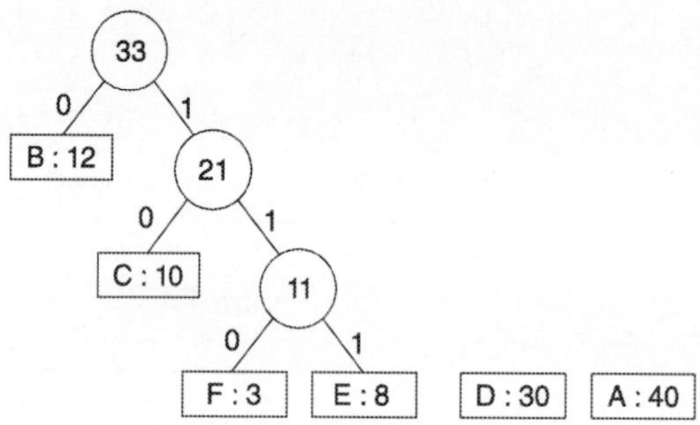

Step 5:

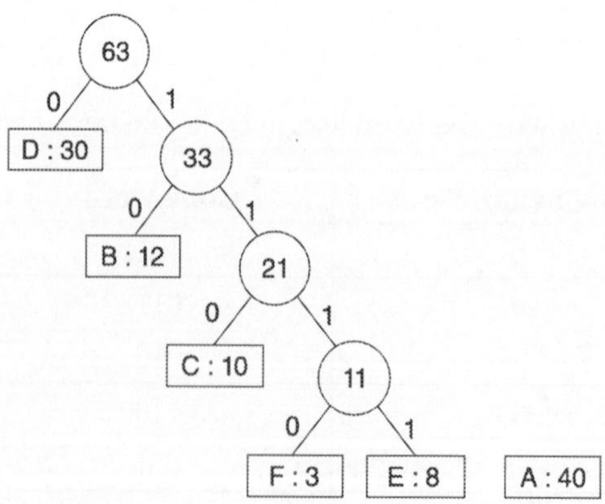

Step 6:

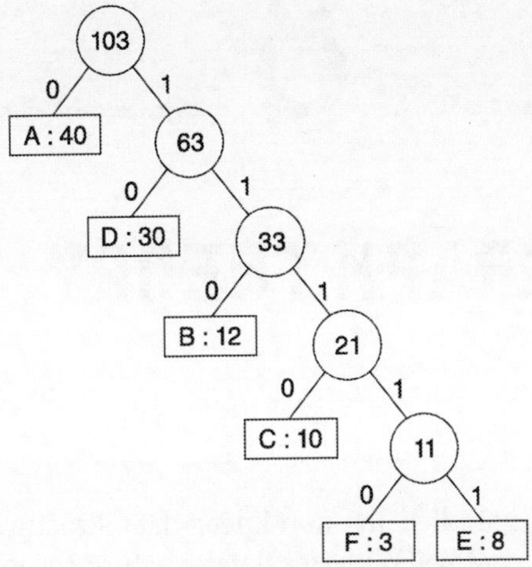

The code words for each symbol are as given below:

Symbol	Code word
A	0
B	110
C	1110
D	10
E	1111
F	11110

If we want to encode a string 'BCCD' then we get **1101110111010** as a code word.

Now we will formulate the number of bits required for both the encoding technique:

Total bits = Frequency * Number of bits used for representation

8

GRAPH THEORY

8.1 INTRODUCTION

In the previous chapter we have studied the non-linear data structure tree. Now we introduce another non-linear data structure, graphs. With tree data structure, the main restriction is that every tree has a unique **root** node. If we remove this restriction we get a more complex data structure i.e. graph. In graph there is no root node at all and so we will get introduced to a more complex data structure. In computer science graphs are used in a wide range. There are many theorems on graphs. The study of graphs in computer science is known as **graph theory.**

One of the first results in graph theory appeared in Leonhard Euler's paper on seven bridges of Konigsberg, published in 1736. It is also regarded as one of the first topological results in geometry. It does not depend on any measurements. In 1945, Gustav Kirchhoff published his Kirchhoff's circuit laws for calculating the voltage and current in electric circuits.

In 1852, Francies Guthrie posed the four color problem which asks if it is possible to color, using only four colors, any map of countries in such a way as to prevent two bordering countries from having the same color. This problem, which was solved only a century later in 1976 by Kenneth Appel and Wolfgang Haken, can be considered the birth of graph theory. While trying to solve it, mathematicians invented many fundamental graph theoretic terms and concepts.

Structures that can be represented as graphs are everywhere, and many practical problems can be represented by graphs. The link structure of a website could be represented by a graph, such that the vertices are the web pages available at the website and there's a directed edge from page X to page Y if and only if X contains a link to Y. Networks have many uses in the practical side of graph theory, network analysis (for example, to model and analyze traffic networks or to discover the shape of the internet).

The difference between a tree and a graph is that a tree is a connected graph having no circuits, while a graph can have circuits. A loop may be a part of a graph but a loop does not take place in a tree.

8.2 DEFINITION OF GRAPH

A graph is a set of objects called vertices (nodes) connected by links called edges (arcs) which can be directed (assigned a direction).

A Graph G = (V, E) consists of the finite non-empty set of objects V, where V (G) = {V_1, V_2, V_3......V_n....} called **vertices,** and another set E, where E (G) = {e_1, e_2, e_3, ...e_n..}, whose elements are called **edges**. A graph may be pictorially represented as shown in Figure 8.1. in which the vertices are represented as points and each edge as a line segment joining its end vertices.

From Figure 8.1 we can represent that:

V (G) = {1, 2, 3, 4, 5, 6}

E (G) = { (1, 2), (2, 1), (2, 3), (3, 2), (1, 4), (4, 1), (4, 5), (5, 4), (5, 6), (6, 5), (3, 6),(6, 3)}

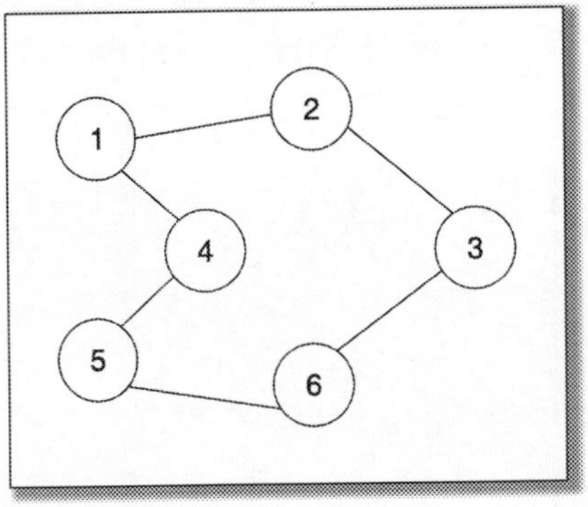

Figure 8.1 A graph.

We could have written (1, 5) and (5, 1) means ordering of vertices is not significant in an undirected graph.

8.3 TERMINOLOGY OF GRAPH

Directed Graph: A graph if in which every edge is identified by an ordered pair of vertices then the graph is said to be a **directed graph**. It is also referred to as **digraph**.

As shown in Figure 8.2, the edges between the vertices are ordered. In this type of graph, the edge E_1 is in between the vertices V_1 and V_2. V_1 is called head and the V_2 is called the tail. Similarly for V_1 head the tail is V_3 and so on.

We can say E_1 is the set of (V_1, V_2) and not of (V_2, V_1). Vertex pair (V_i, V_j) read as V_i - V_j means that an edge is directed from V_i to V_j.

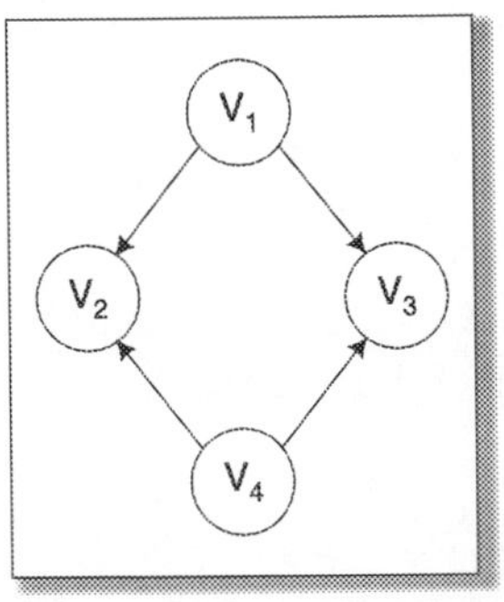

Figure 8.2 A directed graph.

Undirected Graph: A graph is called an undirected graph when the edges of a graph are unordered pairs. If the edges in a graph are undirected or 'two-way' then the graph is known as an **undirected graph**.

By unordered pair of edges we mean that the order in which the 'V_i', 'V_j' occur in the pair of vertices (V_i, V_j) is unrelated for describing the edge. Thus the pair (V_i, V_j) and (V_j, V_i) both represent the same edge that connect the vertices V_i and V_j. Figure 8.3 shows an undirected graph.

Set of vertices $V = \{V_1, V_2, V_3, V_4\}$

Set of edges $E = \{e_1, e_2, e_3, e_4\}$

We can say E_1 is the set of (V_1, V_2) and of (V_2, V_1) represent the same edge.

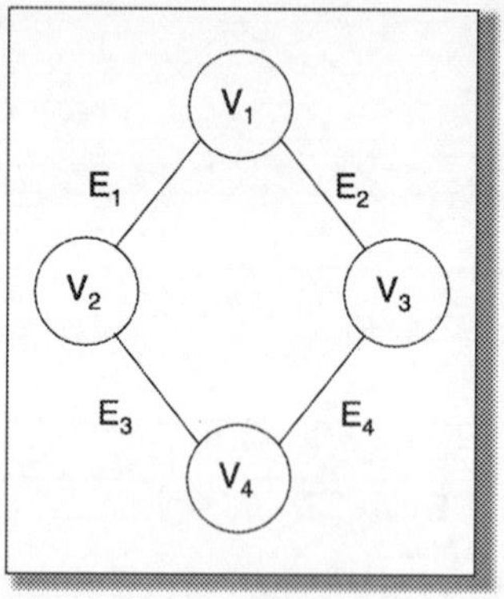

Figure 8.3 An undirected graph.

Complete graph: If an undirected graph of n vertices consists of n (n – 1) /2 number of edges then it is called a complete graph.

The graph shown in Figure 8.4 is a completed graph.

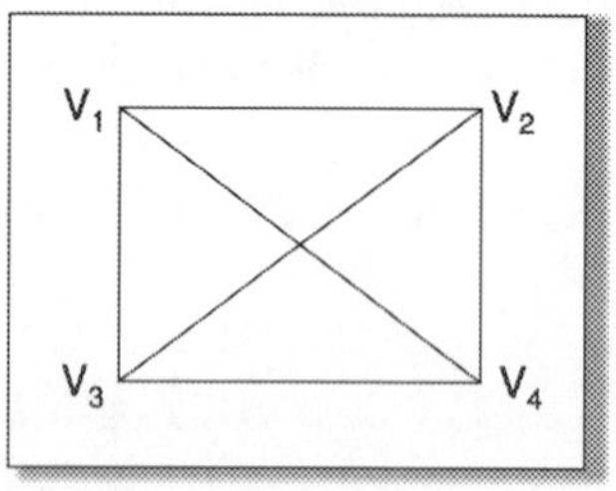

Figure 8.4 A complete graph.

Subgraph: A subgraph G′ of the graph G is a graph such that the set of vertices and the set of the edges of G′ are proper subsets of the set of the edges of G.

The graph shown in Figure 8.5 is a sub-graph.

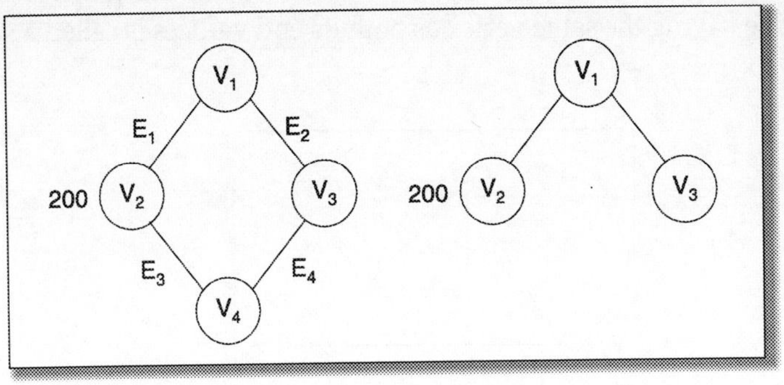

Figure 8.5 A sub-graph.

Connected Graph: An undirected graph is said to be connected if for every pair of distinct vertices V_i and V_j in V(G) there is a graph from V_i and V_j in G. The graph shown in Figure 8.6 is a connected graph.

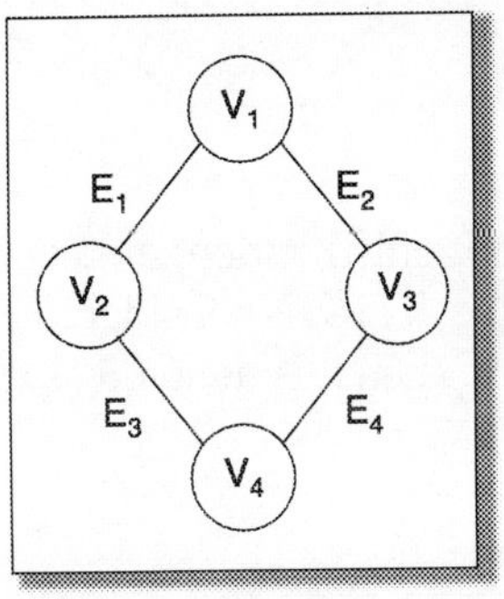

Figure 8.6 A connected graph.

Multigraph: A graph which contains a pair of nodes joined by more than one edge is called a multigraph and such edges are called **parallel edges**. An edge having the same vertex as both its end vertices is called a **self-loop** (or a loop). The graph shown in Figure 8.7 is a multigraph.

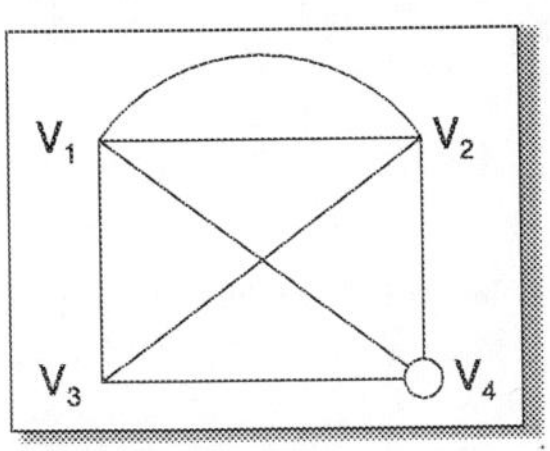

Figure 8.7 A multigraph.

A graph that does not self-loop nor have parallel edges is called a **simple graph.**

Degree: In a graph the degree is defined for a vertex. The degree of a vertex is denoted as $deg_G(V_i)$. It is the total number of edges incident with 'V_i'. It is to be noted that self-loops on a given vertex is counted twice. An edge having the same vertex as both its end vertices is called a **self-loop**.

Consider Figure 8.8.

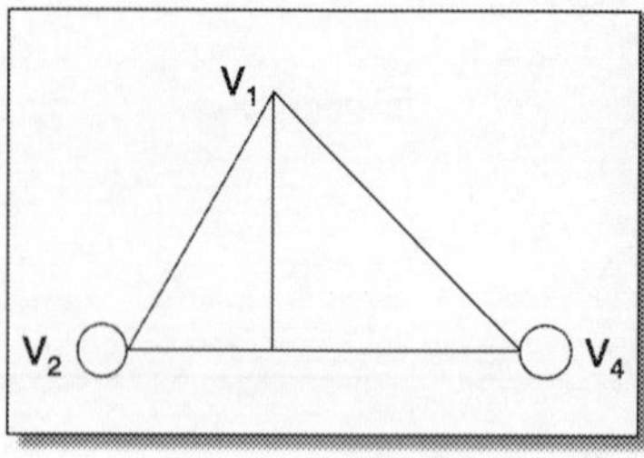

Figure 8.8 A multigraph.

From Figure 8.8, we can calculate the degree of vertices,

$$d_G(V_1) = 3$$
$$d_G(V_2) = 4$$
$$d_G(V_3) = 3$$
$$d_G(V_4) = 4$$

In a directed graph, the edges are not only incident on a vertex but also incident out of vertex and incident into a vertex. In this case, the degree is considered as **out degree** and **in degree**. When the edge is incident out of given vertex V_i then it is denoted as $d_G^+(V_i)$, and when it is incident into a vertex V_i then it is denoted as $d_G^-(V_i)$.

Consider Figure 8.9.

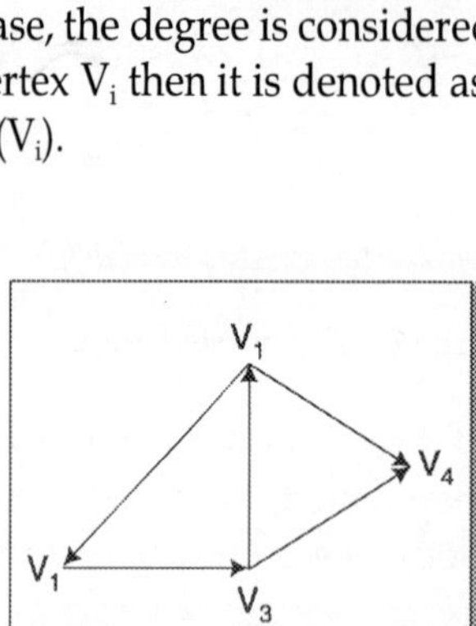

Figure 8.9 A directed graph with four vertices.

For Figure 8.9, the degree of vertices is as follows:

$d_G^+(V_1) = 2$ $\quad d_G^-(V_1) = 1$

$d_G^+(V_2) = 1$ $\quad d_G^-(V_2) = 1$

$d_G^+(V_3) = 2$ $\quad d_G^-(V_3) = 1$

$d_G^+(V_4) = 0$ $\quad d_G^-(V_4) = 2$

As we have observed that for an undirected graph the edge contributes two degrees. A graph 'G' with 'e_k' edges and 'n' vertices $V_1, V_2, \ldots\ldots V_n$, the number of edges is half the sum of the degrees of all vertices.

$$\frac{1}{2}\sum_{i=1}^{n} dg\,(V_i) = e$$

Again, it can be easily calculated that for any directed graph the sum of all in-degrees is equal to the sum of all out-degrees, and each sum is equal to the number of edges in a graph G, thus:

$$\sum_{i=1}^{n} \text{degree in} = \sum_{i=1}^{n} \text{degree out}$$

Null Graph: If a graph contains an empty set of edges and non-empty sets of vertices, the graph is known as a null graph.

The graph shown in Figure 8.10 is null graph.

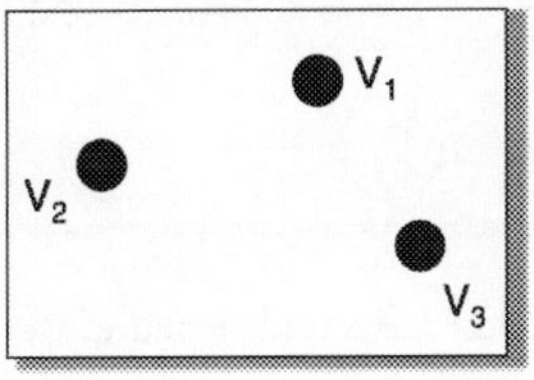

Figure 8.10 A null graph.

Graph Isomorphism

Two graphs, G = {V, E} and G′ = {V, E} are said to be **isomorphic graphs** if there exits one-to-one correspondence between their vertices and between their edges such that the incidence relationship is preserved. Suppose that an edge 'e_k' has end vertices 'V_i' and 'V_j' in G, then the corresponding edge 'e_k' in 'G' must be incident on the vertices 'V_i' and 'V_j' that correspond to 'V_i' and 'V_j' respectively.

Two isomorphic graphs are shown in the figure below.

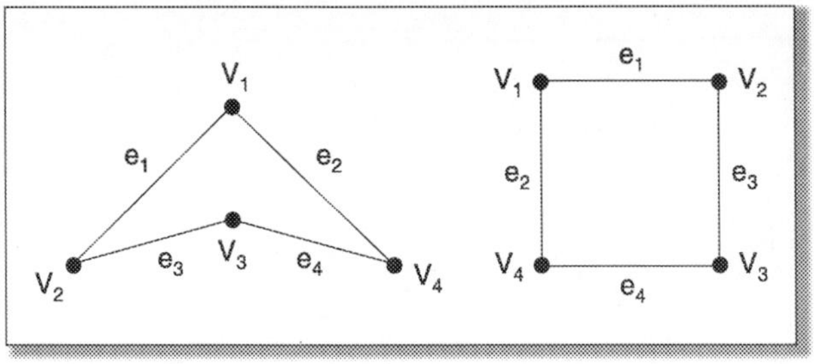

Isomorphic Properties

- Both the graphs G and G′ have the same number of vertices.
- Both the graphs G and G′ have the same number of edges.
- Both the graphs G and G′ have the same degree sequences.

8.4 REPRESENTATION OF GRAPHS

There are two major approaches to represent graphs:

- Adjacency Matrix Representation
- List Representation

Adjacency Matrix Representation

Consider a graph G of n vertices and the matrix M. if there is an edge present between vertices V_i and V_j then M[i][j] = 1 else M[i][j] = 0. Note that for an undirected graph if M[i] [j] =1 then for M[j] [i] is also 1. Here are some graphs shown by adjacency matrix.

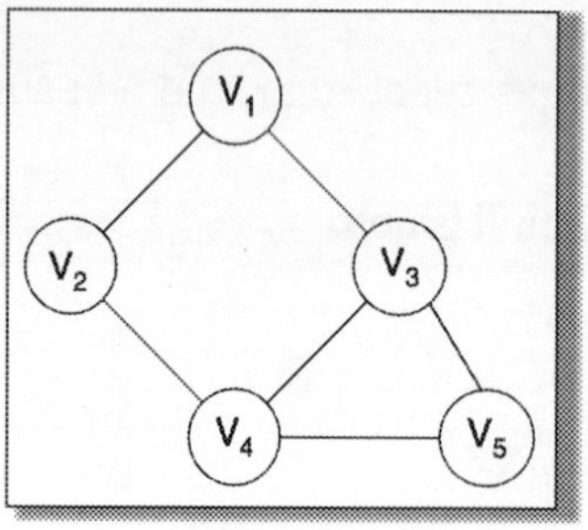

Figure 8.11 An undirected graph.

Adjacency matrix for Figure 8.11, an undirected graph is given below.

	1	2	3	4	5
1	0	1	1	0	0
2	1	0	0	1	0
3	1	0	0	1	1
4	0	1	1	0	1
5	0	0	1	1	0

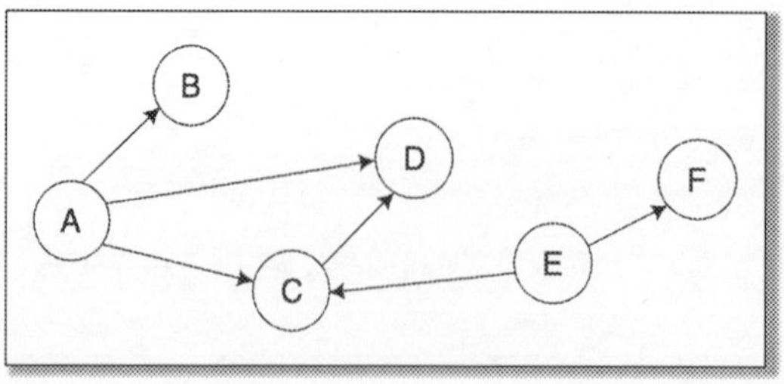

Figure 8.12 A directed graph.

The adjacency matrix A of given graph in Figure 8.12 is as follows:

	A	B	C	D	E	F
A	0	1	1	1	0	0
B	0	0	0	0	0	0
C	0	0	0	1	0	0
D	0	0	0	0	0	0
E	0	0	1	0	0	1
F	0	0	0	0	0	0

Adjacency List Representation

We have seen how a graph can be represented using adjacency matrix. We used array data structure there. But the problems associated with array are still there in the adjacency matrix that there should be some flexible data structure and so we will go for a linked data structure for creation of a graph. The type in which a graph is created with the linked list is called adjacency list.

In this representation, a graph is stored as a linked structure. We will represent a graph using an adjacency list. This adjacency list stores information about only those edges that exist. The adjacency list contains a directory and a set of linked lists. This representation is also known as **node directory representation**. The directory contains one entry for each node of the graph. Each entry in the directory points to a linked list that represents the nodes that are connected to that node. The directory represents the nodes and linked lists represent the edges.

Each node of the linked list has three fields – one is the node identifier, second is an option weight field which contains the weight of the edge and third is the link to the next field.

Nodeid	Next

or

Nodeid	Weight	Next

Figure 8.14 represents the linked list representation of the directed graph as given in Figure 8.13.

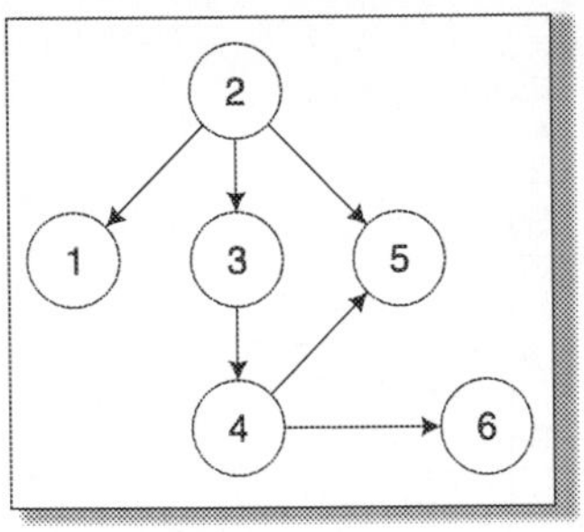

Figure 8.13 A directed graph.

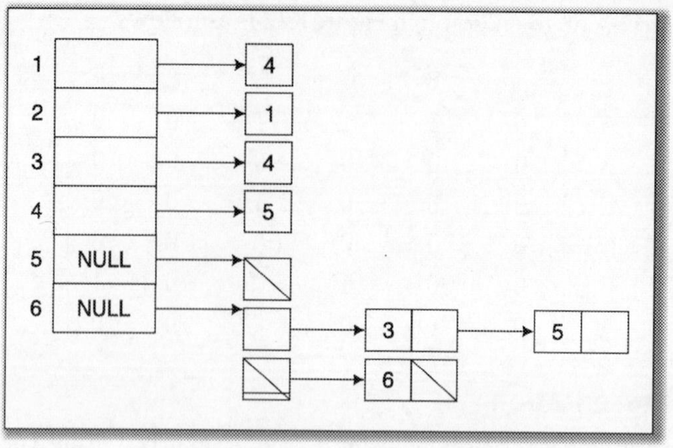

Figure 8.14 Linked list representation of the graph given in Figure 8.13.

An undirected graph of order N with E edges requires N entries in the directory and 2 * E linked list entries. The adjacency list representation of Figure 8.15 is shown in Figure 8.16.

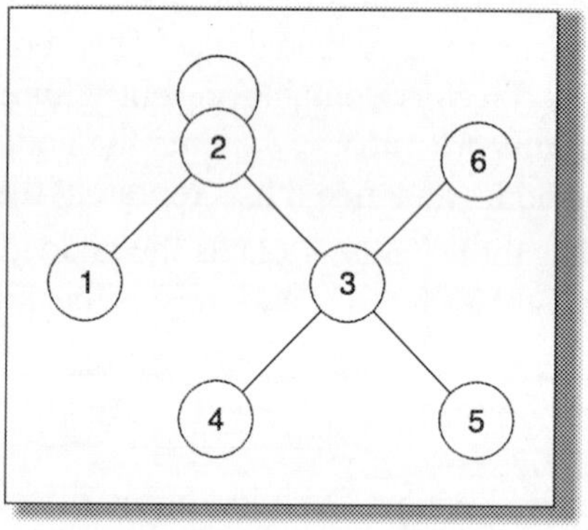

Figure 8.15 An undirected graph.

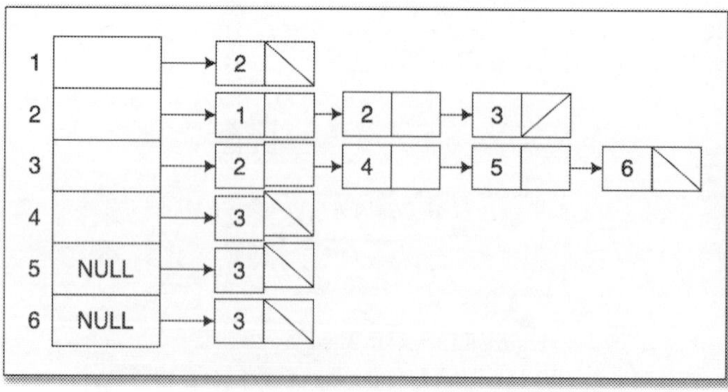

Figure 8.16 Linked list representation of graph shown in Figure 8.15.

Properties of Adjacency Matrix

Except for the self-loop the diagonal element has a value zero. A self-loop at the ith vertex corresponds to $a_{ij} = 1$

An adjacency matrix of an undirected graph is symmetric, as $a_{ij} = a_{ji} = 1$.

The non-zero elements in the matrix represent the number of edges in a graph.

8.5 GRAPH TRAVERSAL

To traverse a graph is to process every node in the graph exactly once. There are many paths leading from one node to another node, the hardest part about traversing a graph is making sure that you do not process the some node twice. So, we have to process the node exactly once. Initially all the nodes are 'unreached'. When the first node is encountered mark it as 'reached' and process that node. So, while traversing the node it is checked every time whether if it is marked 'reached' or not. The graph traversing continues until all the nodes are processed. If we delete the node after processing, then there will be no path leading to that node.

The general technique for graph traversing is given below:

1. Mark all nodes in the graph as **unreached.**
2. Pick a starting node, mark it as **reached** and place it on the **ready** list.
3. Pick a node on the **ready** list, process it. Remove it from **ready,** find all its neighbors those that are **unreached** should be marked as **reached** and added to **ready.**
4. Repeat 3 until the **ready** entries are empty.

Consider the graph shown in Figure 8.17.

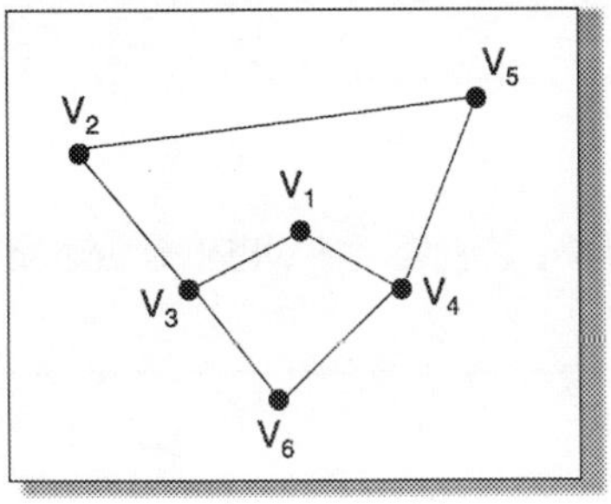

Figure 8.17 Graph with six vertices.

The process of traversing the graph is given below:

$V = \{V_1, V_2, V_3, V_4, V_5, V_6\}$ marked as **unreached.**

V_1 = start vertex.

ready list = $\{V_1\}$ process V_1, place adjacent vertices to vertices to V_1 in ready lists and delete node V_1.

ready list = $\{V_3, V_4\}$ process V_3, place adjacent vertices to V_3, V_2, V_6 as V_1 is deleted so no path from V_3 to V_1.

ready list = $\{V_4, V_2, V_6\}$ process V_4, place adjacent vertices to V_4, V_5, as V_6 is marked as reached and V_4 is deleted.

ready list = { V_2, V_6, V_5} process V_2, place adjacent vertices to V_2 as V_3 is deleted and V_5 is marked as reached and V_2 is deleted.

ready list = {V_6, V_5} process V_6, place adjacent vertices to V_6, as V_3 and V_3 are deleted, V_6 is deleted.

ready list = {V_5} process V_5, as all the adjacent vertices are already deleted so finally delete V_5.

The graph is traversed as V_1, V_3, V_4, V_2, V_6, V_5. Traversing a graph in this manner is done only for connected graphs. For unconnected graph the whole procedure is repeated until all the vertices are marked as 'reached' and then processed.

The graph can be traversed in two ways:

- Depth first search
- Breadth first search

Depth first search traversal (DFS)

Depth first traversal of an undirected graph is similar to pre-order traversal of an ordered tree. The start vertex v is visited first. Let w_1, w_2,...w_k be the vertices adjacent to v. Then the vertex w_1 is visited next. After visiting w_1 all the vertices adjacent to w_1 is visited next. After visiting w_1 all the vertices adjacent to w_1 are visited in depth first manner before returning to traverse w_2, ... w_k. The search terminates when no unvisited vertex can be reached from any of the visited ones. This traversal is formulated as a recursive algorithm.

The algorithm for depth first traversal of undirected graph is given below:

```
visited (v) = TRUE;
visited (v);
for each vertex w adjacent to v do
if not visited (w) then
traverse (w);
end;
```

For example, let a graph is shown in Figure 8.18 which is visited in depth first traversal starting from vertex A.

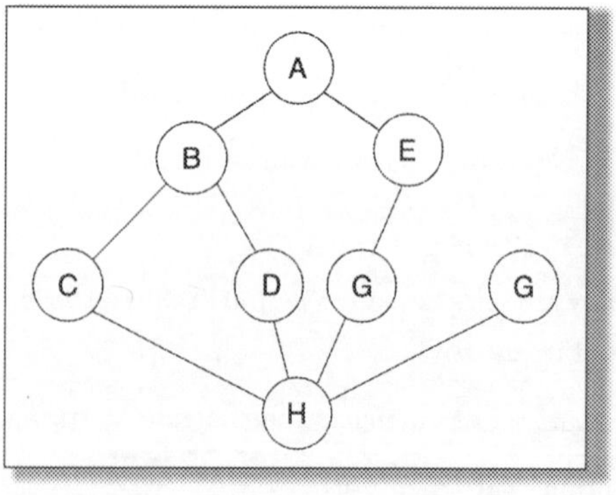

Figure 8.18 An undirected graph.

The sequence of nodes to be visited in depth first search traversal is as follows:

A B C H D E F G

Breadth first search traversal (BFS)

A breadth first traversal differs from depth first traversal in that all unvisited vertices adjacent to v are visited after visiting the starting vertex v and marking it as visited. Next, the unvisited vertices adjacent to these vertices are visited and so on until the entire graph has been traversed. For example, the breadth first traversal of the graph of Figure 8.18 results in visiting the nodes in the following order:

A B E C D F G H

A breadth first search explores the space level by level only when there are no more states to be explored at a given level and the algorithm moves to the next level. We implement BFS using lists open & closed to keep track of progress through the state space.

Algorithm for BFS

```
begin
    open = [start];
    closed = [ ];
    while open ≠ [ ] do
begin
    remove leftmost state from open call it x;
    if x is a goal then return success
    else
begin
    generate children of x;
    put x on closed;
    put children on right end of open;
end
end
return (failure)
end
```

For example, consider the tree shown in Figure 8.19. The open and closed lists maintained by BFS are shown below:

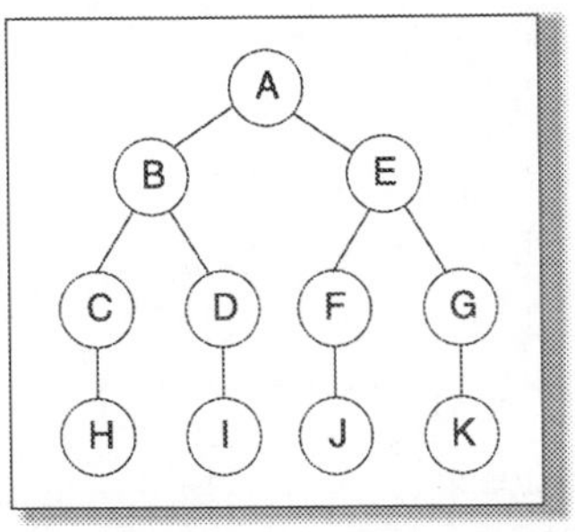

Figure 8.19 An undirected graph.

Open = [A]; Closed = [ ]
Open = [B, E]; Closed = [A]
Open = [E,C,D]; Closed = [A,B]
Open = [C,D,F,G]; Closed = [A,B,E]
Open = [D,F,G,H]; Closed = [A,B,E,C]
Open = [F,G,H,I]; Closed = [A,B,E,C,D]
Open = [G,H,I,J]; Closed = [A,B,E,C,D,F]
Open = [H,I,J,K]; Closed = [A,B,E,C,D,F,G]
Open = [I,J.K]; Closed = [A,B,E,C,D,F,G,H]
Open = [J,K]; Closed = [A,B,E,C,D,F,G,H,I]
Open = [K]; Closed = [A,B,E,C,D,F,G,H,I,J]
Open = [ ];; Closed = [A,B,E,C,D,F,G,H,I,J,K]

To understand DFS, consider Figure 8.20. The open and closed list maintained by DFS is shown below:

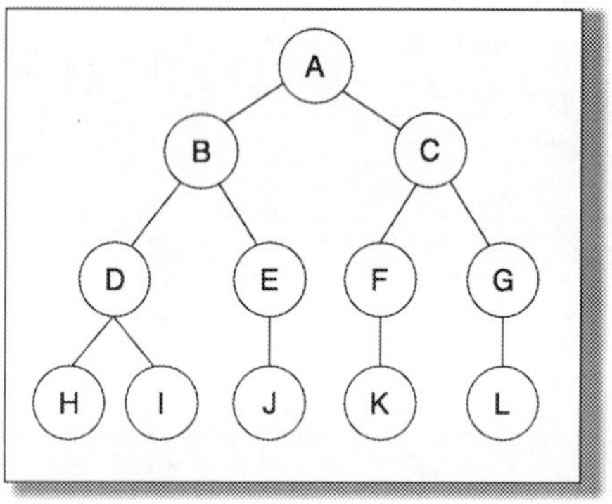

Figure 8.20 An undirected graph.

Open = [A]; Closed = [ ]
Open = [B, C]; Closed = [A]
Open = [D,E,C]; Closed = [A,B]
Open = [H,I,E,C]; Closed = [A,B,D]
Open = [I,E,C]; Closed = [A,B,D,H]
Open = [E,C]; Closed = [A,B,D,H,I]
Open = [J,C]; Closed = [A,B,D,H,I,E]
Open = [C]; Closed = [A,B,D,H,I,E,J]
Open = [F,G]; Closed = [A,B,D,H,I,E,J,C]
Open = [K,G]; Closed = [A,B,D,H,I,E,J,C,F]

Open = [G]; Closed = [A,B,D,H,I,E,J,C,F,K]
Open = [L]; Closed = [A,B,D,H,I,E,J,C,F,K,G]
Open = [ ]; Closed = [A,B,D,H,I,E,J,C,F,K,G,L]

Advantages of BFS

1. BFS will not get trapped on dead-end paths. This constrains with DFS which may follow a single unfruitful path for a long time, before the path actually terminates in a state that has no successor.
2. If there is a solution then BFS guarantees to find it. Furthermore if there are multiple solutions then a minimal solution will be found.

Disadvantage of BFS

Full tree explored so far will have to be stored in the memory.

Advantages of DFS

1. DFS requires less memory since only the nodes on the current path are stored. This contrasts with BFS where all of the tree that have so far been generated must be stored.
2. By chance, DFS may find a solution without examining much of the search space at all. This contrasts with BFS in which all parts of the trees must be examined to level n before any nodes of level n + 1 be examined.

Disadvantages of DFS

1. DFS may be trapped on dead-end paths. DFS follows a single unfruitful path for a long time, before the path is actually terminated in a state that has no successor.
2. DFS may find a long path to a solution in one part of the tree, when a shorter path exists in some other unexpected part of the tree.

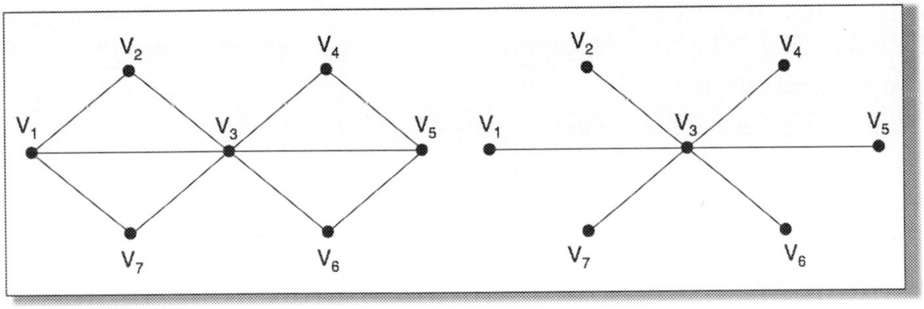

Figure 8.21(a) Undirected graph. **Figure 8.21(b)** Spanning tree.

8.6 SPANNING TREE

Consider a graph G = (V, E). If 'T' is a sub-graph of G and contains all the vertices but no cycle or circuit, then 'T' is said to be a spanning tree. Here we are using the connected graph. The reason for this straight, because a tree is always connected, and in an unconnected graph of 'n' vertices we cannot find a sub-graph with 'n' vertices. For creating the spanning tree of a given graph, we have deleted the edge from the circuit and the resultant obtained tree should be connected. The whole process is repeated if a graph has more number of circuits.

Figure 8.21 (b) illustrates the spanning tree of graph G shown in Figure 8.21(a).

8.6.1 Minimum Spanning Tree

A spanning tree in a graph G is a minimum sub-graph connecting all the vertices of G. if a weighted graph is considered, then the weight of the spanning tree 'T' of graph 'G' can be calculating by summing all the individual weights in the spanning tree T. as we have observed that there exists several spanning trees of a graph 'G' so in the case of weighted graph: different spanning trees of 'G' will have different weights. A spanning tree with the minimum weight in a weighted graph is called **minimal spanning tree** or **shortest spanning tree** or **minimum cost spanning tree.**

There are several methods for finding a minimum spanning tree in a given graph. Two of these are:

- J. Kruskal's Algorithm
- Prim's Algorithm

Kruskal's Algorithm: In Kruskal's algorithm the minimum weight is obtained. Firstly, the list of all the edges of the graph 'G' in order of decreasing weights and then the edge with the shortest of the minimum weight is selected. Next, for each successive step, select from the remaining edges another edge that has the minimum weight and then follow the condition that this edge does not make any circuit with the previously selected edges. The whole process continues till all n-1 edges are selected and these edges will form the desired minimal spanning tree.

Algorithm steps

1. Initialize T = NULL
2. (scan n-1 edges from the given set E)
   Repeat through E_i = 1,2,3,.....n-1, edges
   Set edge = minimum (E_i)
   Set temp = edge [delete edge from the set E]
3. (add temp to T if no circuit is obtained)
   Repeat while E_i does not create cycle
   Set T = temp [minimum weight edges]
4. (no spanning tree)
   If edges of T is less than n-1 edges
   Then message = "No spanning Tree"
5. Exit

Example: Consider a graph G = (V, E, W), an undirected connected weighted graph as shown in Figure 8.22. Kruskal's algorithm on graph 'G' produces the minimum spanning tree shown in Figure 8.23.

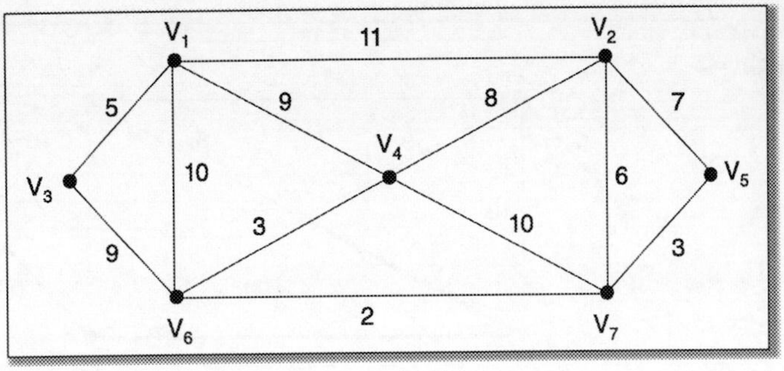

Figure 8.22 Undirected graph G.

Solution The process for obtaining the minimum spanning tree using Kruskal's algorithm is pictorially shown below:

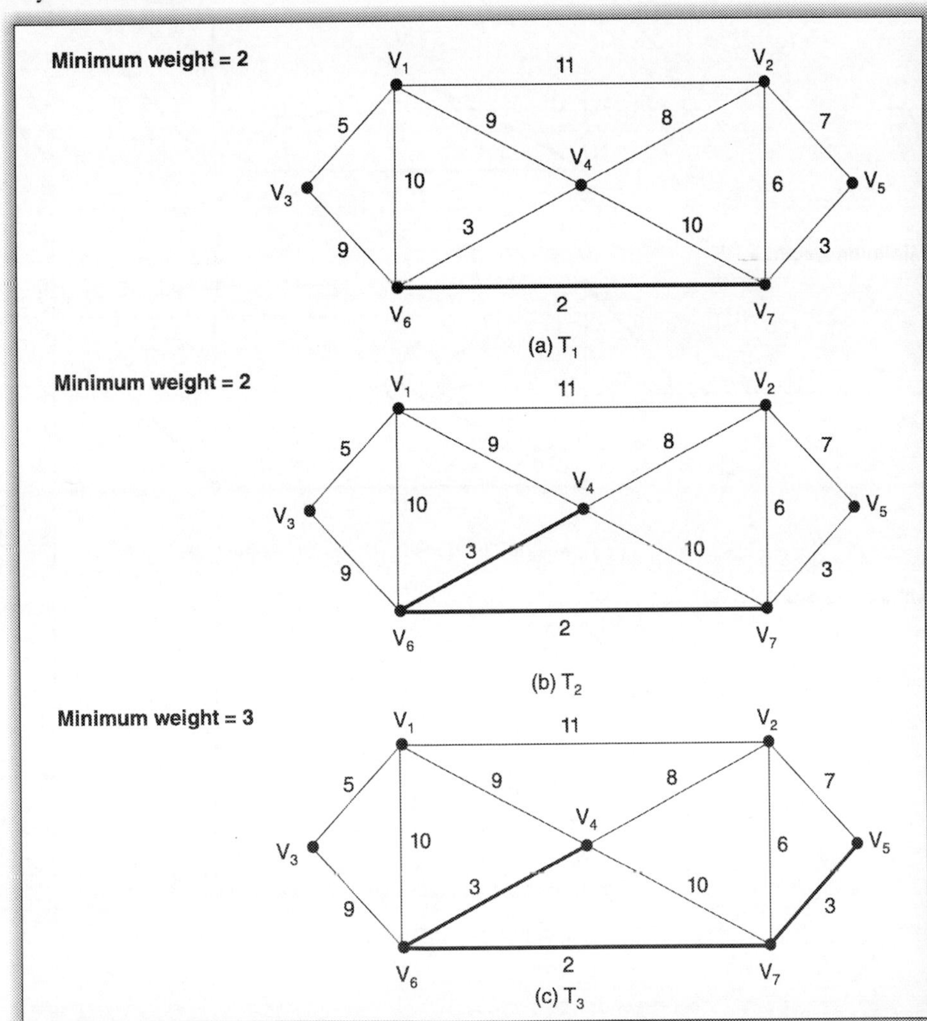

Minimum weight = 5

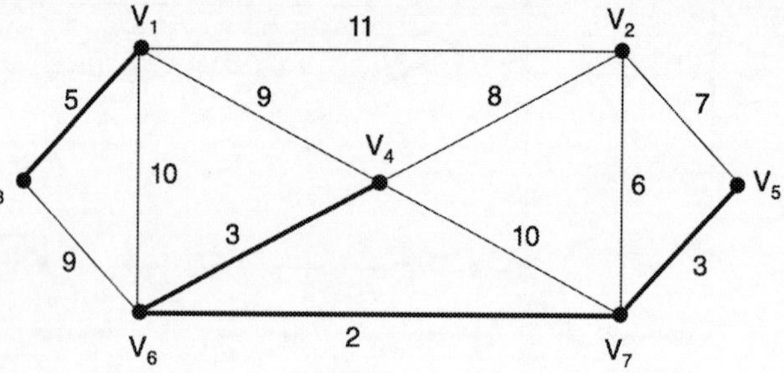

(d) T_4

Minimum weight = 6

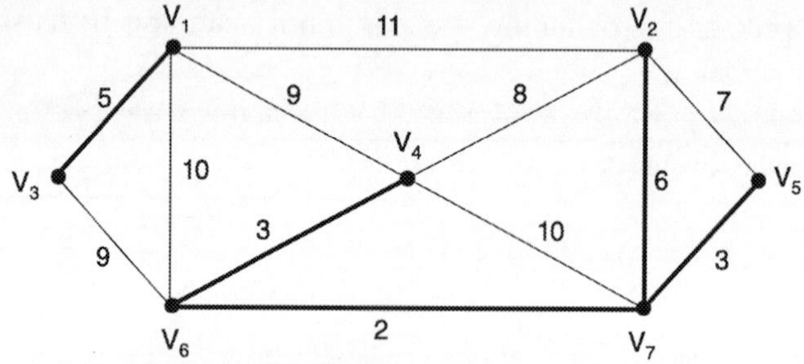

(e) T_5

Minimum weight = 7

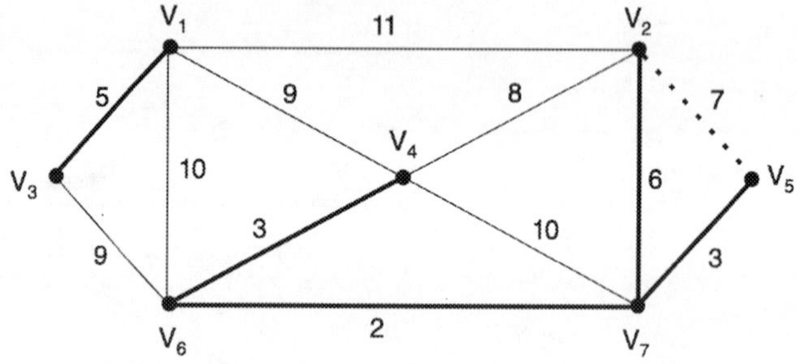

(f) T_6 weight 7 produces cycle so ignore the edge

Minimum weight = 8

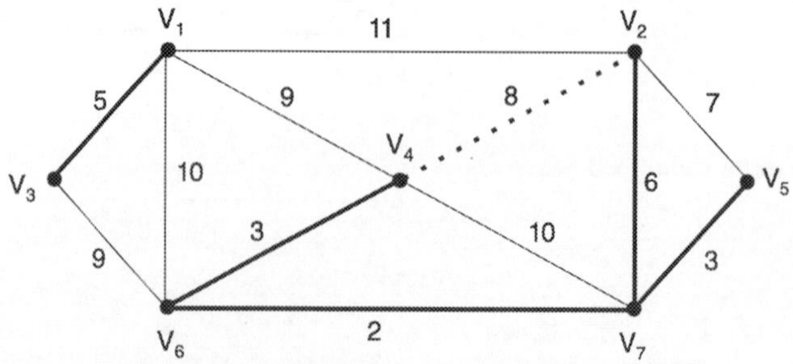

(g) T_7 weight 8 produces cycle so ignore the edge

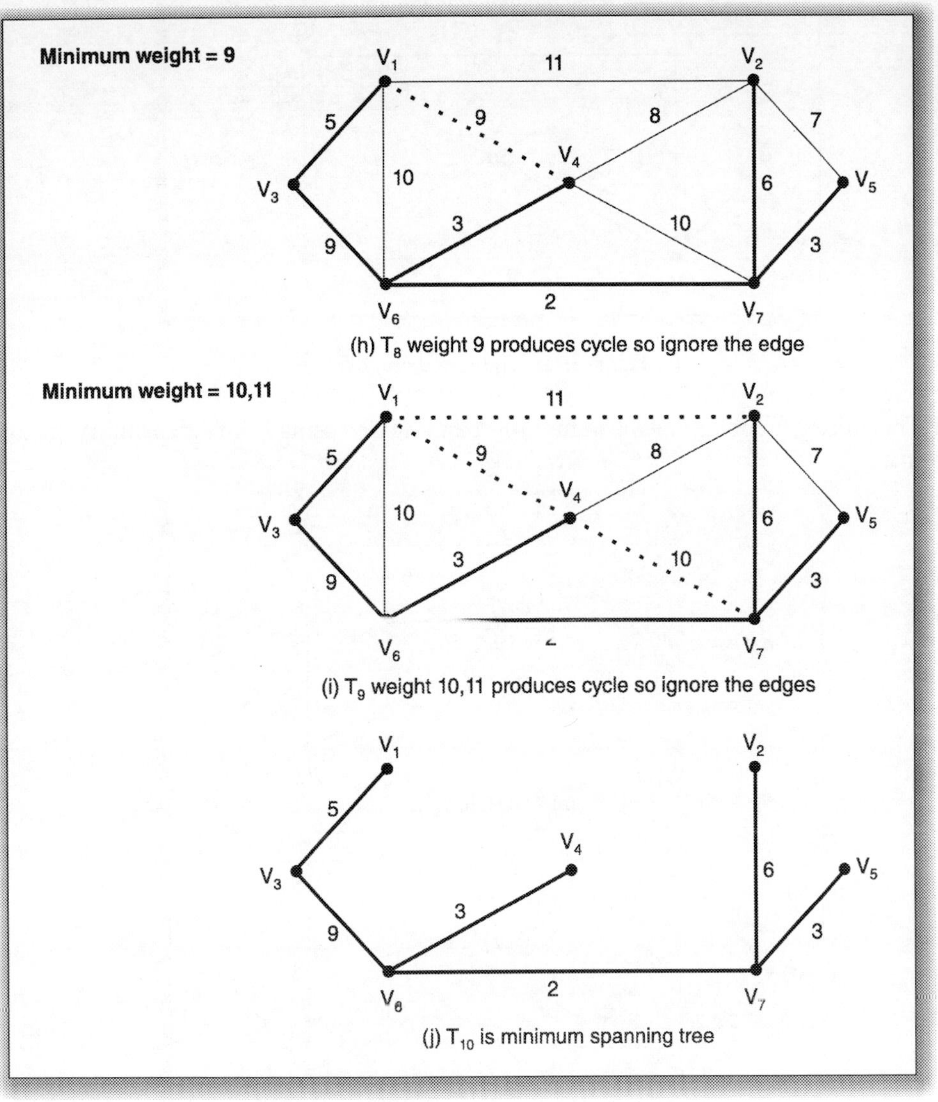

(h) T_8 weight 9 produces cycle so ignore the edge

(i) T_9 weight 10,11 produces cycle so ignore the edges

(j) T_{10} is minimum spanning tree

Figure 8.23 A Minimumspanning tree of Figure 8.22.

Hence, the minimum cost of spanning tree of the given graph using Kruskal's algorithm is $= 2 + 3 + 3 + 5 + 6 + 9 = 28$

Jarnik-Prim's Algorithm: In this algorithm, the pair with the minimum weight is to be chosen. The adjacent to these vertices whichever is the edge having the minimum weight is selected. This process is continued till all the vertices are not covered. The necessary condition in this case is that the **circuit should not be formed.** From Figure 8.24 we will build the minimum spanning tree.

Example: Consider a graph $G = (V, E, W)$, undirected connected weighted graph shown in Figure 8.24. Prim's algorithm on graph 'G' produces the minimum spanning tree shown in Figure 8.25. The arrows on edges indicate the predecessor pointers and the numeric label in each vertex is the key value.

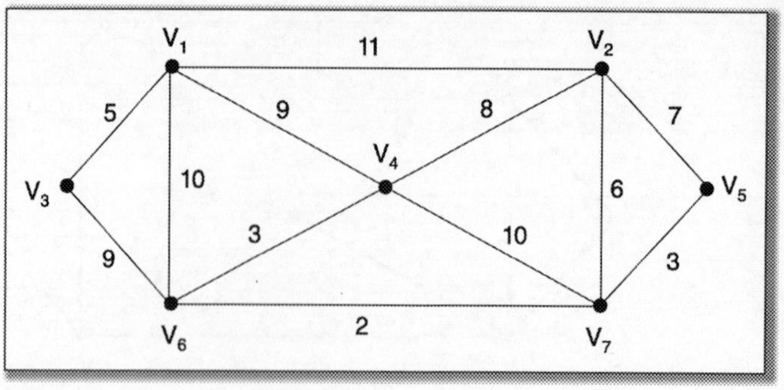

Figure 8.24 Undirected graph G.

Solution The process for obtaining the minimum spanning tree using Prim's algorithm is pictorially shown below:

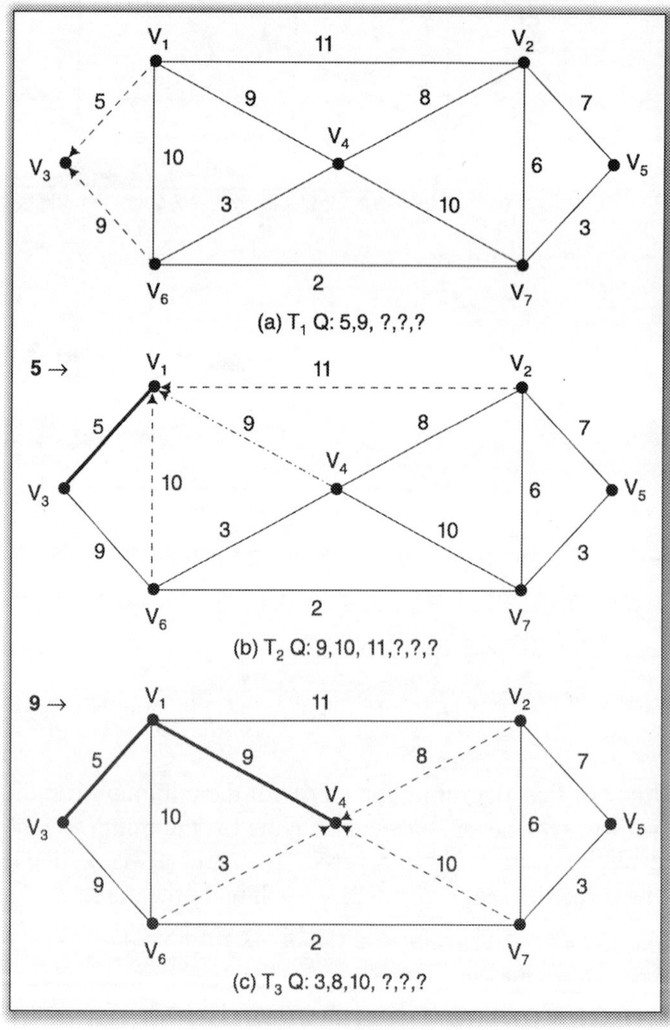

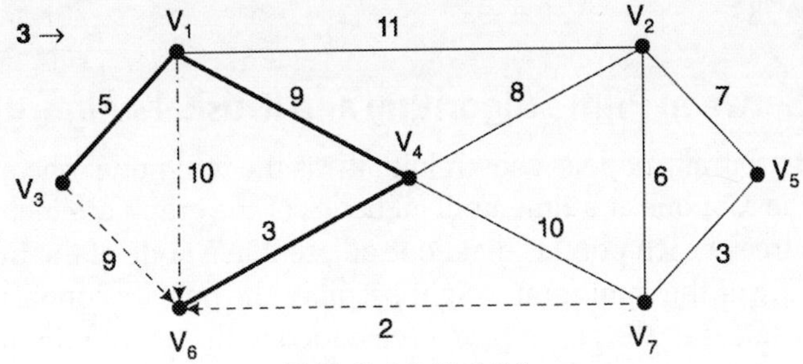

(d) T_4 Q: 2,9,10, ?,?,?

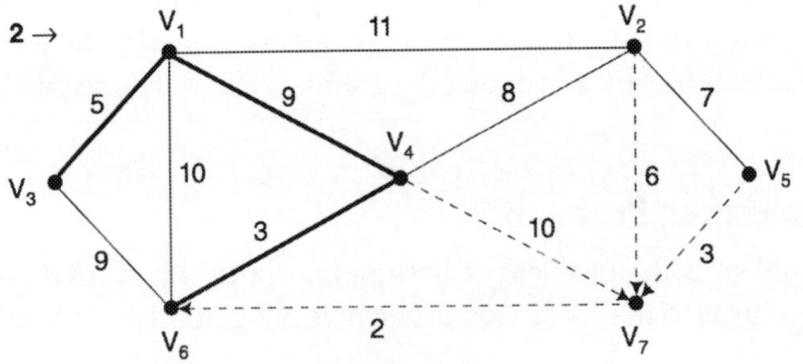

(e) T_5 Q: 3,6,10

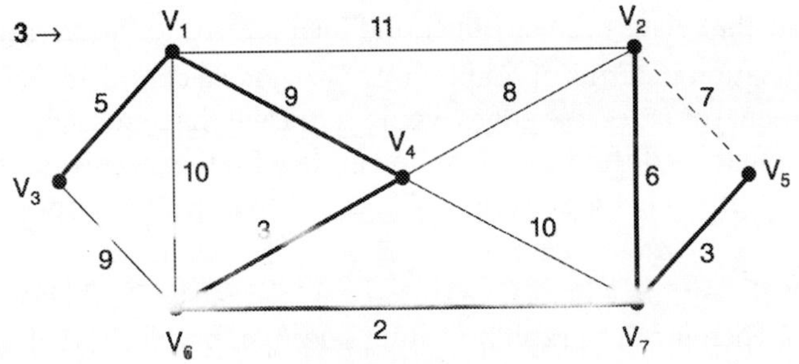

(f) T_6 Q: (empty)

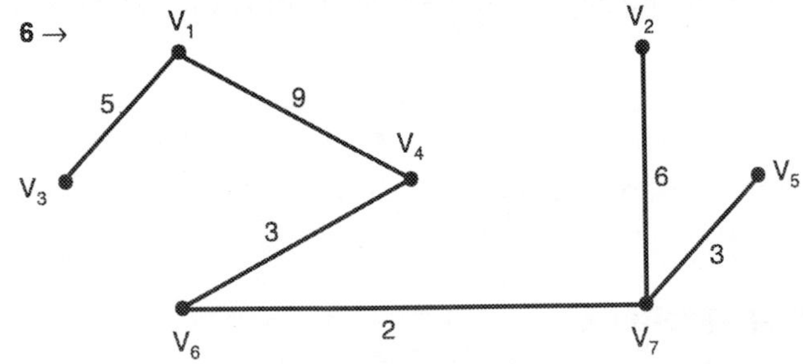

(g) T_7 MST

Figure 8.25

Hence, the minimum cost of spanning tree of the given graph using Prim's algorithm is
= 5 + 9 + 3 + 2 + 3 + 6 = 28

8.6.2 Difference Between Prim's Algorithm and Kruskal's Algorithm

In **Prim's algorithm** an arbitrary node is chosen initially as the root node. The nodes of the graph are then appended to the root one at a time until all nodes of the graph are included. The node of the graph added to the tree at each point is that node adjacent to a node of the tree by an arc of the minimum weight. The arc of the minimum weight becomes the tree arc connecting the new node to the tree. When all the nodes of the graph have been added to the tree, a minimum spanning tree has been considered to be constructed for the graph.

While in **Kruskal's algorithm**, the nodes of the graph are initially considered as n distinct partial trees with one node each. At each step of the algorithm, two distinct partial trees are connected into a single partial tree by an edge of the graph. When only one partial tree exits, it is a minimum spanning tree.

8.6.3 Travelling Salesman Problem

Travelling salesman problem is the problem of finding the shortest path that goes through every node exactly once, and returns to the start. That problem is NP-complete, so an efficient solution is not likely to exist.

Given a number of cities and the costs of traveling from any city to any other city, what is the cheapest round-trip route that visits each city once and then returns to the starting city?

An equivalent formulation in terms of graph theory is: given a complete weight graph (where the vertices would represent the cities, the edges would represent the roads, and the weights would be the cost of distance of that road) find the Hamilton cycle with the least weight. It can be shown that the requirement of returning to the starting city does not change the computational complexity of the problem.

Now, consider a directed graph where edges represent the roads with their weights as distance and vertices as the cities. Then for this graph travelling salesman problem is solved by selecting by selecting all the Hamiltonion circuits and then selecting the shortest one.

The total number of the Hamiltonian circuits present in the graph having 'n' number of vertices can be obtained by:

$$\frac{1}{2}(n-1)!$$

For finding the shortest routes various algorithms are available but none of them have proven to be best.

8.7 SHORTEST PATH PROBLEM

In our daily life everybody faces a problem of choosing the shortest path from one location to another location. Here, the shortest path means the path which has minimum mileage. By minimum spanning tree, we are not able to obtain the shortest path between two nodes (source and destination nodes). We can obtain simply the minimum cost. But by using the shortest path algorithm we can obtain the minimum distance between two nodes. In our laboratories we have local area network for all the computers. Before designing LAN we should always find out the shortest path and thereby we can obtain economical networking.

A solution to the shortest path problem is sometimes called pathing algorithm. The most important algorithms for solving this problem are:

- Dijkstra's algorithm: In this algorithm one solves single source problem if all edge weights are greater than or equal to zero. Without worsening the run time, this algorithm can in fact compute the shortest paths from a given start point to all other nodes.
- Bellman-Ford algorithm: In this algorithm one solves single source problem if the edge weights are negative.
- A*algorithm: A heuristic algorithm for single source shortest paths.
- Floyd-Warshall algorithm: Solves all pairs' shortest paths.
- Johnson's algorithm: In this algorithm one solves all pairs of shortest paths, may be faster than Floyd-Warshall on sparse graphs.

There are weighted and unweighted graph. Based on this category, let us discuss the shortest path algorithm.

1. **Unweighted shortest path:** The unweighted shortest path algorithm gives a path in an unweighted graph which is equal to the number of edges travelled from the source to destination.

   Example: Consider the graph given below Figure 8.26.

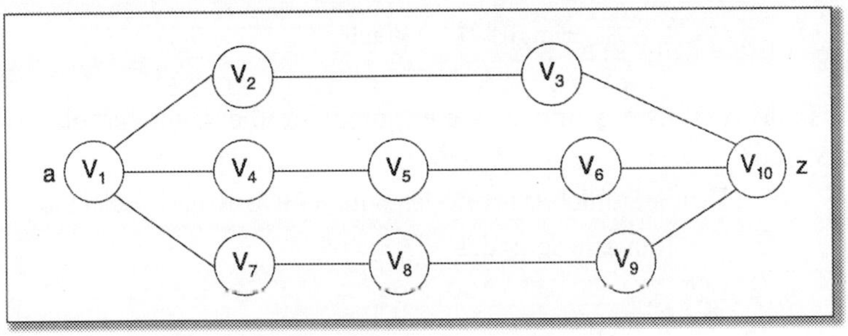

Figure 8.26 Unweighted graph.

The paths between a to z are as below

S.N.	Path	Number of edges
1	$V_1 - V_2 - V_3 - V_{10}$	3
2	$V_1 - V_4 - V_5 - V_6 - V_{10}$	4
3	$V_1 - V_7 - V_8 - V_9 - V_{10}$	4

Out of these the path 1 i.e. $V_1 - V_2 - V_3 - V_{10}$ is shortest one as it consists of only 3 edges from a to z.

2. **Dijkstra's shortest path algorithm:** The Dijkstra's shortest path algorithm suggests the shortest path from some source node to the some other destination node. The source node or the node from where we start measuring the distance is called the start node and the destination node is called the end node. In this algorithm we start finding the distance from the start node and find all the paths from it to neighboring nodes. Among those the path whichever is the nearest node is selected. This process of finding the nearest node is repeated till the end node. This path is called the shortest path.

Since in this algorithm all the paths are tried and then we choose the shortest path among them, this algorithm is solved by a greedy algorithm. One more point is that we are having all the vertices in the shortest path and therefore the graph doesn't give the spanning tree.

Example: Find the shortest distance between a to z for the given in graph shown in Figure 8.27.

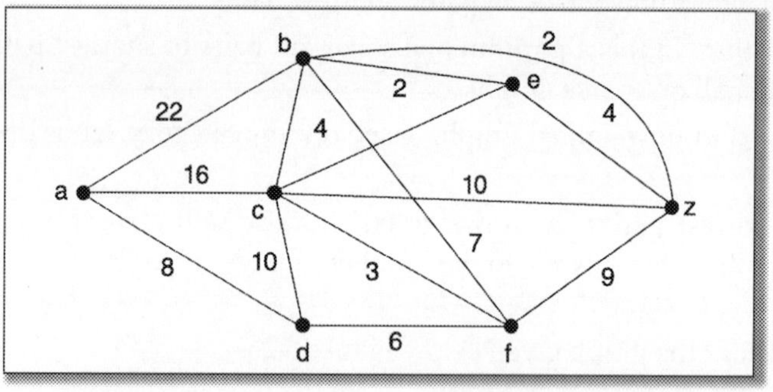

Figure 8.27 A graph.

The shortest distance between a and z is computed for the given graph using Dijkstra's algorithm as follows:

P = Set which is for nodes which have already selected

T = Remaining nodes

Step 1: v = a

P = {a}, T = {b, c, d, e, f, z}

```
distance (b) = min {old distance (b), distance (a) + w (a, b)}
dist (b) = min {∞, 0 + 22}
dist(b) = 22
dist(c) = 16
dist(d) = 8 minimum node
dist(e) = ∞
dist(f) = ∞
dist(z) = ∞
```

so the minimum node is selected in P i.e. node d

Step 2: v = d

P = {a, d}, T = {b, c, e, f, z}

distance (b) = min {old distance (b), distance (a) + w (a, b)}
dist (b) = min {22, 8 + ∞}
dist(b) = 22
dist(c) = min{16, 8 + 10} = 16
dist(e) = min{∞, 8 + ∞} = ∞
dist(f) = min{∞, 8 + 6} = 14 minimum
dist(z) = min{∞, 8 + ∞} = ∞

Step 3: v = f
P = {a, d, f}, T = {b, c, e, z}
distance (b) = min {old distance (b), distance (a) + w (a, b)}
dist (b) = min {22, 14 + 7}= 21
dist(b) = 21
dist(c) = min{16, 14 + 3} = 16 minimum
dist(e) = min{∞, 14 + ∞} = ∞
dist(z) = min{∞, 14 + 9} = 23

Step 4: v = c
P = {a, d, f, c}, T = {b, e, z}
distance (b) = min {old distance (b), distance (a) + w (a, b)}
dist (b) = min {21, 16 + 20} = 21
dist(b) = 21
dist(e) = min{∞, 16 + 4} = 20 minimum
dist(z) = min{23, 16 + 10} = 23

Step 5: v = e
P = {a, d, f, c, e}, T = {b, z}
distance (b) = min {old distance (b), distance (a) + w (a, b)}
dist (b) = min {21, 16 + 20}= 21
dist(b) = 21 minimum
dist(z) = min{23, 20 + 4} = 23

Step 6: v = b
P = {a,d,f,c,e,b}, T = {z}
dist(z) = min{23, 21 + 2} = 23

Now the target vertex for finding the shortest path is z. Hence the length of the shortest path from the vertex a to z is 23.

The shortest path in the given graph is {a, d, f, z}.

Algorithm for shortest path

1. Algorithm shortest paths (v, cost, dist, n)
2. // dist[j], 1≤j≤n, is set to the length of the shortest

```
// path from vertex v to vertex j in a diagraph G
// with n vertices dist[v] is set to zero, G is
// represented by its cost adjacency matrix cost[1 : n, 1 : n]
{
For i: =1 to n do
{// initialize S
S [i]: = false; dist[v] = cost [v,i];
}
S [v]: = true; dist[v] = 0.0; // put v in S.
For num: = 2 to n-1 do
{
// determine n -1 paths from v
Choose u from among those vertices not in S such
That dist[u] is minimum;
S[u]: = true; // put u in S
For (each w adjacent to u with S[w] = false do
If(dist[w] < (dist[u] + cost[u,w])) then
Dist [w]; = dist[u] + cost [u,w];
}
}
```

8.8 APPLICATIONS OF GRAPH

The graph theory is used in the computer science very widely. There are many interesting applications of graph. We will list out few applications.

- In computer networking such as Local Area Network (LAN), Wide Area Networking, Inter-networking.
- In telephone cabling graph theory is effectively used.
- In job scheduling algorithms.
- In study of molecules in science, in condensed matter physics, the three dimensional structure of the complicated atomic structures can be studied quantitatively by gathering statistics on graph-theoretic properties.
- Konigsberg bridge problem.
- Seating problem.
- Problem related to electric networks.
- Time table or schedule of periods.
- Utilities problem.

A graph can also be used to represent the physical situation involving discrete objects and a relationship among them.

9

SORTING AND SEARCHING

9.1 INTRODUCTION

The sorting and searching operation plays a very important role in various applications. For most of them the database applications involve a large amount of data. Consider a payroll system for a multidimensional company, having several departments; each department having many employees. Now if we want to see the salary of a particular employee, it will very difficult for us to see each and every record of the employee. If the data is organized according to the employee's salary i.e. either in ascending (increasing) or in descending (decreasing) order of the employee Id the employee record is arranged then the searching of the desired data will be an easy task.

Another application of systematic arrangement of the data is our university student records. In any university there are many colleges having several courses, having several departments. Each department has many students. If we want to see the result of a particular student it will very difficult. So organizes student's data according to the student's enrolment number. Another example of telephone directory – where the phone numbers are stored along with person's name, and the surnames are arranged in an alphabetical order. So to find a person's telephone number, you just search it by his surname. Imagine how difficult it would have been if the telephone directory is with the non-systematic arrangement of the numbers. Above examples are based on two techniques – sorting and searching.

Sorting is a systematic arrangement of the data. Systematic arrangement means based on some key the data should be arranged in an ascending or descending order.

9.2 INTERNAL & EXTERNAL SORTING

Sorting can be of two types – internal sorting and external sorting.

Internal sorting is a sorting in which the data resides in the main memory of the computer. For many applications it is not possible to store the entire data in the main memory for two reasons. First, the size of main memory available is smaller than the amount of data. Secondly, the main memory is a volatile device so it will loose the data when the power is shut down. To overcome these problems the data is sorted in the secondary storage devices.

The technique which is used to sort the data which resides in the secondary storage (auxiliary storage) devices is called **external sorting.**

A sort takes place either on the records themselves or an auxiliary table of pointers.

9.2.1 Basic Terminology of Sorting

Before learning the sorting techniques let us understand some basic terminology which is used in sorting.

9.2.1.1 Order

Sorting is a technique by which we expect the list of elements to be arranged as we expect. Sorting order is the arrangement of the elements in some specific manner. Usually sorting is of two types:

Descending Order: It is the sorting order in which the elements are arranged in the form of high to low value. In other words elements are in a decreasing order.

Example: 15, 35, 45, 25, 55, 10
can be arranged in descending order after applying some sorting methods as

55, 45, 35, 25, 15, 10

Ascending Order: It is the sorting order in which the elements are arranged in the form of low to high value. In other words elements are in an increasing order.

Example: 15, 35, 45, 25, 55, 10
can be arranged in ascending order after applying some sorting methods as

10, 15, 25, 35, 45, 55

9.2.1.2 Efficiency and passes

One of the major issues in the sorting algorithms is its efficiency. If we can efficiently sort the records then that adds value to the sorting algorithm. We generally denote the efficiency of a sorting algorithm in terms of time complexity. The time complexities are given in terms of big-O notations.

Commonly there are $O(n^2)$ and O(nlogn) time complexities for various algorithms. The sorting techniques such as bubble sort, insertion sort, selection sort, shell sort has the time complexity $O(n^2)$ and the techniques such as merge sort, quick sort, heap sort has time complexities such as O(nlogn). Efficiency also depends on number of records to be sorted. A sorting efficiency means how much time that algorithm have taken to sort the elements.

Sorting the elements in some specific order gives a group of arrangement of elements. The phases in which the elements move to acquire their proper position are called **passes.**

Example: 10, 30, 20, 50, 40

Pass 1: 10, 20, 30, 50, 40

Pass 2: 10, 20, 30, 40, 50

In the above method we can see that data is getting sorted in two definite passes. By applying the logic of comparison of each element with its adjacent elements gives us the result in two passes.

9.3 SORTING TECHNIQUES

Sorting is an important activity and every time we insert or delete the data we need to sort the remaining data. Various sorting algorithms are developed for sorting elements such as:

- Bubble sort
- Insertion sort
- Selection sort
- Merge sort
- Quick sort
- Heap sort
- Radix sort

9.3.1 Bubble Sort

Bubble sort also called 'sorting by exchange', as in order to find the successive smallest elements the whole method relies closely on the exchange of the adjacent element. This approach of sorting requires 'n-1' passes to sort the given list in some proper order.

Consider the number of 'n' elements present in an array 'A'. The first pass starts with the comparison of the keys of nth and $(n-1)^{th}$ element. If the 'n^{th}' key element is smaller than the $(n-1)^{th}$ key element then the two elements are interchanged. The smaller key is compared with the key of the $(n-2)^{th}$ element. And if required, the elements are interchanged to place the smaller among the two in the $(n-2)^{th}$ position. This sorting technique will cause the elements with small key to move or 'bubble up'. The whole process is continued in this manner and the first pass ends with the comparison and possible exchange of elements A[1] and A[0]. The whole sorting method terminated with '(n-1)' passes, thereby resulting into a sorted list.

Example: Consider 6 unsorted elements:

45, 55, 35, 90, 70, 30

Suppose an array 'A' consists of 6 elements as –

45	55	35	90	70	30
A_0	A_1	A_2	A_3	A_4	A_5

Pass 1:

In this pass each element will be compared with its neighboring element.

45	55	35	90	70	30
A_0	A_1	A_2	A_3	A_4	A_5

Compare A[0] = 45 and A[1] = 55. Is 45 > 55 is false so no interchange.

45	55	35	90	70	30
A_0	A_1	A_2	A_3	A_4	A_5

Compare A[1] = 55 and A[2] = 35. Is 55 > 35 is true so interchange. A[1] = 35 and A[2] = 55.

45	35	55	90	70	30
A_0	A_1	A_2	A_3	A_4	A_5

Compare A[2] = 55 and A[3] = 90. Is 55 > 90 is false so no interchange.

45	35	55	90	70	30
A_0	A_1	A_2	A_3	A_4	A_5

Compare A[3] = 90 and A[4] = 70. Is 90 > 70 is true so interchange. A[3] = 70 and A[4] = 90.

45	35	55	70	90	30
A_0	A_1	A_2	A_3	A_4	A_5

Compare A[4] = 90 and A[5] = 30. Is 90 > 30 is true so interchange. A[4] = 30 and A[4] = 90.

45	35	55	70	30	90
A_0	A_1	A_2	A_3	A_4	A_5

After the first pass the array will hold the elements which are sorted to some level.

Pass 2:

45	35	55	70	30	90
A_0	A_1	A_2	A_3	A_4	A_5

Compare A[0] = 45 and A[1] = 35. Is 45 > 35 is true so interchange. A[0] = 35 and A[1] = 45.

35	45	55	70	30	90
A_0	A_1	A_2	A_3	A_4	A_5

Compare A[1] = 45 and A[2] = 55. Is 45 > 55 is false so no interchange.

35	45	55	70	30	90
A_0	A_1	A_2	A_3	A_4	A_5

Compare A[2] = 55 and A[3] = 70. Is 55 > 70 is false so no interchange.

35	45	55	70	30	90
A_0	A_1	A_2	A_3	A_4	A_5

Compare A[3] = 70 and A[4] = 30. Is 70 > 30 is true so interchange. A[3] = 30 and A[4] = 70.

35	45	55	30	70	90
A_0	A_1	A_2	A_3	A_4	A_5

Compare A[4] = 70 and A[5] = 90. Is 70 > 90 is false so no interchange.

35	45	55	30	70	90
A_0	A_1	A_2	A_3	A_4	A_5

After the second pass the array will hold the elements which are sorted to some level.

Pass 3:

35	45	55	30	70	90
A_0	A_1	A_2	A_3	A_4	A_5

Compare A[0] = 35 and A[1] = 45. Is 35 > 45 is false so no interchange.

35	45	55	30	70	90
A_0	A_1	A_2	A_3	A_4	A_5

Compare A[1] = 45 and A[2] = 55. Is 45 > 55 is false so no interchange.

35	45	55	30	70	90
A_0	A_1	A_2	A_3	A_4	A_5

Compare A[2] = 55 and A[3] = 30. Is 55 > 30 is true so interchange. A[2] = 30 and A[3] = 55.

35	45	30	55	70	90
A_0	A_1	A_2	A_3	A_4	A_5

Compare A[3] = 55 and A[4] = 70. Is 55 > 70 is false so no interchange.

35	45	30	55	70	90
A_0	A_1	A_2	A_3	A_4	A_5

Compare A[4] = 70 and A[5] = 90. Is 70 > 90 is false so no interchange.

35	45	30	55	70	90
A_0	A_1	A_2	A_3	A_4	A_5

After third pass the array will hold the elements which are sorted to some level.

Pass 4:

35	45	30	55	70	90
A_0	A_1	A_2	A_3	A_4	A_5

Compare A[0] = 35 and A[1] = 45. Is 35 > 45 is false so no interchange.

35	45	30	55	70	90
A_0	A_1	A_2	A_3	A_4	A_5

Compare A[1] = 45 and A[2] = 30. Is 45 > 30 is true so interchange. A[1] = 30 and A[2] = 45.

35	30	45	55	70	90
A_0	A_1	A_2	A_3	A_4	A_5

Compare A[2] = 45 and A[3] = 55. Is 45 > 55 is false so no interchange.

35	30	45	55	70	90
A_0	A_1	A_2	A_3	A_4	A_5

Compare A[3] = 55 and A[4] = 70. Is 55 > 70 is false so no interchange.

35	30	45	55	70	90
A_0	A_1	A_2	A_3	A_4	A_5

Compare A[4] = 70 and A[5] = 90. Is 70 > 90 is false so no interchange.

35	30	45	55	70	90
A_0	A_1	A_2	A_3	A_4	A_5

After the fourth pass the array will hold the elements which are sorted to some level.

Pass 5:

35	30	45	55	70	90
A_0	A_1	A_2	A_3	A_4	A_5

Compare A[0] = 35 and A[1] = 30. Is 35 > 30 is true so interchange. A[0] = 30 and A[1] = 35.

30	35	45	55	70	90
A_0	A_1	A_2	A_3	A_4	A_5

Compare A[1] = 35 and A[2] = 45. Is 35 > 45 is false so no interchange.

30	35	45	55	70	90
A_0	A_1	A_2	A_3	A_4	A_5

Compare A[2] = 45 and A[3] = 55. Is 45 > 55 is false so no interchange.

30	35	45	55	70	90
A_0	A_1	A_2	A_3	A_4	A_5

Compare A[3] = 55 and A[4] = 70. Is 55 > 70 is false so no interchange.

30	35	45	55	70	90
A_0	A_1	A_2	A_3	A_4	A_5

Compare A[4] = 70 and A[5] = 90. Is 70 > 90 is false so no interchange.

30	35	45	55	70	90
A_0	A_1	A_2	A_3	A_4	A_5

Finally, at the end of the last pass the array will hold the entire sorted element like this

30	35	45	55	70	90
A_0	A_1	A_2	A_3	A_4	A_5

Since the comparison positions look like bubbles, it is called **bubble sort**.

Algorithm of Bubble Sort

Step 1: Read the total number of elements say n.

Step 2: Store the elements in an array.

Step 3: Set the initial element i = 0.

Step 4: Compare the adjacent elements.

Step 5: Repeat step 4 for all n elements.

Step 6: Increment the value of i by 1 and repeat step 4, 5 for i < n.

Step 7: Print the sorted list of elements.

Step 8: Stop

Program for sorting the elements by bubble sort algorithm

```
# include <iostream.h>
# include<conio.h>
void main()
{
int a[100],n, i, j, temp;
clrscr( );
cout <<"How many element you want to sort =";
cin >> n;
cout <<endl <<"Enter the element of array" <<endl;
for (i=0; i <=n-1; i++)
{
cin >> a[i];
}
for (i=0; i<=n-1; i++)
{
for (j=0; j<=n-1; j++)
{
if (a[j] > a[j+1])
{
```

```
temp = a[j];
a[j] = a[j+1];
a[j+1] = temp;
}
}
cout << endl<<"Element of array after the sorting are : ";
for (i=0; i<=n; i++)
{
cout <<a[i] <<endl;
}
getch( );
}
}
```

Output of the program

```
How many element you want to sort = 5
Enter the element of array
30
20
50
40
10
Element of array after the sorting are: 10 20 30 40 50
```

Analysis

The complexity of sorting depends on the number of comparisons. The number of passes necessary may vary from 1 to (n – 1), but the number of comparisons required in a pass is not dependent on data. For the ith pass, the number of comparisons required is (n – 1).

In the **best case**, the bubble sort performs only one pass, which gives O(n) complexity. The number of comparison required is obviously (n – 1). This case arises when the given list of array is sorted.

In the **worst case,** performance of the bubble sort is given by:

$$\sum_{i=1}^{n-1} (n-i) = \frac{1}{2} n (n-1) = O(n^2)$$

9.3.2 Insertion Sort

Insertion sort technique is based on the concept of inserting records into an existing file. To insert a record, we must find the proper place where the insertion is to be made. To find this place, we need to search. Once we have found the correct place, we need to move the records to make a place for the new record. In this sorting, we combine the two operations – searching and sorting.

Now we consider an unsorted array. In this we take one entry at a time and insert it into an initially empty new array. We always keep the entries in the new list in the proper order.

Example: Consider 6 unsorted elements:

30, 70, 20, 50, 40, 10

Suppose an array 'A' consists of 6 elements as:

30	70	20	50	40	10
A_0	A_1	A_2	A_3	A_4	A_5

Pass 1: Compare A[1] > A[0] or 70 > 30. True, so the position of the elements remain same.

30	70	20	50	40	10
A_0	A_1	A_2	A_3	A_4	A_5

Pass 2: Compare A[2] > A[1] or 20 > 70. False, so interchange the position of the elements. And A[1] > A[0] or 20 > 30. False, so interchange the position of the elements.

20	30	70	50	40	10
A_0	A_1	A_2	A_3	A_4	A_5

Pass 3: Compare A[3] > A[2] or 50 > 70. False, so interchange the position of the elements. And A[2] > A[1] or 50 > 30. True, so the position of the elements remain same.

20	30	50	70	40	10
A_0	A_1	A_2	A_3	A_4	A_5

Pass 4: Compare A[4] > A[3] or 40 > 70. False, so interchange the position of the elements. And A[3] > A[2] or 40 > 50. False, so interchange the position of the elements. A[2] > A[1] or 40 > 30. True, so the position of the elements remain same.

20	30	40	50	70	10
A_0	A_1	A_2	A_3	A_4	A_5

Pass 5: Compare A[5] > A[4] or 10 > 70. False, so interchange the position of the elements. And A[4] > A[3] or 10 > 50. False, so interchange the position of the elements. A[3] > A[2] or 10 > 40. False, so interchange the position of the elements. A[2] > A[1] or 10 > 30. False, so interchange the position of the elements. And A[1] > A[0] or 10 > 20. False, so interchange the position of the elements.

10	20	30	40	50	70
A_0	A_1	A_2	A_3	A_4	A_5

Finally, at the end of the last pass the array will hold the entire sorted element like this

10	20	30	40	50	70
A_0	A_1	A_2	A_3	A_4	A_5

Algorithm of Insertion Sort

Step 1: Read the total number of elements say n.

Step 2: Store the elements in an array.

Step 3: Set the initial element i = 1.

Step 4: Compare the key (which we want insert) to the last element of the array.
If key ≤ array
Then
Move down the last array element by one.
Else
Insert the key into array.

Step 5: Repeat step 4 for all n elements.

Step 6: Increment the value of i by 1 and repeat step 4, 5 for i < n.

Step 7: Print the sorted list of elements.

Step 8: Stop.

Program for sorting the elements by insertion sort algorithm

```
# include<iostream.h>
# include<conio.h>
void main()
{
clrscr( );
int a[100],n, i, j, temp;
clrscr( );
cout <<"How many element you want to sort =";
cin >> n;
cout <<endl <<"Enter the element of array" <<endl;
for (i=0; i <=n-1; i++)
{
cin>>a[i];
 }
cout<<"Elements before sorting is"<<"\n";
for(i=0;i<n-1;i++)
 {
 cout<<a[i]<<endl;
 }
for(i=0;i<n-1;i++)
 {
 temp=a[i];
```

```
j=i-1;
while(j>=0&&a[j]>temp)
{
a[j+1]=a[j];
j=j-1;
}
a[j+1]=temp;
}
cout<<"Elements after sorting are"<<"\n";
for(i=0;i<n-1;i++)
{
cout<<a[i]<<endl;
}
getch( );
}
```

Output of the program

```
How many element you want to sort = 6
Enter the element of array
Elements before sorting is
30
70
20
50
40
10
Elements after sorting are
10
20
30
40
50
70
```

Analysis

When an array of elements is almost sorted then it is **best case** complexity. The best case time complexity of insertion sort is **O(n).**

If an array is randomly arranged then it results in **average case** time complexity which is **$O(n^2)$.**

If the list of elements is arranged in a descending order and if we want to sort the elements in ascending order then it results in **worst case** time complexity which is **$O(n^2)$.**

9.3.3 Selection Sort

In the selection sort method, the scan starts from the first element and searches the entire array list until it finds the minimum value and swaps it with the first element. The sort places the minimum value in the first place, selects the second element and searches for the second smallest element. This process continues until the complete list is sorted.

Example: Consider 6 unsorted elements:

70, 45, 25, 50, 90, 20

Suppose an array 'A' consists of 6 elements as:

Initially set array list

70	45	25	50	90	20
A_0	A_1	A_2	A_3	A_4	A_5
↑	↑				
min	j				

Pass 1:

70	45	25	50	90	20
A_0	A_1	A_2	A_3	A_4	A_5
↑	↑ scan from A1 in array find the smallest				
min	element to min value				

70	45	25	50	90	20
A_0	A_1	A_2	A_3	A_4	A_5
↑					↑
i			smallest element to min value		

Now swap A[i] with smallest element. Then we get the array list,

20	45	25	50	90	70
A_0	A_1	A_2	A_3	A_4	A_5

Pass 2:

20	45	25	50	90	70
A_0	A_1	A_2	A_3	A_4	A_5
	↑ i,	↑ scan from A2 find smallest			
	min	element to min value			

20	45	25	50	90	70
A_0	A_1	A_2	A_3	A_4	A_5
	↑ i	↑ smallest element to i value			

Now swap A[i] with smallest element. Then we get the array list,

20	25	45	50	90	70
A_0	A_1	A_2	A_3	A_4	A_5

Pass 3:

20	25	45	50	90	70
A_0	A_1	A_2	A_3	A_4	A_5
		↑ i, min	↑ scan from A3 find smallest element		

As there is no smallest element than 45 we will increment pointer i.

20	25	45	50	90	70
A_0	A_1	A_2	A_3	A_4	A_5
			↑ i		

Then we get the array list,

20	25	45	50	90	70
A_0	A_1	A_2	A_3	A_4	A_5

Pass 4:

20	25	45	50	90	70
A_0	A_1	A_2	A_3	A_4	A_5
			↑ i,	↑ scan from A_4 find smallest element to i value	

As there is no smallest element than 50 we will increment pointer i.

20	25	45	50	90	70
A_0	A_1	A_2	A_3	A_4	A_5
				↑ i	

Then we get the array list,

20	25	45	50	90	70
A_0	A_1	A_2	A_3	A_4	A_5

Pass 5:

20	45	25	50	90	70
A_0	A_1	A_2	A_3	A_4	A_5
				↑	↑
				i,	smallest

Now swap A[i] with smallest element. Then we get the array list,

20	25	45	50	70	90
A_0	A_1	A_2	A_3	A_4	A_5

This is the sorted array list.

Algorithm of Selection Sort

Step 1: Read the total number of elements say n.

Step 2: Store the elements in an array.

Step 3: Set the initial element i = 0 or min.

Step 4: Repeat step 9 while (i < n)

Step 5: j = i + 1

Step 6: Repeat step 8 while (j < n)

Step 7: if A[i] > A[j] then
temp = A[i]
A[i] = A[j]
A[j] = temp

Step 8: j = j + 1

Step 9: i = i + 1

Step 10: Print the sorted list of elements.

Step 11: Stop.

Program for sorting the elements by selection sort algorithm

```
# include<iostream.h>
# include<conio.h>
void main()
{
```

```
clrscr( );
int a[100],n, i, j, temp, current = 0;
clrscr( );
cout <<"How many element you want to sort =";
cin >> n;
cout <<endl <<"Enter the element of array" <<endl;
for(i=0;i<n-1;i++)
 {
 cin>>a[i];
 }
cout<<"Elements before sorting is"<<"\n";
for(i=0;i<n-1;i++)
   {
   cout<<a[i];
   cout<<endl;
   }
while(current<n-1)
     {
     j=current+1;
     while(j<n-1)
 {
    if(a[current]>a[j])
{
    temp=a[current];
    a[current]=a[j];
    a[j]=temp;
  }
     j=j+1;
 }
     current=current+1;
     }
cout<<"Elements after sorting are"<<"\n";
for(i=0;i<n-1;i++)
   {
   cout<<a[i];
   cout<<endl;
   }
getch();
}
```

Output of the program

```
How many element you want to sort = 6
Enter the element of array
Elements before sorting are
70
 45
 25
 50
```

```
 90
 20
Elements after sorting are
20
25
45
50
70
90
```

Analysis

When an array of elements is almost sorted then it is **best case** complexity. The best case time complexity of insertion sort is **O(n).**

If an array is randomly arranged then it results in **average case** time complexity which is $O(n^2)$.

If the list of elements is arranged in descending order and if we want to sort the elements in ascending order then it results in **worst case** time complexity which is $O(n^2)$.

Advantage

- Selection sort is faster than bubble sort.
- If an item is in its correct final position, then it will never be moved.
- The selection sort has better predictability, that is, the worst case time will differ little from its best case time .

9.3.4 Merge Sort

The merge sort is sorting algorithms that uses the divide and conquer method. Merge sort on an input array with n elements consists of three steps:

Divide: Partition array into two sublists S1 and S2 with n/2 elements each.

Conquer: Then sort sub list S1 and S2.

Combine: Merge S1 and S2 into a unique sorted group.

Example: The whole process of merge sort is as follows-

[5] [7] [3] [6] [2] [8] [4] [1]

Pass 1: [5 7] [3 6] [2 8] [4 1]

Pass 2: [3 5 6 7] [1 2 4 8]

Pass 3: [1 2 3 4 5 6 7 8]

Sorted element: 1 2 3 4 5 6 7 8

When merge sort apply two or more list

Merging is the process of combining two or more sorted files into a third sorted file. Let 'A' be a sorted list combining 'X' number of elements and 'B' be a sorted list containing 'Y' number of elements. Then the operation that combines the elements A and B into new sorted list C with Z = X + Y number of elements is called merging.

Compare the smallest elements of A and B. After finding the smallest, put it into new list C. The process is repeated until either list A or B is empty. Now place the remaining elements of A (or perhaps B) in C. The new list C contain the sorted elements which is equal to the total sum of elements of A and B lists.

Algorithm

Given two sorted lists A and B that consist of 'X' and 'Y' number of elements respectively. These algorithms merge the two lists and produce a new sorted list C.

Variables 'P_a' and 'P_b' keep track the location of smallest element in A and B. Variable P_c refers to the location in C to be filled.

Step 1: Set $P_a = 1$;
$P_b = 1$;
$P_c = 1$;

Step 2: loop comparisons
Repeat while ($P_a \le X$ and $P_b \le Y$)
If ($A[P_a] < B[P_b]$) then
Set $C[P_c] = A[P_a]$
Set $P_c = P_c + 1$
Set $P_a = P_a + 1$
else
$C[P_c] = B[P_b]$
Set $P_c = P_c + 1$
Set $P_b = P_b + 1$

Step 3: Append C list with remaining elements in A (or B)
If ($P_a > X$) then
Repeat for i = 0, 1, 2........, Y – P_b.
Set $C[P_c + i] = B[P_b + i]$
End loop
Repeat for i = 0, 1, 2........, Y – Pa.
Set $C[P_c + i] = B[P_a + i]$
End loop

Step 4: Finished.

Example: Consider two sorted lists A and B is as follows:

A:	1	5	10	20	25
B:	7	14	21	28	35

The process of merging and sorting illustrated below, which will produce a new sorting list C.

Initially: $P_a = 1;$

$P_b = 1;$

$P_c = 1;$

Step 1: Compare $A[P_a]$ and $B[P_b]$ or (A[1] and B[1])

$A[P_a] < B[P_b]$, $(1 < 7)$ so put 1 in $C[P_c]$

A:	1	5	10	20	25
B:	7	14	21	28	35
C:	1				

$P_a = P_a + 1$

$P_a = 2$

$P_b = 1$

$P_c = P_c + 1$

$P_c = 2$

Step 2: Compare $A[P_a]$ and $B[P_b]$ or (A[2] and B[1])

$A[P_a] < B[P_b]$, $(5 < 7)$ so put 5 in $C[P_c]$

A:	~~1~~	~~5~~	10	20	25
B:	7	14	21	28	35
C:	1	5			

$P_a = P_a + 1$

$P_a = 3$

$P_b = 1$

$P_c = P_c + 1$

$P_c = 3$

Step 3: Compare $A[P_a]$ and $B[P_b]$ or (A[3] and B[1])

$A[P_a] > B[P_b]$, $(10 > 7)$ so put 7 in $C[P_c]$

A:	~~1~~	~~5~~	10	20	25
B:	~~7~~	14	21	28	35
C:	1	5	7		

$P_a = 3$
$P_b = P_b + 1$
$P_b = 2$
$P_c = P_c + 1$
$P_c = 4$

Step 4: Compare $A[P_a]$ and $B[P_b]$ or (A[3] and B[2])

$A[P_a] < B[P_b]$, (10 < 14) so put 10 in $C[P_c]$

A:	~~1~~	~~5~~	~~10~~	20	25
B:	~~7~~	14	21	28	35
C:	1	5	7	10	

$P_a = P_a + 1$
$P_a = 4$
$P_b = 2$
$P_c = P_c + 1$
$P_c = 5$

Step 5: Compare $A[P_a]$ and $B[P_b]$ or (A[4] and B[2])

$A[P_a] > B[P_b]$, (20 > 14) so put 14 in $C[P_c]$

A:	~~1~~	~~5~~	~~10~~	20	25
B:	~~7~~	~~14~~	21	28	35
C:	1	5	7	10	14

$P_a = 4$
$P_b = P_b + 1$
$P_b = 3$
$P_c = P_c + 1$
$P_c = 6$

Step 6: Compare $A[P_a]$ and $B[P_b]$ or (A[4] and B[3])

$A[P_a] < B[P_b]$, (20 < 21) so put 20 in $C[P_c]$

A:	~~1~~	~~5~~	~~10~~	~~20~~	25	
B:	~~7~~	~~14~~	21	28	35	
C:	1	5	7	10	14	20

$P_a = P_a + 1$
$P_a = 5$
$P_b = 3$
$P_c = P_c + 1$
$P_c = 7$

Step 7: Compare $A[P_a]$ and $B[P_b]$ or (A[5] and B[3])

$A[P_a] > B[P_b]$, (25 > 21) so put 21 in $C[P_c]$

A:	~~1~~	~~5~~	~~10~~	~~20~~	25		
B:	~~7~~	~~14~~	~~21~~	28	35		
C:	1	5	7	10	14	20	21

$P_a = 5$
$P_b = P_b + 1$
$P_b = 4$
$P_c = P_c + 1$
$P_c = 8$

Step 8: Compare $A[P_a]$ and $B[P_b]$ or (A[5] and B[4])

$A[P_a] < B[P_b]$, (25 < 28) so put 25 in $C[P_c]$

A:	~~1~~	~~5~~	~~10~~	~~20~~	~~25~~			
B:	~~7~~	~~14~~	~~21~~	28	35			
C:	1	5	7	10	14	20	21	25

$P_a = P_a + 1$
$P_a = 6$
$P_b = 4$
$P_c = P_c + 1$
$P_c = 9$

Step 9: Append the elements of B in C

As $P_a > x$ so, put all the remaining elements of B in C and increment P_b and P_c respectively by 1 until the list B is also empty.

A:	~~1~~	~~5~~	~~10~~	~~20~~	~~25~~				
B:	~~7~~	~~14~~	~~21~~	~~28~~	35				
C:	1	5	7	10	14	20	21	25	28

$P_a = 6$
$P_b = P_b + 1$
$P_b = 5$
$P_c = P_c + 1$
$P_c = 10$

A:	~~1~~	~~5~~	~~10~~	~~20~~	~~25~~					
B:	~~7~~	~~14~~	~~21~~	~~28~~	~~35~~					
C:	1	5	7	10	14	20	21	25	28	35

$P_a = 6$

$P_b = P_b + 1$

$P_b = 6$

$P_c = P_c + 1$

$P_c = 11$

Now, $P_b > y$. This shows that B is also empty finally we have a sorted new list C as follows:

$$C = 1, 5, 7, 10, 14, 20, 21, 25, 28, 35$$

Analysis

When an array of elements is almost sorted then it is **best case** complexity. The best case time complexity of insertion sort is **$O(n \log_2 n)$.**

If an array is randomly arranged then it results in **average case** time complexity which is **$O(n \log_2 n)$.**

If the list of elements is arranged in descending order and if we want to sort the elements in an ascending order then it results in **worst case** time complexity which is **$O(n \log_2 n)$.**

9.3.5 Quick Sort

The quick sort algorithm is based on the divide and conquer design technique. In this at every step each element is placed in its proper position. It performs well on a longer list. The three steps of quick sort are as follows:

Divide: Divide the array list into two sub-lists such that each element in the left sub-array is less than or equal the middle element and each element in the right sub-array is greater than the middle element. The splitting of the array into two sub-arrays is based on the pivot element. All the elements that are less than the pivot should be in left sub-array and all the elements that are more than the pivot should be in right sub-array.

Conquer: Recursively sort the two sub-arrays.

Combine: Combine all the sorted elements in a group to form a list of sorted elements.

Working of Quick Sort

First select a random 'pivot value' from the array (list). Then partition the list into elements that are less than the pivot and greater than the pivot. The problem of sorting a given list is reduced to the problem of sorting two sublists. By scanning that last element of the list from the right to the left, and checks with the element. The comparisons of elements with the first element stops when we obtain the elements smaller than the first element. Thus, in this case an exchange of both the elements takes place. The whole procedure continues until all the elements of the list are arranged in such a way that on the left side of the element (pivot), the elements are lesser and on the right side, the elements are greater than the pivot. Thus, the list is subdivided into two lists. The working of quick sort is illustrated in Figure 9.1.

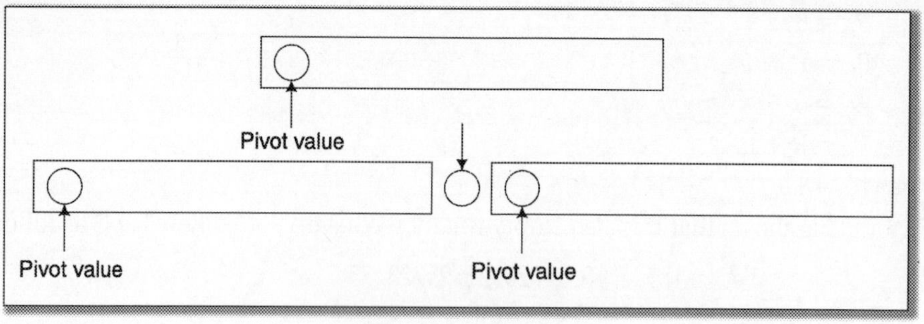

Figure 9.1 Quick sort.

Example: Consider a list 25, 10, 35, 5, 60, 12, 58, 18, 49, 19 we have to sort the list using quick sort techniques.

Solution Given

A_0	A_1	A_2	A_3	A_4	A_5	A_6	A_7	A_8	A_9
(25) →	10	35	5	60	12	58	18	49	← (19)

We use the first number 25. Beginning with the last number, 19, scanning from the right to left, comparing each number with 25 and stopping at the first number having a value of less than 25. The first number visited that has a value less than 25 is 19. Thus, exchange both of them.

A_0	A_1	A_2	A_3	A_4	A_5	A_6	A_7	A_8	A_9
(19)	10	35	5	60	12	58	18	49	(25)

Scanning from left to right, the first number visited that has a value greater than 25 is 35. Thus, exchange both of them.

A_0	A_1	A_2	A_3	A_4	A_5	A_6	A_7	A_8	A_9
19	10	(25)	5	60	12	58	18	49	(35)

Scanning from right to left, the first number visited that has a value less than 25 is 18. Thus, exchange both of them.

A_0	A_1	A_2	A_3	A_4	A_5	A_6	A_7	A_8	A_9
19	10	(18)	5	60	12	58	(25)	49	35

Scanning from left to right, the first number visited that has a value greater than 25 is 60. Thus, exchange both of them.

A_0	A_1	A_2	A_3	A_4	A_5	A_6	A_7	A_8	A_9
19	10	18	5	(25)	12	58	(60)	49	35

Scanning from right to left, the first number visited that has a value less than 25 is 12. Thus, exchange both of them.

A_0	A_1	A_2	A_3	A_4	A_5	A_6	A_7	A_8	A_9
19	10	18	5	(12)	(25)	58	60	49	35

Thus 25 is correctly placed in its final position, and we get two sublist. Sublist1 and Sublist2. Sublist1 has lesser value than 25 while Sublist2 has greater values.

A_0	A_1	A_2	A_3	A_4	A_5	A_6	A_7	A_8	A_9
19	10	18	5	12	(25)	58	60	49	35
←		Sublist1		→		←	Sublist2		→

Now sorting of first Sublist1

A_0	A_1	A_2	A_3	A_4
(19)	10	18	5	(12)

Beginning with the last number, 12, scanning from the right to left, comparing each number with 19 and stopping at the first number having a value less than 19. The first number visited that has a value less than 19 is 12. Thus, exchange both of them.

A_0	A_1	A_2	A_3	A_4
(12)	10	18	5	(19)

Now, 19 is correctly placed in its final position. Therefore, we sort the remaining Sublist1 beginning with 12. We scan the list from right to left. The first number having a value less than 12 is 5. We interchange 5 and 12 to obtain list.

A_0	A_1	A_2	A_3
(5)	10	18	(12)

Beginning with 5 we scan the list from left to right. The first number having a value greater than 12 is 18. We interchange 12 and 18 to obtain the list.

A_0	A_1	A_2	A_3
5	10	(12)	(18)

Hence first Sublist1 has been sorted as

A_0	A_1	A_2	A_3	A_4
5	10	12	18	19

Now sorting of first Sublist2

A_6	A_7	A_8	A_9
(58)	60	49	(35)

Beginning with 58 we scan the list right to left. The first number having a value less than 58 is 35. We interchange 58 and 35 and obtain the list.

A_6	A_7	A_8	A_9
(35)	60	49	(58)

Beginning with 35 we scan the list from left to right. The first number having a value greater than 58 is 60. We interchange 58 and 60 to obtain the list.

A_6	A_7	A_8	A_9
35	(58)	49	(60)

Beginning with 60 we scan the list right to left. The first number having a value less than 58 is 49. We interchange 58 and 49 and obtain the list.

A_6	A_7	A_8	A_9
35	(49)	(58)	60

Hence, the second Sublist2 has been sorted as

A_6	A_7	A_8	A_9
35	49	58	60

The resulted sorted list is as follows:

A_0	A_1	A_2	A_3	A_4	A_5	A_6	A_7	A_8	A_9
5	10	12	18	19	25	35	49	58	60

Algorithm for quick sort

The quick sort algorithm is performed using following two important functions- Quick and partition.

Algorithm: **Quick (A[0....n-1], low, high)**

This algorithm performs sorting of the elements given an array A[0.....n-1] in which unsorted elements are given. The low indicates the leftmost element in the list and high indicates the rightmost element in the list.

Step 1: **checking**

If(low < high) then

Calling partition function

m ← partition(A[low....high)] // m is mid of array

First Sublist

Quick(A[low.......m-1])

Second Sublist

Quick(A[m+1.......high])

The algorithm partitioning the given list is given below.

Algorithm: **Partition (A[low.......high])**

Step 1: Initialization

pivot ← A[low]

i ← low

j ← high +1

Step 2: Checking

While (i < = j) do

While (A[i] < = pivot) do

i ← i +1

while (A[j] > = pivot) do

j ← j-1

if (i < = j) then

swap (A[i], A[j])

swap (A[low], A[j])

return j

Program for sorting the elements by Quick sort algorithm

```
#include<process.h>
#include<iostream.h>
#include<conio.h>
#include<stdlib.h>
int Partition(int low,int high,int arr[]);
void Quick_sort(int low,int high,int arr[]);

void main()
{
int *a,n,low,high,i;
clrscr();
cout<<"/*********Quick Sort Algorithm Implementation**************/";
cout<<"Enter number of elements:";
```

```
cin>>n;
a=new int[n];
/* cout<<"enter the elements:";
for(i=0;i<n;i++)
cin>>a;*/
for(i=0;i<n;i++)
a[i]=rand()%100;
clrscr();
cout<<"Initial Order of elements";
 for(i=0;i<n;i++)
 cout<<a[i]<<"        ";
cout<<" ";
high=n-1;
low=0;
Quick_sort(low,high,a);
cout<<"Final Array After Sorting:";
  for(i=0;i<n;i++)
 cout<<a[i]<<"        ";
getch();
}

/*Function for partitioning the array*/

int Partition(int low,int high,int arr[])
{ int i,high_vac,low_vac,pivot/*,itr*/;
   pivot=arr[low];
   while(high>low)
{ high_vac=arr[high];

  while(pivot<high_vac)
  {
    if(high<=low) break;
    high--;
    high_vac=arr[high];
  }

  arr[low]=high_vac;
  low_vac=arr[low];
  while(pivot>low_vac)
  {
    if(high<=low) break;
    low++;
    low_vac=arr[low];
  }
  arr[high]=low_vac;
}
  arr[low]=pivot;
   return low;
}
void Quick_sort(int low,int high,int arr[])
{
```

```
   int Piv_index,i;
   if(low<high)
   {
    Piv_index=Partition(low,high,arr);
    Quick_sort(low,Piv_index-1,arr);
    Quick_sort(Piv_index+1,high,arr);
   }
}
```

Output

```
/*********Quick Sort Algorithm Implementation***************/

Enter number of elements: 9
enter the elements:
Initial Order of elements 50 30 10 90 80 20 40 70
Final Array after Sorting: 10 20 30 40 50 70 80 90
```

Analysis

When the pivot is chosen such that the array gets divided at the middle then it gives the **best case** complexity. The best case time complexity of insertion sort is **$O(n \log_2 n)$**.

If an array is randomly arranged then it results in **average case** time complexity which is **$O(n \log_2 n)$**.

The worst case for quick sort occurs when the pivot is minimum or maximum of all the elements in the list. Then it results in **worst case** time complexity which is **$O(n^2)$**.

9.3.6 Heap Sort

The term heap can be defined as a heap of size n is a binary tree of n nodes that satisfies the two important properties regarding heap.

The heap must be either 'almost complete binary tree' or 'complete binary tree'.

- **Almost complete binary tree:**

  The almost complete binary tree is a tree in which-

  1. Each node has a left child whenever it has a right child.
  2. The leaf in a tree must be present at height h or h -1. That means all the leaves are on two adjacent levels.

  Example:

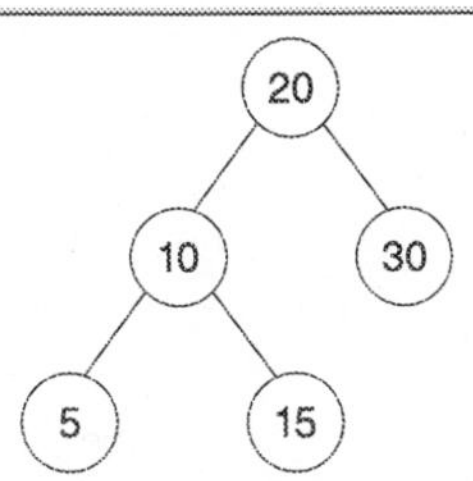

Almost complete binary tree

- **Complete binary tree:** The complete binary tree is a binary tree in which all levels are at the same depth or total number of nodes at each level i is 2^i.

  For example:

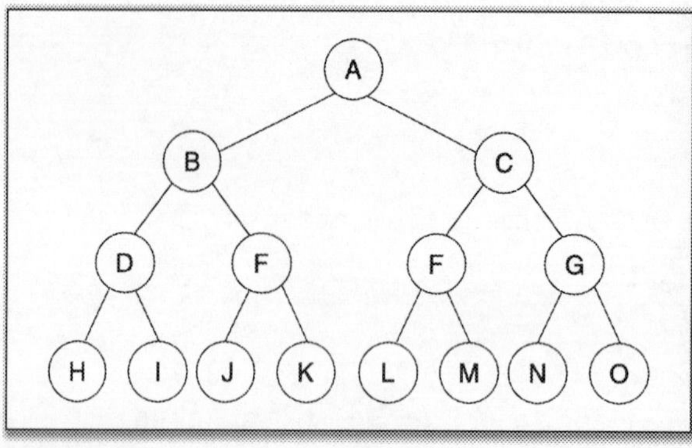

The heap must be either max heap (i.e. the parent is greater than all its children nodes) or min heap (i.e. parent node is lesser than all children nodes).

Heap sort is a sorting method discovered by J.W.J. Williams. It works in two stages, **heap construction** and **processing the heap**.

Heap construction: heap is a tree data structure in which every parent node must be either greater than or lesser than its children nodes. Such heaps are called as max heap and min heap respectively.

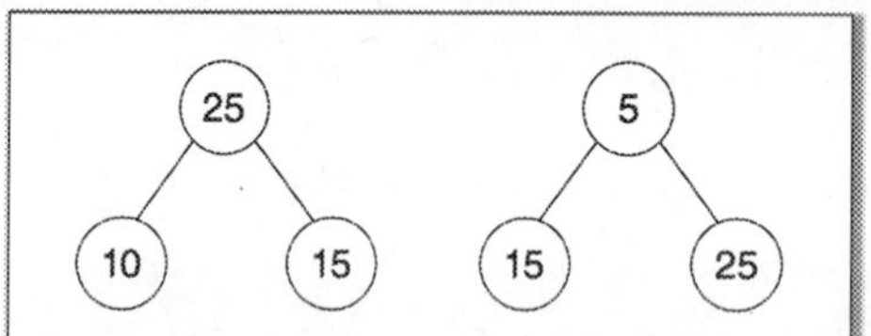

Max. heap Min. heap

Example: Consider a list 5, 15, 11, 9, 7, 13. Construct a heap.

Solution We will first create a complete binary tree or almost complete binary tree.

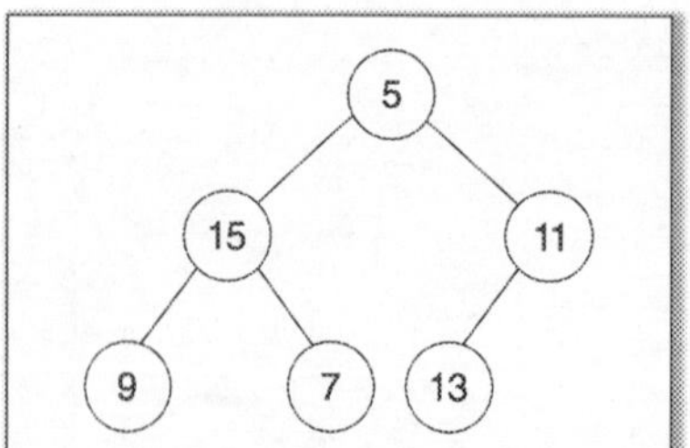

Almost complete binary tree

Now we will scan the tree from bottom and check parental property in order to build max heap.

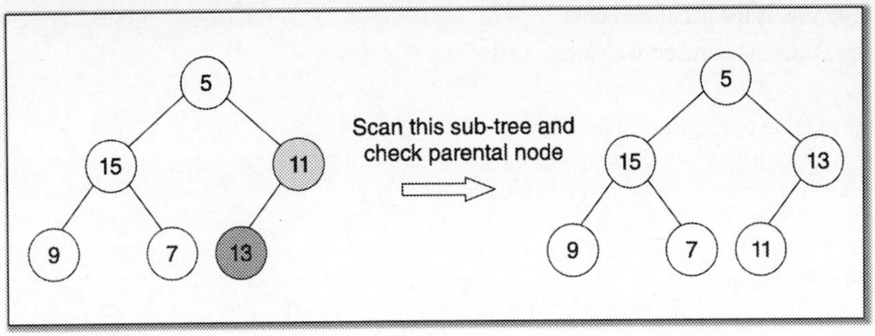

As the parent is greater than its children no need to exchange it.

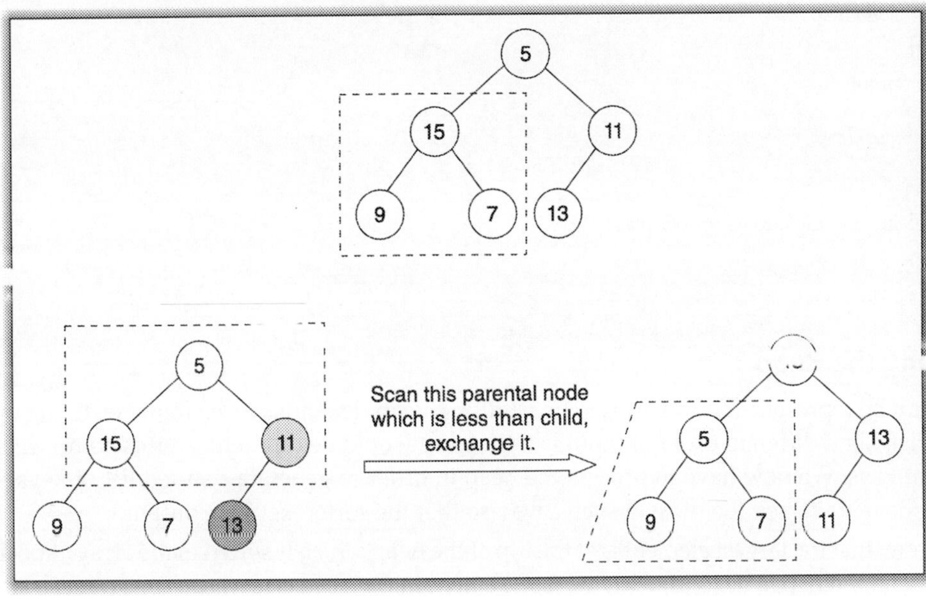

Thus, the help is getting constructed

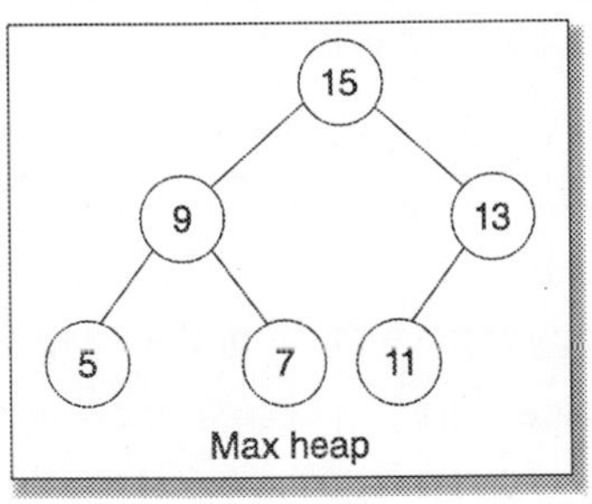

Algorithm to create a heap

Create_heap (list, n)

Where list = represents the list of elements

n = represents the number of elements in the list

[build heap]

Repeat through the number of elements in the list

[initialize]

i = k

temp = list[k]

[obtain parent of new element]

i = i/2

[place new element in the existing heap]

Repeat through step (vi) while (i > 1) and (temp > list[j])

[interchange elements]

list[i] = list[j]

[obtain next parent]

i = j

j = i/2

if (j < i) then j=1

[copy new element value into its proper place]

list[i] = temp

Return.

Processing the Heap

A heap may be represented as an array. The resulting heap depends on the initial ordering of the unsorted list. For a different order of input list, the heap would be different. At this point, we have the heap of keys. We now have to process the heap in order to generate a sorted list of keys. This means we have traversed the heap in such a way so that the sorted keys are output.

We know that the largest element is at the top of the heap which is sorted in the array at position heap [0]. We interchange heap [0] with the last element in the heap array heap [maxnodes], so that heap [0] is in the proper place. We then adjust the array to be a heap of size n-1. Again interchange heap [0] with heap [n-2], adjusting the array to be a heap of size n-2 and so on. At the end, we get an array which contains the keys in the sorted order.

A_0	A_1	A_2	A_3	A_4	A_5
15	9	13	5	7	11

Array representation of a heap

Now the figure below shows below the processing of heap. The nodes which are moved to their final positions in the array are shown with dashed circle as they are no longer part of the heap. A dashed line shows an edge whose two nodes have been interchanged to adjust the tree to be a heap again.

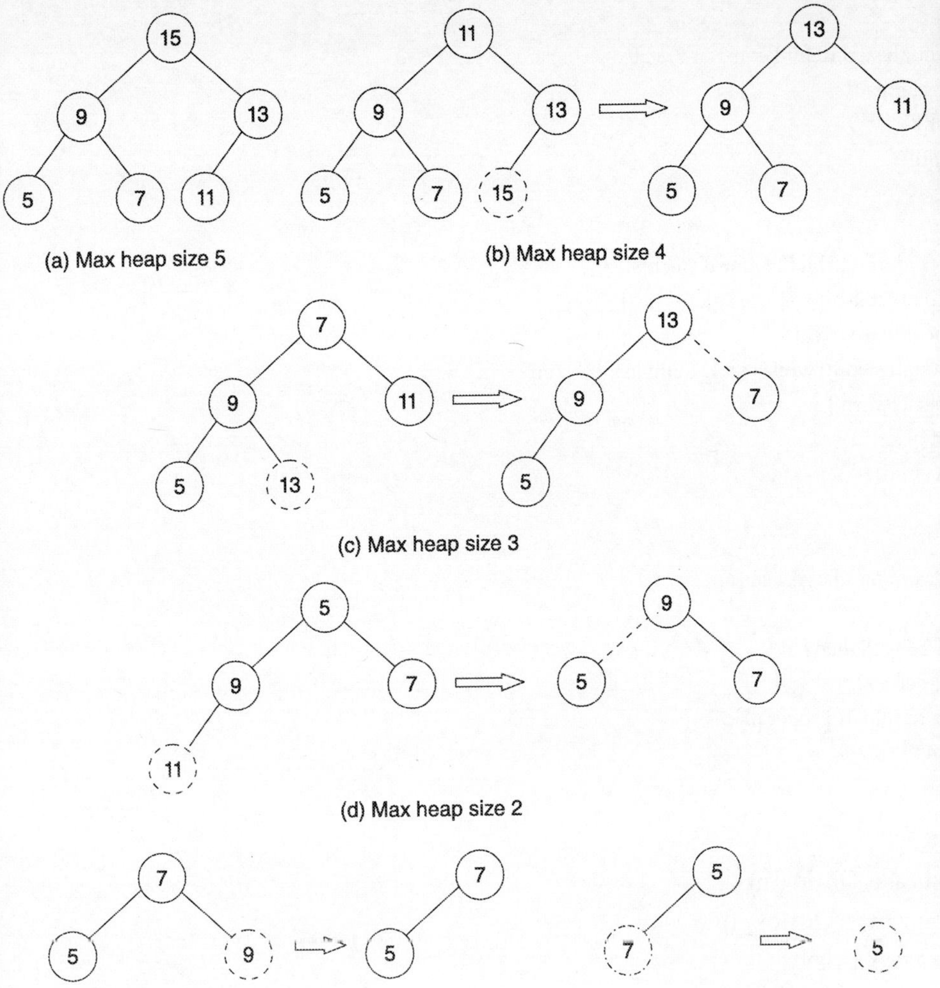

(a) Max heap size 5

(b) Max heap size 4

(c) Max heap size 3

(d) Max heap size 2

(e) Max heap size 1

(f) Max heap size 0

Now the sorted heap sort array is:

A_0	A_1	A_2	A_3	A_4	A_5
5	7	9	11	13	15

Algorithm to Processing a heap

Heap _sort (list, n)

Where list = represents the list of elements

n = represents the number of elements in the list

[initial heap]
Call create_heap(list, n)
[start sort]
Repeat through step 10 for k = n-1, n-2, ...0.
[exchange element]
list[0] = list[k]
temp = list[0])
i = 1
j = 2
[find index of largest child of new elements]
If j + 1 < k then, if list [j + 1] > list [j] then j = j+1
[reconstruct the new heap]
Repeat through step 10 while j <= k-1 and list[j] > temp.
[interchange element]
list[i] = list [j]
[obtain left child]
i = j
j = 2 * i
[obtain index of next largest child]
If j+1 < k
If list [j+ 1] > list [j] then j =j+1
Else if j >n then j =1
[copy element into its proper place]
list [j] = temp
Exit.

Analysis

Worst case: $O(n\log_2 n)$
Average case: $O(n\log_2 n)$
Best case: $O(n\log_2 n)$

9.3.7 Radix Sort

In Radix sort the sorting can be done digit by digit and thus all the elements can be sorted.

Example: Consider the unsorted array of 9 elements:
348, 143, 361, 423, 538, 128, 321, 543, 366

Step 1: In the first pass, sort the element according the units digits.

Unit digit	0	1	2	3	4	5	6	7	8	9
Elements		361, 321		143, 423, 543			366		348, 538, 128	

Now sort this number

Unit Digits	Element
0	
1	321, 361
2	
3	143, 423, 543
4	
5	
6	366
7	
8	128, 348, 538
9	

Elements after the first pass: 321, 361, 143, 423, 543, 366, 128, 348, 538

Step 2: In the second pass, sort the elements according the tens digits.

Tens Digits	Element
0	
1	
2	321, 423, 128
3	538
4	143, 543, 348
5	
6	361, 366
7	
8	
9	

Elements after the second pass: 321, 423, 128, 538, 143, 543, 348, 361, 366

Step 3: In the third or final pass, sort the elements according the hundreds digits.

Hundreds Digits	Element
0	
1	128, 143
2	
3	321, 348, 361, 366
4	423

5	538, 543
6	
7	
8	
9	

Elements after the third pass: 128, 143, 321, 348, 361, 366, 123, 538, 543.

Thus, finally the sorted list by radix sort method will be:

128, 143, 321, 348, 361, 366, 123, 538, 543.

Algorithm for Radix sort

1. Read the total number of elements in the array.
2. Store the unsorted elements in the array.
3. Now sort the elements by digit by digit.
4. Sort the elements according to the unit digit than tens digit than hundred and so on.
5. Thus the elements should be sorted for up to the most significant bit.
6. Store the sorted element in the array and print them.
7. Stop.

9.4 SEARCHING

The technique for finding the particular or desired data element that has been stored with specific given identification is referred to as **searching.** Every day in our daily life, most the people spend their time in searching their keys. We are using **key** as the identification of the data, which has to be searched.

While searching, we are asked and to find a record that contains other information associated with the key. For example, given a name we are asked to find the telephone number, or given an account number and we are asked to find the balance in that account. Such a key is called an **internal key** or an **embedded key**. There may be a separate table of keys that includes pointer to records, and then it will be necessary to store the records in the secondary storage. This kind of searching where most of the table is kept in the secondary storage is called **external searching**. Searching where the table to be searched is stored entirely in the main memory is called **internal searching**.

There are two searching methods: **linear search** and **binary search.**

9.4.1 Linear or Sequential Searching

The sequential or linear search is the simplest search techniques. In this technique, we start at a beginning of a list or a table search for the desired data by examining each subsequent record until the desired data is found or the list is exhausted.

Algorithm for Linear search

In the set of N data items is given having k respective keys. If the desired data 'target' is located that contains the key then the search is successful; otherwise unsuccessful. We assume that N > = 1.

```
Initialization i = 0;
Comparison while ( i < = N)
    {
    If (target = = k[i])
    {
    Print: "successful search";
    Go to step 4.
    }
    Else
    i++;
    }
No match then
    Print "unsuccessful search";
Exit
```

Example: Given a set contains 6 data items:

25, 30, 13, 20, 37, 26

A0	A1	A2	A3	A4	A5
25	30	13	20	37	26

From the set we have to search the data item target = 13. The sequential search is as follows:

Step 1: target ≠ A0, here i = 0 (as 13 ≠ 25) so i++

Step 2: target ≠ A1 here i = 1 (as 13 ≠ 30) so i++

Step 3: target ≠ A2 here i = 1 (as 13 = 13)

The search is successful and it requires 3 comparisons.

Program for linear search algorithm

```
#include <iostream.h>
#include <apvector.h>
int main(void)
{
      apvector <int> array(10);
      //"drudge" filling the array
      array[0]=20; array[1]=40; array[2]=100; array[3]=80; array[4]=10;
```

```
    array[5]=60; array[6]=50; array[7]=90; array[8]=30; array[9]=70;
    cout<< "Enter the number you want to find (from 10 to 100)…"<<endl;
    int key;
    cin>> key;
    int flag = 0;     // set flag to off

    for(int i=0; i<10; i++)     // start to loop through the array
   {
         if (array[i] == key)    // if match is found
         {
               flag = 1;    // turn flag on
               break ;     // break out of for loop
         }
    }
         if (flag)     // if flag is TRUE (1)
         {
         cout<< "Your number is at subscript position " << i <<".\n";
         }
       else
       {
        cout<< "Sorry, I could not find your number in this array."<<endl<<endl;
       }
   return 0;
}
```

Output

```
Enter the number you want to find (from 10 to 100)…
10
Your number is at subscript position 4
```

Analysis

Worst case: O(n)
Average case: O(n)
Best case: O(1)

Advantages of Linear Search

- It is a simple and easy method.
- It is efficient for small lists.
- No sorting of items is required.

Disadvantages of Linear Search

- It is not suitable for large list of elements.
- It is requires more comparisons.

9.4.2 Binary Search

Algorithm for Linear search:

Binary_search (K, N,X)

Given an array K, consisting of N elements in an ascending order, this algorithm searches the structure for a given element whose value is given by X. The variables LOW, MIDDLE and HIGH denote lower, middle and upper limits respectively.

Initialize

LOW = 1

HIGH = N

Perform Search

Repeat through step 4 while

LOW ≤ HIGH

Obtain index of midpoint of interval

MIDDLE = (LOW + HIGH) / 2

Compare

If X < K[MIDDLE]

Then HIGH = MIDDLE -1

Else if X > K[MIDDLE]

Then LOW = MIDDLE + 1

Else Print ("successful search")

Return (MIDDLE)

Unsuccessful search

Print "unsuccessful search"

Return(0)

Example: Given an ordered set contains 8 data items (in an ascending order):

5 10 15 20 25 30 35 40

From the set we have to search the data item with X = 10, the binary search is as follows.

Solution Initially,

LOW = 1

HIGH = 8

The data items are arranged in the following manner along with their respective keys:

A_1	A_2	A_3	A_4	A_5	A_6	A_7	A_8
5	10	15	20	25	30	35	40

Step 1: MIDDLE = (LOW + HIGH) / 2

MIDDLE = (1 + 8) / 2 = 4

Now, K[MIDDLE] = 20

X ≠ K[MIDDLE] (10 ≠ 20)

X < K[MIDDLE], therefore

HIGH = MIDDLE -1

Now,

HIGH = 4 -1 = 3

Step 2: MIDDLE = (LOW + HIGH) / 2

MIDDLE = (1 + 3) / 2 = 2

Now, K[MIDDLE] = 10

X = K[MIDDLE] = 10

The search is successful as it searched the desired data item. For the successful search it required 2 comparisons.

Program for Binary search algorithm

```
#include<iostream.h>
#include<conio.h>
int bsearch(int AR[], int N, int VAL);
int main()
{
int AR[100],n,val,found;
cout<<"Enter number of elements you want to insert ";
cin>>n;
cout<<"Enter element in ascending order\n";
for(int i=0;i<n;i++)
{
cout<<"Enter element "<<i+1<<":";
cin>>AR[i];
}
cout<<"\nEnter the number you want to search ";
cin>>val;
found=bsearch(AR,n,val);
if(found==1)
cout<<"\nItem found";
else
```

```
cout<<"\nItem not found";
getch();
return 0;
}
int bsearch(int AR[], int N, int VAL)
{
int Mid,Lbound=0,Ubound=N-1;

while(Lbound<=Ubound)
{
Mid=(Lbound+Ubound)/2;
if(VAL>AR[Mid])
Lbound=Mid+1;
else
if(VAL<AR[Mid])
Ubound=Mid-1;
else
return 1;
}
return 0;
}
```

Output

```
SAMPLE RUN # 1
Enter number of elements you want to insert 5
Enter element in ascending order
Enter element 1: 13
Enter element 2: 19
Enter element 3: 23
Enter element 4: 50
Enter element 5: 67
Enter the number you want to search 23
Item found
SAMPLE RUN # 2
Enter number of elements you want to insert 3
Enter element in ascending order
Enter element 1: 33
Enter element 2: 59
Enter element 3: 63
Enter the number you want to search 30
Item not found
```

Analysis

Worst case: $O(\log_2 n)$

Average case: $O(\log_2 n)$

Best case: $O(1)$

Advantages of Binary Search

- It is more efficient than linear search for large number of elements in the list.
- It requires less number of comparisons.

Disadvantages of Binary Search

- It requires sorting of items.
- The ratio of insertion time or deletion time to search item is quite high for this method.

10

TABLES

10.1 INTRODUCTION

In this chapter, we examine the simplest of all data types of 'table'. The values in a table, like the values in a sorted list, have two parts, a key and a data part. As the specification shows, there are only 3 non-trivial operations: insert, delete and retrieve. Retrieve operation takes a key and returns a Boolean indicating if the table contains a value with that key and if the Boolean is true, returns the appropriate data part.

10.2 EXAMPLES

A familiar example is a telephone book. A value is an entry for a person or business. The key is the person's name, the data part is the other information (address and phone number). Another example is a tax table issued with the income tax guide. The key is the amount of taxable income, the data parts include the amount of federal and provincial tax you must pay.

However, these examples are actually sorted lists, not tables in the pure sense. The difference is that in a list, the elements are arranged in a sequence. There is a first element, a second one, etc. for every element (except the last). Also, there is a unique 'next' element.

In a table, there is no order given to the elements. There is no notion of 'next'. Tables with no particular order arise fairly often in everyday life. A very familiar example is a table for converting two kinds of units between themselves, such as metric units (of measure) and English units. The key is the unit of measure that you currently have, the data is the unit in the other system and the conversion formula. There is no particular order given to the entries in this table. Although it happens that the entry for kilograms is written directly after the entry for meters, this is an arbitrary ordering which has no intrinsic meaning. An abstract type 'table' reflects the fact that, in general, there is no intrinsic order among the entries of a table.

A table most closely resembles the abstract type 'collection'. Indeed, there is only one important difference between the two. While we have an operation for traversing a collection (MAP) there is no such operation for tables which means there is no way to examine the entry contents of a table. You can lookup individuals with the 'retrieve' operation – e.g. you can find out how to convert grams to kilograms – but there is no operation that will list all the values in a table. Indeed there is not even an operation reporting how many values a table contains.

10.3 REPRESENTING TABLES

We have studied a couple of data structures that could be used to implement tables relatively efficiently. A heap would be good for insertion and deletion but terrible for retrieval. In most applications, retrieval is the principal operation. You build up a table initially with a sequence of insertions, and then do a large number of retrievals. Deletion is usually rare. The importance of retrieval makes heaps poor way to implement tables.

The best choices are binary search trees (especially if balanced), or B-trees, giving O (logN) insertion, deletion and retrieval. We will look at a technique called hashing that aims to make these operations in constant time. That may seem impossible, but hashing does indeed come very close to achieving this goal.

We can access any position of an array in constant time. We think of the subscript as the key, and the value stored in the array as the data. Given the key, we can access the data in constant time. For example, suppose we want to store the student details in a table class. We could use an array of size 100, say, and assign to each student a particular position in the array. We tell this number to the student calling it his/her student record. We have used a student number as a subscript in the array.

This is the basic idea behind a hash table. In fact, the only flaw in the strategy is that there is a need to be addressed is the steps which tell you what the 'student number' is. In practice, we usually do not control the key values: the set of possible keys is given to us as the part of the problem, and we must accommodate it. To carry on with our example, suppose that circumstances forced us to use some part of student personal data as the key – say the students social insurance number as an array subscript, and you stored your information in the position that it is indexed.

- The set of possible key values is very large. This set might even be unbounded. Imagine that the student name was to be used as the key: there are an infinite number of different names.
- The the set of actual key values is quite small.
- To get constant-time operations, we must use an array to store the information.

The array cannot possibly be large enough to have a different position for every possible key. And, in any case we must be able to accommodate keys of types (such as real numbers or strings) that are not legitimate (in C) as array subscripts.

10.4 HASHING

The search techniques are based exclusively on comparing keys. The organization of the file and the order in which the keys are inserted affect the number of keys that must be examined before getting the desired one. If the location of the record within the table depends only on the values of the key and not on the locations of the keys, we can retrieve each key in a single access. The most efficient way to achieve this is to store each record at a single offset from the base application of the table. This suggests the use of arrays. If the record keys are integers, the keys themselves can serve as the index to the array. There is a one-to-one correspondence between keys and array index.

The perfect relationship between the key value and the location of an element is not easy to establish or maintain. Consider, if an institute uses its students' five digit ID number as the primary key. Now, the range of key values is from 00000 to 99999. It is clear that it will be impractical to setup an array of 1,00,000 elements each if only 100 are needed. What if we keep the array size down to the size that we actually need (array of 100 elements) and just use the last two digits of the key to identify each student? For instance, the element of student 53374 is in student record [74].

Position	Key	Record
0	31300	
1	49001	
2	52202	
.	.	
.	.	
99	01999	

Hashing is an approach to convert a key into an integer within a limited range. This key to address transformation is known as hashing function which maps the key space (K) into an address space (A). Thus, a hash function H produces a table address where the record may be located for the given key value (K).

Hashing function can be denoted as:

$$H : K \rightarrow A$$

Ideally no two keys should be converted into the same address. Unfortunately, there exists no hash function that guarantees this. This situation is called collision. For example, the hash function in the preceding example is h(k) = key % 100. The function key % 100 can produce any integer between 0 and 99, depending on the value of key.

10.4.1 Hash Table

In computer science, a hash table, or a hash map is a data structure that associate keys with values. The primary operation it supports efficiently is a lookup: e.g., given a key (e.g. person's name), find the corresponding value (e.g. that person's telephone number). It works by transforming the key using a hash function into a hash, a number that the hash table uses to locate the desired value.

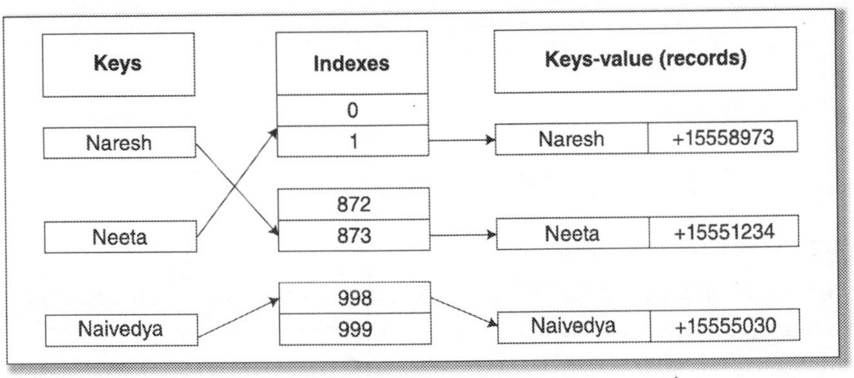

Figure 10.1 A small phone book as a hash table.

- A hash table is used for storing and retrieving data every quickly. Insertion of data in the hash table is based on the key value. Hence, every entry in the hash table is associated with some key. For example, for storing an employee record in the hash table the employee ID will work as a key.
- Using the hash key the required piece of data can be searched in the hash table by few or more key comparisons. The searching time is then dependent upon the size of the hash table.
- Effective representation of directory can be done using a hash table. We can place the dictionary entries (key and value pair) in the hash table using the hash function.

10.4.2 Hash Function

A hash function is a function which is used to put the data in a hash table. Hence one can use the same hash function to retrieve the data from the hash table. Thus, the hash function is used to implement the hash table. The integer returned by the hash function is called the hash key.

Example: Consider that we want place some employee records in the hash table. The record of employee is placed with the help of key: employee ID. The employee ID is a 7 digit number for placing the record in the hash table. To place the record, the key 7 digit number is converted into 3 digits by taking only the last three digits of the key.

If the key is 496700 it can be stored at 0th position. The second key is 8421002, the record of this key is placed at the 2nd position in the array.

Hence the hash function will be:

$$H(key) = key \% 1000$$

Where key % 1000 is a hash function and key obtained by hash function is called the hash key. The hash table will be:

	Employee ID	Record
0	496800	
1		
2	7421002	
.	.	
.	.	
998	7886998	
999	1245999	

10.4.3 Types of Hash Function

There are various types of hash functions that are used to place the record in the hash table.

1. **Division method:** The hash function depends upon the remainder of the division. Typically the divisor is the table length. For example:

   If the record 54, 72, 89, 37 is to be placed in the hash table and if the table size is 10 then

$$H(key) = record \% table\ size$$

4 = 54 % 10
2 = 72 % 10
9 = 89 % 10
7 = 37 % 10

2. **Mid square:** In the mid square method, the key is squared and the middle or mid part of the result is used as the index.
   If the key is a string, it has to pre-process to produce a number.
   Consider that if we want to place a record 3111 then
   $3111^2 = 9678321$
   For the hash table size 1000
   H(3111) = 783 (the middle 3 digits)
3. **Multiplicative hash function:** The given record is multiplied by some constant value. The formula for computing the hash key is:
   H(key) = floor(p * fractional part of key * A)) where p is integer constant and A is constant real number.
   Knuth suggests to use constant A = 0.61803398987
   If key 107 and p = 50 then
   H(key) = floor (50 * 107 *0.61803398987)
   = floor(3306.4818458045)
   = 3306
   At location 3306 in the hash table the record 107 will be placed.
4. **Digit folding:** The key is divided into separate parts, and using some simple operation these parts are combined to produce the hash key.
   For example, consider a record 12365412. Then it is divided into separate parts as 123 654 12 and these are added together:
   H(key) = 123 + 654 + 12
   = 789
   The record will be placed at location 789 in the hash table.
5. **Digit Analysis:** The method forms addresses by selecting and shifting digits of the original key for a given key set. The same positions in the key and the same rearrangement pattern must be used. The digit positions are analyzed and the ones having the most uniform distributions are selected.

For example: a key 7654321 is transformed to address 1247 by selecting digits in positions 1, 2, 4 and 7 then by reversing their order. There are many other hash functions which may be used depending on the set of the keys to be hashed. If a set of keys does not contain integers they must be converted into integers before applying any of the hashing functions explained earlier such as if a key consists of letters, each letter may be converted to digits by using 1-26 corresponding to letters A to Z.

10.5 COLLISION

The hash function is a function that returns the key value using which the record can be placed in the hash table. Thus this function helps us in placing the record in the hash table at an appropriate position and due to this we can retrieve the record directly form that location. This function needs to be designed very carefully and it should not return the same hash key address for two different records. This is undesirable in hashing.

The situation in which the hash function returns the same hash key for more than one record is called collision and the two identical hash keys returned for different records are called synonyms.

When there is no room for a new pair in a hash table such a situation is called an overflow. Sometimes when we handle collision it may lead to overflow conditions. Collision and overflow show poor hash functions.

Example: Consider a hash function. H(key) = key % 10 having the hash table of size 10.

The record keys to be placed are 131, 44, 43, 78, 19, 36, 57 and 77

Index	Key
0	
1	131
2	
3	43
4	44
5	
6	36
7	57
8	78
9	19

Now if we try to place 77 in the hash table then we get the hash key to be 7, and at index 7 the record key 57 is in place already. This situation is called **collision.** From the index 7 if we look for next vacant position at subsequent indices 8, 9 then we find that there is no room to place 77 in the hash table. This situation is called an **overflow.**

Characteristics of Good Hashing Function

1. The hash function should be simple to compute.
2. Number of collisions should be less while placing the record in the hash table. Ideally no collision should occur. Such a function is called a perfect hash function.
3. Hash functions should produce such a key which will get distributed uniformly over an array.
4. The function should depend upon every bit of the key. Thus the hash function that simply extracts the portion of a key is not suitable.

10.6 COLLISION RESOLUTION TECHNIQUES

If two keys hash to the same index, the corresponding records cannot be stored in the same location. So, if it's already occupied, we must find another location where the new record can be stored, and do it so that we can find it when we look it up later on. An idea for the collision resolution strategy is that if collision occurs then it should be handled by applying some techniques. Such a technique is called collision handling technique.

There are two methods for detecting collisions and overflows in the hash table:

- Chaining
- Linear probing

Two more difficult collision handling techniques are:

- Quadratic probing
- Double hashing

10.6.1 Chaining

In collision handling method chaining is a concept which introduces an additional field with data i.e. chain. A separate chain is maintained for the colliding data. When collision occurs then a linked list (chain) is maintained at the home bucket.

Chaining involves maintaining two tables in the memory. First of all, as before, there is a table in the memory which contains the records except that now it has an additional field Link, which is used so that all records in the table with same hash address H may be linked together to form a linked list. Second there is a hash address table list, which contains pointers to the linked list in the table.

Chaining hash tables have advantages over open addressed hash tables in that the removal operation is simple, and resizing the table can be postponed for a much longer time because performance degrades more gracefully even when every slot is used.

Example: Consider the keys to be placed in their home buckets are: 3, 4, 61, 131, 24, 9, 8, 7, 97, 21

We will apply a hash function as:

$$H(key) = key \ \% \ D$$

where D is size of table. (Here D = 10) The hash table will be:

10.6.2 Linear Probing (Open Addressing)

This is the easiest method of handling collisions. When a collision occurs, when two records demand for the same location in the hash table then the collision can be solved by placing the second record linearly down whenever an empty location is found. When we use linear probing the hash table is represented as a one-dimensional array with indices that range from 0 to the desired table size – 1. Before inserting any element into this table we must initialize the table to represent the situation where all slots are empty. This allows us to detect overflows and collisions when we insert elements into the hash table.

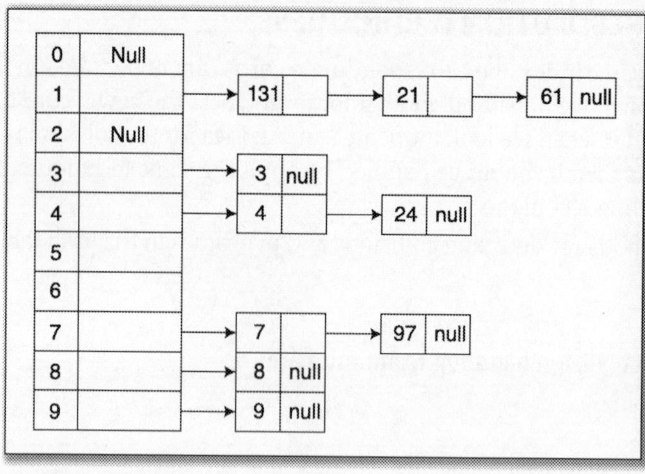

Figure 10.2 Chaining.

Example: Consider the keys to be placed in their home buckets are: 3, 4, 61, 131, 21, 24, 9, 8, 7

We will apply a hash function. We will use the division hash function. That means the keys are placed using the formula:

H(key) = key % tablesize

H(key) = key % 10

For instance the element 61 can be placed at:

H(key) = 61 % 10

= 1

Index 1 will be the home bucket for 61. Continuing in this fashion we will place 3, 4, 8, 7.

0	Null
1	61
2	Null
3	3
4	4
5	Null
6	Null
7	7
8	8
9	9

Now the next key to be inserted is 131. According to the hash function

H(key) = 131 % 10

H(key) = 1

But the index 1 location is already occupied by 61 i.e. collision occurs. To resolve this collision we will linearly move down and at the next empty location. Therefore 131 will be placed at index 2. 21 is placed at index 5 and 24 at index 6.

0	Null
1	61
2	131
3	3
4	4
5	21
6	24
7	7
8	8
9	9

10.6.3 Chaining Without Replacement

In the collision handling method chaining is a concept which introduces an additional field with data i.e chain. A separate chain is maintained for the colliding data. When collision occurs we store the colliding data by the linear probing method. The address of this colliding data can be stored with first colliding element in the chain table, without replacement.

Example: Consider the elements: 131, 3, 4, 21, 61, 6, 71, 8, 9

Index	Data	Chain
0	–1	–1
1	131	2
2	21	5
3	3	–1
4	4	–1
5	61	7
6	6	–1
7	71	–1
8	8	–1
9	9	–1

Figure 10.3 Chaining without replacement.

We can see that the chain is maintained at the number which demands for location 1. When the first number 131 comes we will place it at index 1. Next comes 21 but collision occurs so by linear probing we will place 21 at index 2, and the chain is maintained by writing 2 in the chain table at index 1. Similarly next comes 61 by linear probing. We can place 61 at place 61 at index 5 and the chain will be maintained at index 2. Thus, any element which gives hash key as 1 will be stored by linear probing at an empty location but a chain is maintained so that traversing the hash table will be efficient.

The drawback of this method is in finding the next empty location. We are least bothered about the fact that when the element which actually belongs to that empty location cannot obtain its location. This means that the logic of hash function gets disturbed.

10.6.4 Chaining with Replacement

As previous method has a drawback of losing the meaning of the hash function. To overcome this drawback the method known as changing with replacement is introduced. Let us discuss the example to understand the method. Suppose we have to store following elements: 131, 21, 31, 4, 5

0	-1	-1
1	131	2
2	21	3
3	31	-1
4	4	-1
5	5	-1
6		
7		
8		
9		

Now next element is 2. The hash function will indicate the hash key as 2. We have stored element 21 already at index 2. But we also know that 21 is not of that position at which currently it is placed. Hence we will replace 21 by 2 and accordingly the chain table will be updated. See the table:

Index	Data	Chain
0	-1	-1
1	131	6
2	2	-1
3	31	-1
4	4	-1
5	5	-1
6	21	3

7	-1	-1
8	-1	-1
9	-1	-1

The value -1 in the hash table and chain table indicate the empty location.

The advantage of this method is that the meaning of hash function is preserved. But each time some logic is needed to test the element, whether it is at its proper position or not.

10.6.5 Quadratic Probing

Quadratic probing operates by taking the original hash value and adding successive values of an arbitrary quadratic polynomial to the starting value. This method uses the following formula

$$H_i(\text{key}) = (\text{Hash (key)} + i^2) \ \% \ m$$

where m can be a table size or any prime number.

Example: We have to insert following elements in the hash table with table size 10: 27, 80, 65, 22, 11, 17, 49, 87.

We will fill the hash table step by step

27 % 10 = 7

80 % 10 = 0

65 % 10 = 5

22 % 10 = 2

11% 10 = 1

0	90
1	11
2	22
3	
4	
5	65
6	
7	27
8	
9	

Now if we want to place 17 a collision will occur as 17 % 10 = 7 and buckets 7 has already an element 27. Hence we will apply quadratic probing to insert this record in the hash table.

$$H_i(\text{key}) = (\text{Hash (key)} + i^2) \ \% \ m$$

Consider i = 0 then

$(17 + 0^2) \ \% \ 10 = 7$

$(17 + 1^2) \ \% \ 10 = 8$ when i = 1

The bucket 8 is empty hence we will place the element at index 8.

Then comes 49 which will be placed at index 9.

49 % 10 = 9

Now to place 87 we will use quadratic probing.

$(87 + 0) \% 10 = 7$

$(87 + 1) \% 10 = 8$ but already used

$(87 + 2^2) \% 10 = 1$ already used

$(87 + 3^2) \% 10 = 6$

It is observed that if we want to place all the necessary elements in the hash table, the size of divisor (m) should be twice as large as total number of elements.

0	90
1	11
2	22
3	
4	
5	65
6	87
7	27
8	17
9	49

10.6.6 Double Hashing

Double hashing is a method in which a second hash function is applied to the key when a collision occurs. By applying the second hash function we will get the number of positions from the point of collision to insert.

There are two important rules to be followed for the second function:

- It must never be evaluated to zero
- It must make sure that all cells can be probed.

The formula to be used for double hashing is

$$H_1(\text{key}) = \text{key mod tablesize}$$
$$H_2(\text{key}) = M - (\text{key mod } M)$$

where M is a prime number smaller than the size of the table.

Let the following elements to be placed in the hash table size 10: 37, 90, 45, 22, 17, 49, 55

Initially insert the elements using the formula for $H_1(\text{key})$.

Insert 37, 90, 45, 22

$$H_1(37) = 37 \% 10 = 7$$
$$H_1(90) = 90 \% 10 = 0$$

0	90
1	
2	22

3	
4	
5	45
6	
7	37
8	
9	49

$$H_1(45) = 45 \% 10 = 5$$
$$H_1(22) = 22 \% 10 = 2$$
$$H_1(49) = 49 \% 10 = 9$$

Now if 17 is to be inserted, then:

$$H_1(17) = 17 \% 10 = 7$$
$$H_2(\text{key}) = M - (\text{key mod } M)$$

Here M is a prime number smaller than the size of the table. A prime number that is smaller than the table size of 10 is 7.

$$\text{Hence, } M = 7$$
$$H_2(17) = 7 - (17 \text{ mod } 7) = 7 - 3 = 4$$

That means we have to insert the element 17 at 4 places from 37. In short we have to take 4 jumps. Therefore, 17 will be placed at index 1.

Now to insert 55,

$$H_1(55) = 55 \% 10 = 5$$
$$H_2(55) = 7 - (55 \text{ mod } 7) = 7 - 6 = 1$$

That means we have take one jump from index 5 to place 55. Finally, the hash table will be:

0	20
1	17
2	22
3	
4	
5	45
6	55
7	37
8	
9	49

Difference between quadratic probing and double hashing

- Double hashing is more complex to implement than quadratic probing. Quadratic probing is a faster technique than double hashing.

- Double hashing requires another hash function whose efficiency is same as some other hash function required when handling a random collision.

10.6.7 Rehashing

Rehashing is a technique in which the table is resized. The size of the table is doubled by creating a new table. It is preferable to have the total size of table as a prime number. There are situations in which the rehashing is required which are:

- When the table is completely full
- With quadratic probing when the table is filled half
- When insertions fail due to overflow

In such situations, we will have to transfer entries from the old table to the new table by recomputing their positions using suitable hash functions.

Consider that we have to insert the elements 37, 90, 55, 22, 17, 49, and 87. The table size is 10 and will use hash function,

$$H(\text{key}) = \text{key mod table size}$$

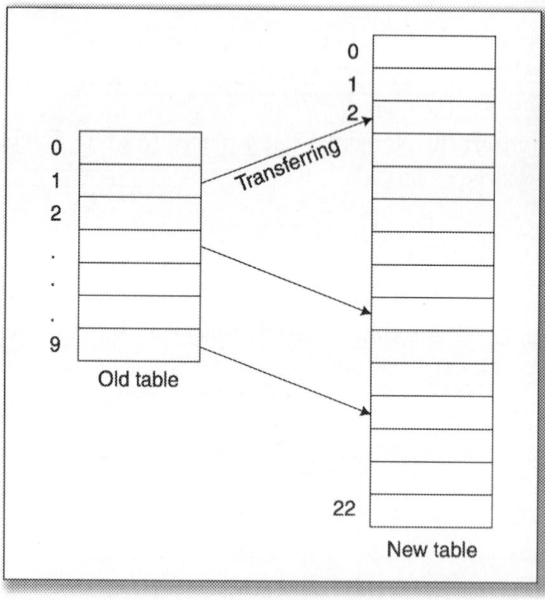

Figure 10.4 Rehashing.

37 % 10 = 7

90 % 10 = 0

55 % 10 = 5

22 % 10 = 2

17 % 10 = 7 collision solved by linear probing

49 % 10 = 9

0	90
1	
2	22
3	
4	
5	55
6	
7	37
8	17
9	49

Now this table is almost full and if we try to insert more elements collisions will occur and eventually further insertion will fail. Hence we will rehash by doubling the table size. The old table size is 10 then we should this size for new table, which becomes 20. But 20 is not a prime number. We will prefer to make table size as 23. Now hash function will be

H(key) = key mod 23
37 % 23 = 14
90 % 23 = 21
55 % 23 = 9
22 % 23 = 22
17 % 23 = 17
49 % 23 = 3
87 % 23 = 18

0	
1	
2	
3	49
4	
5	
6	
7	
8	
9	55
10	
11	
12	
13	
14	37
15	
16	
17	17
18	87
19	
20	

21	90
22	22

Now the hash table is sufficiently large to accommodate new insertions.

Advantages

- This technique provides the programmer a flexibility to enlarge the table size if required.
- Only the space gets doubled with the simple hash function which avoids occurrence of collisions.

10.7 APPLICATIONS OF HASHING

1. Hash tables are commonly used for symbol tables, caches and sets.
2. In compiler it is used to keep a track of declared variables.
3. For online spelling checking hashing functions are used.
4. Hashing helps in game playing programs to store the moves made.
5. For a browser program while caching the web pages, hashing is used.
6. In computer chess, a hash table is generally used to implement the transposition table.

10.8 SYMBOL TABLE

A symbol table is a data structure in which information is stored in the form of name-value pair. A symbol table arises frequently in computer science, when building loaders, assemblers, compilers, or any keyboard driven translator. In these contexts a symbol table is a set of name-value pairs. In the table, each name is associated with an attribute, a collection of attributes or some directions about what further processing is needed. The operations that can be performed on symbol tables are:

- Ask if a particular name is already present
- Retrieve the attributes of that name
- Insert a new name and its value
- Delete a name and its value

A tree table is a data structure in which hierarchical data is displayed in a tabular form. There are two types of tree table.

1. Static tree table
2. Dynamic tree table

Static Tree Table: In a static tree table all the hierarchical information is stored in a tabular form for all the nodes, at once. We can obtain the final tree structure after processing the tabular information. The typical example of static tree table is **Optimal Binary Search Tree (OBST).**

Dynamic Tree Table: A dynamic tree table is the tree table in which all the nodes are not specified already. Instead, the rules are specified for arranging the nodes in a tree form. Hence, the nature of the tree which is getting built is changing on insertion of each node. A typical example of dynamic tree table is **AVL tree**. Dynamic tables may also be maintained as a **binary search tree**.

Index